USING MATHEMATICS
Book 3

ANDRIA P. TROUTMAN
Professor, University of South Florida
Tampa, Florida

JAMES J. BEZDEK
Professor of Education, North Texas State University
Denton, Texas

CATHERINE TOBIN
Educational Consultant
Newtonville, Massachusetts

TEACHER–CONSULTANTS

Philip E. Bertoni
Teacher, John F. Kennedy High School
Anaheim Union High School District
La Palma, California

Caroline L. Chin
Teacher, Nathan Hale School
Boston Public Schools
Roxbury, Massachusetts

Lula P. Smith
Teacher, Mahalia Jackson School
Chicago Public Schools
Chicago, Illinois

Alma E. Wright
Teacher, Trotter School
Boston Public Schools
Boston, Massachusetts

LAIDLAW BROTHERS • PUBLISHERS
A Division of Doubleday & Company, Inc.
RIVER FOREST, ILLINOIS

Irvine, California   Chamblee, Georgia   Dallas, Texas   Toronto, Canada

The USING MATHEMATICS Program

USING MATHEMATICS Kindergarten

USING MATHEMATICS Book 1	USING MATHEMATICS Book 5
USING MATHEMATICS Book 2	USING MATHEMATICS Book 6
USING MATHEMATICS Book 3	USING MATHEMATICS Book 7
USING MATHEMATICS Book 4	USING MATHEMATICS Book 8

ACKNOWLEDGMENTS

EDITORIAL STAFF

Project Director: Albert F. Kempf   *Staff Editor:* David B. Spangler   *Production Director:* LaVergne G. Niequist
Art Director: Gloria J. Muczynski   *Assistant to the Art Director:* Dennis Horan   *Production Supervisor:* Mary C. Steermann
Production Associate: Kathryn L. Meyers   *Photo Researcher:* William A. Cassin

ILLUSTRATORS

George Hamblin; Paul Hazelrigg; Rick Incrocci; Sergei Itomlenskis/John D. Firestone & Associates, Inc.; Donald C. Meighan; Keith Neely; Joseph Rogers; Sam Sirdofsky; Linda B. Weller/Carol Bancroft & Friends

PHOTOGRAPHERS

Cover photograph by Cary Wolinsky/Stock Boston; other photographs credited where each photograph appears.

ISBN 0-8445-1203-6

23456789 10 11 12 13 14 15   10987654

CONTENTS

1 Addition-Subtraction Facts

2 Numeration

3 Addition and Subtraction

4 Multiplication Facts

5 Geometry

6 Measurement

7 Addition

8 Subtraction

9 Time, Weight, and Capacity

10 Multiplication

11 Division

12 Fractions and Decimals

13 Graphs

Review and Practice 296–327

1 Addition-Subtraction Facts

Michael D. Sullivan

7

Adding

He made 6 sand towers. She made 4. How many did they make in all?

You can add this way: $6 + 4 = 10$

or this way:
$$\begin{array}{r} 6 \\ +4 \\ \hline 10 \end{array}$$

They made 10 towers.

Exercises

1.
$$\begin{array}{r} 4 \\ +5 \\ \hline \end{array}$$

2.
$6 + 0 = \square$

3. $3 + 3 = \square$ 4. $2 + 5 = \square$ 5. $5 + 4 = \square$

6. $4 + 6 = \square$ 7. $4 + 4 = \square$ 8. $5 + 5 = \square$

9. $1 + 7 = \square$ 10. $7 + 3 = \square$ 11. $0 + 9 = \square$

12.
$$\begin{array}{r} 6 \\ +2 \\ \hline \end{array}$$
13.
$$\begin{array}{r} 2 \\ +7 \\ \hline \end{array}$$
14.
$$\begin{array}{r} 1 \\ +9 \\ \hline \end{array}$$
15.
$$\begin{array}{r} 5 \\ +2 \\ \hline \end{array}$$
16.
$$\begin{array}{r} 8 \\ +0 \\ \hline \end{array}$$
17.
$$\begin{array}{r} 2 \\ +8 \\ \hline \end{array}$$

18.
$$\begin{array}{r} 9 \\ +1 \\ \hline \end{array}$$
19.
$$\begin{array}{r} 8 \\ +1 \\ \hline \end{array}$$
20.
$$\begin{array}{r} 3 \\ +6 \\ \hline \end{array}$$
21.
$$\begin{array}{r} 4 \\ +3 \\ \hline \end{array}$$
22.
$$\begin{array}{r} 3 \\ +7 \\ \hline \end{array}$$
23.
$$\begin{array}{r} 0 \\ +7 \\ \hline \end{array}$$

24.

5 + 3 = ☐

25.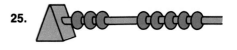

3 + 5 = ☐

Are your answers the same?

26. Which way would you add 4 and 5?
Are both ways correct?

$$\begin{array}{c} 4 \\ +5 \end{array} \text{ or } \begin{array}{c} 5 \\ +4 \end{array}$$

27. 6 pupils were playing.
3 more came. How many
are playing?

28. 7 eggs hatched.
1 more hatched.
How many eggs hatched?

29. She had 4 books.
She got 3 more. How many
books does she have now?

30. 5 planes were flying.
4 more took off. How many
planes are flying now?

31. He had 8 cars. He bought 2
more. How many cars does he
have?

32. Ava found 8 shells. Ida found 1
more than that. How many did
Ida find?

Who Am I?

1. Add me to myself.
You still have me.

2. Add me to myself.
You get 8.

3. Add me to 3.
You get 9.

4. Add me to 0.
You still have me.

Subtracting

5 kites went up.
Then 3 came down.
How many stayed up?

You can subtract this way:

$$5 - 3 = 2$$

or this way:
$$\begin{array}{r} 5 \\ -3 \\ \hline 2 \end{array}$$

2 kites stayed up.

Exercises

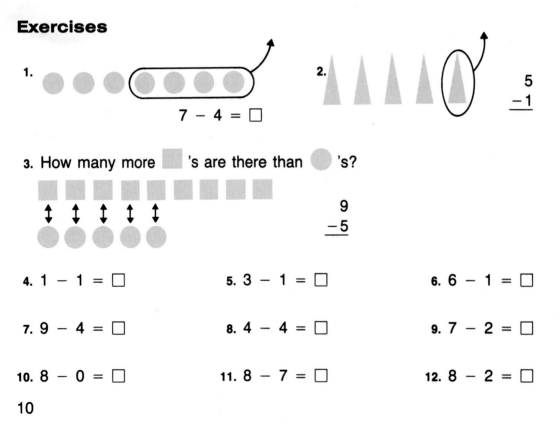

1. $7 - 4 = \square$

2. $\begin{array}{r} 5 \\ -1 \\ \hline \end{array}$

3. How many more ■'s are there than ●'s?

$\begin{array}{r} 9 \\ -5 \\ \hline \end{array}$

4. $1 - 1 = \square$ **5.** $3 - 1 = \square$ **6.** $6 - 1 = \square$

7. $9 - 4 = \square$ **8.** $4 - 4 = \square$ **9.** $7 - 2 = \square$

10. $8 - 0 = \square$ **11.** $8 - 7 = \square$ **12.** $8 - 2 = \square$

13. 8 −4	14. 7 −5	15. 6 −3	16. 9 −9	17. 9 −1	18. 8 −3
19. 5 −4	20. 9 −2	21. 9 −8	22. 5 −0	23. 7 −3	24. 8 −6
25. 8 −1	26. 6 −4	27. 9 −7	28. 7 −0	29. 6 −6	30. 6 −5
31. 9 −6	32. 8 −5	33. 7 −6	34. 6 −2	35. 7 −1	36. 9 −3

37. She needs 9¢. She has 7¢. How much more does she need?

38. Paul is 9 years old. Gertrude is 2 years old. How much older is Paul?

39. 8 pupils said they would come. So far 5 pupils have arrived. How many more are still coming?

40. 8 newspapers were on a shelf. 0 were sold. How many were left?

41. I have some pennies. If I had 4 more, I would have 7 pennies. How many pennies do I have?

42. Ed had 7 peanuts. He gave 4 to the elephant and 3 to the giraffe. How many did Ed have left?

Who Am I?

1. Subtract 4 from me. You get 4.

2. Subtract 9 from me. You get 0.

3. Subtract me from 6. You get me back again.

4. Subtract me from myself. You get 0.

Addition Facts

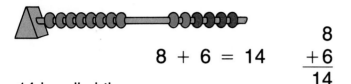

$$8 + 6 = 14 \qquad \begin{array}{r} 8 \\ +6 \\ \hline 14 \end{array}$$

14 is called the **sum**.

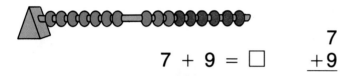

$$7 + 9 = \square \qquad \begin{array}{r} 7 \\ +9 \end{array}$$

Using 10 makes addition easy.

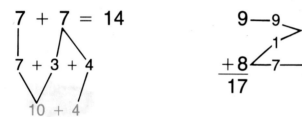

$$7 + 7 = 14$$

$$7 + 3 + 4$$

$$10 + 4$$

$$\begin{array}{r} 9 \\ +8 \\ \hline 17 \end{array} \quad \begin{array}{c} 9 \\ 1 \\ 7 \end{array} \begin{array}{c} 10 \\ 7 \end{array}$$

Exercises

1. 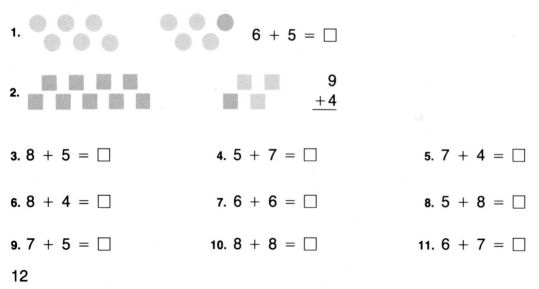 $6 + 5 = \square$

2. $\begin{array}{r} 9 \\ +4 \end{array}$

3. $8 + 5 = \square$ 　　4. $5 + 7 = \square$ 　　5. $7 + 4 = \square$

6. $8 + 4 = \square$ 　　7. $6 + 6 = \square$ 　　8. $5 + 8 = \square$

9. $7 + 5 = \square$ 　　10. $8 + 8 = \square$ 　　11. $6 + 7 = \square$

12

12. 9 +2	13. 5 +6	14. 3 +8	15. 2 +9	16. 7 +6	17. 4 +8
18. 4 +9	19. 3 +9	20. 5 +9	21. 4 +7	22. 6 +9	23. 7 +7
24. 9 +7	25. 8 +5	26. 9 +3	27. 9 +5	28. 7 +8	29. 8 +7
30. 9 +6	31. 7 +9	32. 9 +8	33. 6 +8	34. 8 +9	35. 9 +9

36. 8 books were in a stack.
5 more were put on top.
How many are in the stack?

37. 9 turtles are on a log.
5 turtles are on a rock.
How many turtles are there?

38. 8 crayons are in a box.
7 crayons are on a desk.
How many crayons are there?

39. A pencil costs 8¢. A folder
costs 9¢ more than that.
How much does a folder cost?

Suppose the time is 7 o'clock.

40. What time will it be in 2 hours?

41. What time will it be in 4 hours?

42. What time will it be in 5 hours?

Adding Three Numbers

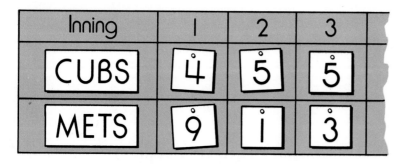

Inning	1	2	3	
CUBS	4	5	5	
METS	9	1	3	

How many runs have the Cubs scored?

Here are some ways to find the answer.

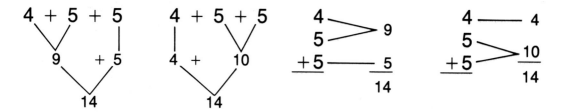

How would you find the number of runs for the Mets? How many runs have the Mets scored?

Exercises

1. $3 + 5 + 2 = \square$ **2.** $6 + 4 + 2 = \square$

3. $7 + 2 + 8 = \square$ **4.** $9 + 0 + 8 = \square$

5. $5 + 2 + 7 = \square$ **6.** $6 + 3 + 7 = \square$

7. $1 + 9 + 0 = \square$ **8.** $4 + 4 + 5 = \square$

14

9.	9	10.	3	11.	5	12.	0	13.	2	14.	3
	1		4		5		6		5		4
	+5		+3		+5		+6		+4		+6

15.	7	16.	3	17.	4	18.	5	19.	7	20.	9
	2		6		2		3		2		9
	+7		+3		+8		+5		+6		+0

21.	4	22.	7	23.	3	24.	8	25.	6	26.	6
	4		1		4		1		2		3
	+4		+8		+5		+9		+6		+5

27. 8 books are on the shelf, and 2 books are on the table. She is holding 7 books. How many books are there?

28. A cat had 5 kittens this year, 4 last year, and 6 the year before that. How many kittens did the cat have?

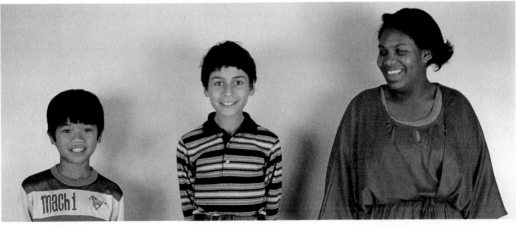

Connie and P. C. Peri

Skip is 8 years old.

Ira is 2 years older than Skip.

Bonnie is 4 years older than Ira.

29. How old is Ira?

30. How old is Bonnie?

31. How old will Ira be in 5 years?

32. How old will Bonnie be in 5 years?

Solving Problems

Bernard and Sylvia are helping their father make pancakes.

1. How many eggs are there?

2. How many ounces of strawberries are there?

3. Father and Sylvia will each make 8 pancakes. How many will they make in all?

4. 2 cups of milk will be used in the pancakes. They have 8 cups. How much milk will be left?

5. Father will eat 5 pancakes, Bernard 4, and Sylvia 2. How many will they eat in all?

6. Mother will eat 5 pancakes, Father 5, and Bernard 4. How many will they eat in all?

7. Mother put 6 plates, 2 bowls, and 8 glasses on the table. How many items did she put on the table?

8. The time is 8 minutes after 9. In 5 minutes the pancakes will be ready. At what time will the pancakes be ready?

16

Using a Calculator

When you push a key, you tell the calculator what to do.

8	+	4	=	12
Start with this number.	Add	this number.	Show the answer.	Answer

What was the other number key?

1. 7 + ? = 9   2. 8 − ? = 3

3. 9 − ? = 9   4. 7 + ? = 16

Was the + or the − pushed?

5. 6 ? 2 = 4   6. 8 ? 7 = 15

7. 5 ? 9 = 14   8. 9 ? 1 = 8

What pairs of number keys could be pushed?

9. ? + ? = 5   10. ? − ? = 6

11. ? − ? = 3   12. ? + ? = 15

17

Families of Facts

What do you notice about the three numbers used in each of the facts shown?

Exercises

Write a numeral for each □.

1. 6 + 3 = □   9 − 3 = □   2. 3 + 6 = □   9 − 6 = □

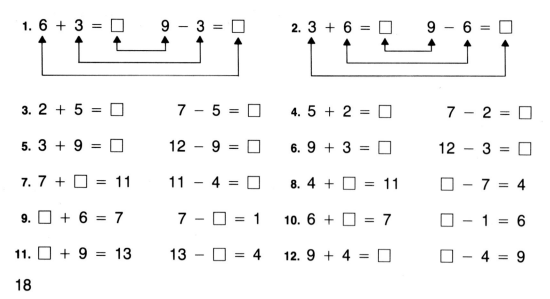

3. 2 + 5 = □   7 − 5 = □   4. 5 + 2 = □   7 − 2 = □

5. 3 + 9 = □   12 − 9 = □   6. 9 + 3 = □   12 − 3 = □

7. 7 + □ = 11   11 − 4 = □   8. 4 + □ = 11   □ − 7 = 4

9. □ + 6 = 7   7 − □ = 1   10. 6 + □ = 7   □ − 1 = 6

11. □ + 9 = 13   13 − □ = 4   12. 9 + 4 = □   □ − 4 = 9

18

13. $5 + 8 = \square$

14. $13 - 8 = \square$

15. $8 + \square = 13$

16. $13 - 5 = \square$

17. $9 + 7 = \square$

18. $16 - \square = 9$

19. $\square + 9 = 16$

20. $\square - 9 = 7$

21. $9 + \square = 14$

22. $\square - 5 = 9$

23. $5 + 9 = \square$

24. $14 - \square = 5$

25. $\square + 8 = 10$

26. $\square - 8 = 2$

27. $8 + \square = 10$

28. $10 - \square = 8$

29. $9 + \square = 14$

30. $14 - \square = 9$

31. $5 + 9 = \square$

32. $\square - 9 = 5$

33. $8 + 7 = \square$

34. $\square - 7 = 8$

35. $\square + 8 = 15$

36. $15 - 8 = \square$

37. The sum of two numbers is 8. One of the numbers is 0. Find the other number.

38. The sum of two numbers is 12. One of the numbers is 3. Find the other number.

39. When you subtract this number from 9 you get 1. Find the number.

40. When you subtract 6 from this number you get 8. Find the number.

41. These numbers are in a family. Write four sentences with the numbers. 5, 7, 12

Who Am I?

1. I'm the smallest number in my family. The other two are 11 and 6.

2. I'm the largest number in my family. The other two are 4 and 9.

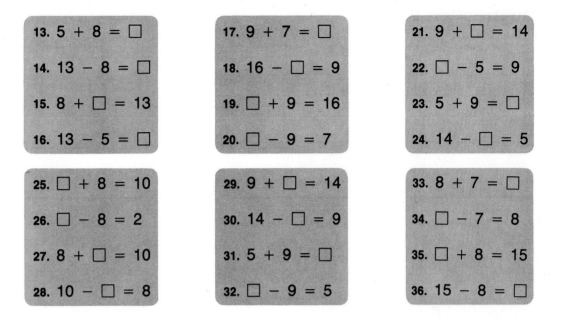

Subtraction Facts

Dom had 14 buttons. He gave 6 buttons to his sister. How many did he have left?

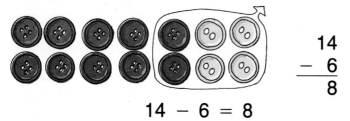

$$14 - 6 = 8$$

$$\begin{array}{r} 14 \\ -\ 6 \\ \hline 8 \end{array}$$

He had 8 buttons left.

Subtract enough to make 10. Then subtract the rest.

Exercises

1. $10 - 2 = \square$ 2. $12 - 4 = \square$ 3. $12 - 2 = \square$

4. $13 - 5 = \square$ 5. $11 - 5 = \square$ 6. $11 - 3 = \square$

7. $13 - 3 = \square$ 8. $15 - 6 = \square$ 9. $13 - 5 = \square$

10. $\begin{array}{r} 12 \\ -\ 5 \\ \hline \end{array}$
11. $\begin{array}{r} 11 \\ -\ 4 \\ \hline \end{array}$
12. $\begin{array}{r} 11 \\ -\ 8 \\ \hline \end{array}$
13. $\begin{array}{r} 12 \\ -\ 7 \\ \hline \end{array}$
14. $\begin{array}{r} 10 \\ -\ 3 \\ \hline \end{array}$
15. $\begin{array}{r} 14 \\ -\ 7 \\ \hline \end{array}$

16. $\begin{array}{r} 11 \\ -\ 6 \\ \hline \end{array}$
17. $\begin{array}{r} 13 \\ -\ 8 \\ \hline \end{array}$
18. $\begin{array}{r} 16 \\ -\ 6 \\ \hline \end{array}$
19. $\begin{array}{r} 15 \\ -\ 7 \\ \hline \end{array}$
20. $\begin{array}{r} 12 \\ -\ 3 \\ \hline \end{array}$
21. $\begin{array}{r} 13 \\ -\ 6 \\ \hline \end{array}$

| 22. | 15
 − 5 | 23. | 14
 − 4 | 24. | 13
 − 7 | 25. | 13
 − 9 | 26. | 10
 − 1 | 27. | 18
 − 8 |

22. 15 − 5 **23.** 14 − 4 **24.** 13 − 7 **25.** 13 − 9 **26.** 10 − 1 **27.** 18 − 8

28. 17 − 8 **29.** 11 − 9 **30.** 14 − 8 **31.** 16 − 9 **32.** 17 − 7 **33.** 12 − 8

34. 15 − 9 **35.** 16 − 8 **36.** 18 − 9 **37.** 16 − 7 **38.** 17 − 9 **39.** 19 − 9

40. How much farther does the car have to go?

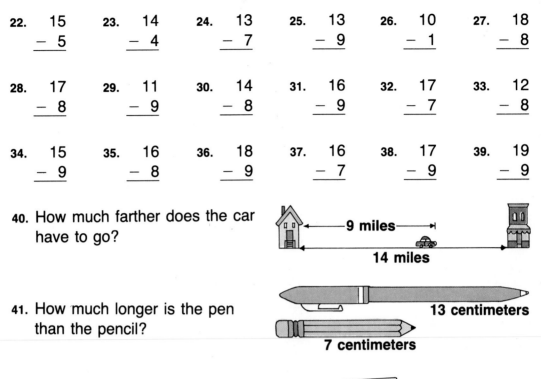

9 miles

14 miles

41. How much longer is the pen than the pencil?

13 centimeters

7 centimeters

42. You buy the ball. How much change should you get?

8¢

43. You are holding 17¢. 9¢ is in one hand. How much is in the other hand?

44. Jamie counted 15 stars. Gwen counted 8 stars. How many more did Jamie count?

Who Am I?

1. Subtract 8 from me. You get 8.

2. Subtract me from 13. You get 13.

3. Subtract me from 14. You get me back again.

4. Subtract 6 from me. Then add 2. You get 8.

Using Numbers

6 beads were on a string.

4 fell off.

3 were put back on.

How many are on the string now?

Do what is in the ( ) first.

$(6 - 4) + 3 = \square$

$(6 - 4) + 3$

$2 + 3$

5

Ed Hoppe Photography

Exercises

Find each result.

1. $(5 + 2) - 4$

___ $- 4$

___

2. $(9 - 6) + 5$

___ $+ 5$

___

3. $(3 + 4) - 4$

___ $- 4$

___

4. $(4 - 3) + 6$

___ $+ 6$

___

5. $(2 + 6) - 7$

___ $- 7$

___

6. $(9 - 7) + 4$

___ $+ 4$

___

7. $(8 - 6) + 6 = \square$

8. $(5 + 4) - 9 = \square$

9. $(7 - 3) + 5 = \square$

10. $(5 + 3) - 6 = \square$

11. $(4 + 2) - 1 = \square$

12. $(9 - 4) + 2 = \square$

13. $(6 - 3) + 4 = \square$

14. $(1 + 6) - 5 = \square$

15. $(2 + 7) - 6 = \square$

16. $(8 - 4) + 3 = \square$

17. 3 owls sat in a tree. 5 more came. Then 6 went away. How many are in the tree now?

18. 8 kites were flying. 3 came down. Then 2 went back up. How many kites are flying?

19. 2 ants came out. 7 more came out. 4 went back in. How many are out now?

20. How many runs do the Sox need to tie the score?

21. Leona brought 8 records. Joy brought 7 records. They played 6 of them. How many were not played?

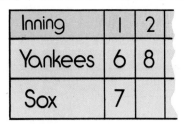

Inning	1	2
Yankees	6	8
Sox	7	

Bookworms

Warren read 5 books. Willa read 3 books.

Could they do this with

8 different books?

only 7 different books?

only 6 different books?

only 5 different books?

Solving Problems

The first team to score 15 points wins.

1. How many more points have the Rockets scored than the Jets?

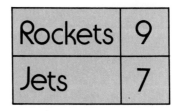

Rockets	9
Jets	7

2. How many more points do the Rockets need to win?

3. How many more points do the Jets need to win?

4. How many points have been scored in all?

5. 14 players are on the Jets. 4 of them did not play today. How many did play today?

6. So far the Rockets have played 15 games and won 6 of them. How many have they lost?

Artstreet

7. 9 children were playing. 6 of them went home. Then 4 more came to play. How many children are there now?

8. 4 children were playing. 5 more came to play. Then 4 went home. How many children are there now?

Addition-Subtraction Practice

Add.

1. 6 +3	**2.** 1 +7	**3.** 4 +5	**4.** 5 +5	**5.** 2 +7	**6.** 9 +1
7. 7 +6	**8.** 8 +7	**9.** 9 +5	**10.** 4 +9	**11.** 6 +8	**12.** 9 +9
13. 6 2 +1	**14.** 8 2 +6	**15.** 4 5 +5	**16.** 7 3 +4	**17.** 9 6 +4	**18.** 7 1 +9

Subtract.

19. 6 −4	**20.** 5 −5	**21.** 7 −6	**22.** 8 −3	**23.** 9 −2	**24.** 9 −7
25. 11 − 3	**26.** 14 − 7	**27.** 12 − 6	**28.** 13 − 9	**29.** 15 − 5	**30.** 11 − 6
31. 12 − 8	**32.** 14 − 6	**33.** 16 − 9	**34.** 13 − 7	**35.** 18 − 8	**36.** 15 − 8
37. 19 − 9	**38.** 17 − 8	**39.** 16 − 7	**40.** 15 − 7	**41.** 14 − 8	**42.** 18 − 9

Find each result.

43. $(6 + 2) - 8 = \square$

44. $(9 - 7) + 5 = \square$

More or Less

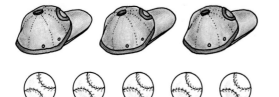 

Are there less caps or baseballs?

3 is less than 5.

3 < 5

Are there more gloves or bats?

3 is more than 2.

3 > 2

< points to the smaller number. So does >.

Exercises

Write < or > for each ●.

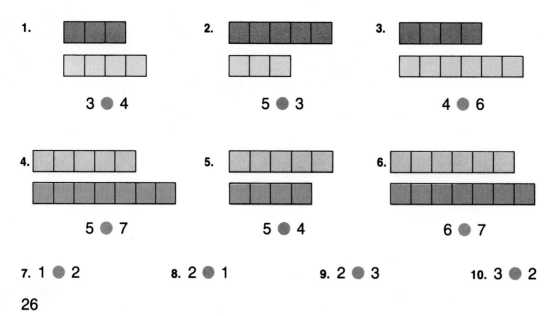

1. 3 ● 4

2. 5 ● 3

3. 4 ● 6

4. 5 ● 7

5. 5 ● 4

6. 6 ● 7

7. 1 ● 2

8. 2 ● 1

9. 2 ● 3

10. 3 ● 2

26

11. 3 ● 5   12. 8 ● 5   13. 5 ● 1   14. 6 ● 9

15. 7 ● 4   16. 2 ● 6   17. 3 ● 4   18. 8 ● 7

19. 0 ● 9   20. 6 ● 8   21. 9 ● 7   22. 12 ● 8

23. 13 ● 6   24. 10 ● 0   25. 5 ● 17   26. 16 ● 9

27. Who has more, Mr. Red or Mr. Blue?

28. Which book has fewer pages, *Cats* or *Dogs?*

29. Which costs more, a lemon or a lime?

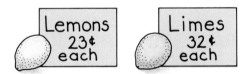

30. A car is going 18 miles an hour. Is it going too fast?

31. Ricky is 12 years old. Should he buy an adult ticket or a student ticket?

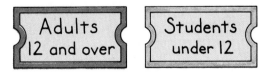

32. 7 is how much less than 13?

33. 19 is how much more than 9?

CHAPTER REVIEW

Add.

1. 3 + 7 = ___

2. 8 + 0 = ___

3. 9 + 3 = ___

4. $\begin{array}{r} 8 \\ +6 \\ \hline \end{array}$

5. $\begin{array}{r} 7 \\ +9 \\ \hline \end{array}$

6. $\begin{array}{r} 9 \\ +9 \\ \hline \end{array}$

7. $\begin{array}{r} 4 \\ 3 \\ +2 \\ \hline \end{array}$

8. $\begin{array}{r} 4 \\ 5 \\ +4 \\ \hline \end{array}$

9. $\begin{array}{r} 6 \\ 3 \\ +5 \\ \hline \end{array}$

Write a numeral for each □.

10. 8 + 9 = □

11. 17 − □ = 8

12. □ + 8 = 17

13. □ − 8 = 9

14. I read 8 pages yesterday and 5 pages today. How many pages did I read?

15. 14 fish are in a bowl. 7 of them are guppies. How many are not guppies?

Subtract.

16. 7 − 0 = ___

17. 9 − 4 = ___

18. 12 − 4 = ___

19. $\begin{array}{r} 13 \\ -\ 7 \\ \hline \end{array}$

20. $\begin{array}{r} 16 \\ -\ 8 \\ \hline \end{array}$

21. $\begin{array}{r} 10 \\ -\ 3 \\ \hline \end{array}$

22. $\begin{array}{r} 18 \\ -\ 8 \\ \hline \end{array}$

23. $\begin{array}{r} 16 \\ -\ 9 \\ \hline \end{array}$

24. $\begin{array}{r} 18 \\ -\ 9 \\ \hline \end{array}$

Find each result.

25. (9 − 2) + 6 = □

26. (8 + 1) − 6 = □

Write < or > for each ●.

27. 7 ● 4

28. 0 ● 3

29. 6 ● 16

30. 10 ● 1

2 Numeration

Joe Outland

Ordinals

Numbers can tell order.

A   B   C   D   E   F   G   H   I   J

first   second   third   fourth   fifth   sixth   seventh   eighth   ninth   tenth

Exercises

1. The rabbit is ___.

2. The cat is ___.

3. The dog is ___.

4. The ___ is fifth.

5. The ___ is seventh.

A blue whale is the largest animal that ever lived.

As you read the sentence, tell which word is

6. third

7. second

8. seventh

9. sixth

10. eighth

11. tenth

12. fifth

13. ninth

14. fourth

30

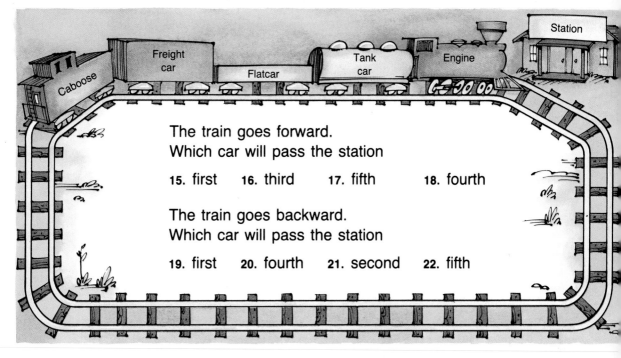

The train goes forward.
Which car will pass the station

15. first   **16.** third   **17.** fifth   **18.** fourth

The train goes backward.
Which car will pass the station

19. first   **20.** fourth   **21.** second   **22.** fifth

Math Contest

Pupil	Points	Place
Mark	38	second
23. Diane	42	
24. Bob	27	
25. Tom	35	

Sunday is the first day of the week.

26. Which day is second?

27. Which day is fourth?

28. Which day is seventh?

29. Which day is Tuesday?

Biggest Ocean

CLUES: P __ __ __ __ __ __

The fourth and sixth letters are *I*.
The third and seventh letters are *C*.
The second letter is the first letter in *AND*.
The fifth letter is the sixth letter in the alphabet.

Extra Practice—Set A, page 298   **31**

Tens and Ones (11–39)

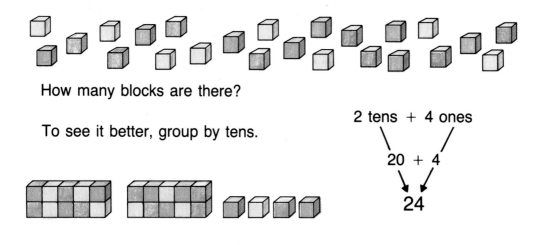

How many blocks are there?

To see it better, group by tens.

2 tens + 4 ones

20 + 4

24

Exercises

Write a numeral for each ___.

1.

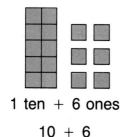

1 ten + 6 ones

10 + 6

———

2.

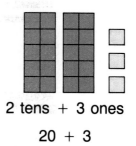

2 tens + 3 ones

20 + 3

———

3.

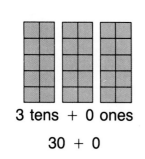

3 tens + 0 ones

30 + 0

———

4.

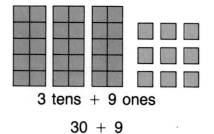

3 tens + 9 ones

30 + 9

———

5. twelve = 10 + 2 = ___

6. fifteen = 10 + 5 = ___

7. seventeen = 10 + 7 = ___

8. eighteen = 10 + 8 = ___

9. twenty = 20 + 0 = ___

10. thirty = 30 + 0 = ___

11. twenty-one = 20 + 1 = ___

12. thirty-one = 30 + 1 = ___

13. twenty-two = 20 + 2 = ___

14. thirty-two = 30 + 2 = ___

15. twenty-three = 20 + 3 = ___

16. thirty-three = 30 + 3 = ___

17. twenty-four = 20 + 4 = ___

18. thirty-four = 30 + 4 = ___

19. twenty-five = 20 + 5 = ___

20. thirty-five = 30 + 5 = ___

21. twenty-six = 20 + 6 = ___

22. thirty-six = 30 + 6 = ___

23. twenty-seven = 20 + 7 = ___

24. thirty-seven = 30 + 7 = ___

25. twenty-eight = 20 + 8 = ___

26. thirty-eight = 30 + 8 = ___

27. twenty-nine = 20 + 9 = ___

28. thirty-nine = 30 + 9 = ___

What Is Covered?

1. 25, 26, [ ] 28

2. 37, 36, 35, [ ]

3. 10, 15, [ ] 25

4. 35, 30, 25, [ ]

5. 5, [ ] 25, 35

6. 30, 20, [ ] 0

Tens and Ones (40–99)

5 tens + 3 ones

50 + 3

53

Exercises

Write a numeral for each ___.

1.

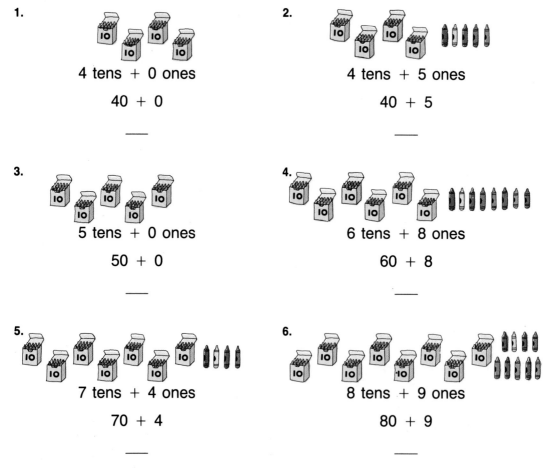

4 tens + 0 ones

40 + 0

___

2.

4 tens + 5 ones

40 + 5

___

3.

5 tens + 0 ones

50 + 0

___

4.

6 tens + 8 ones

60 + 8

___

5.

7 tens + 4 ones

70 + 4

___

6.

8 tens + 9 ones

80 + 9

___

7. forty = 40 + 0 = ___

8. fifty = 50 + 0 = ___

9. sixty = 60 + 0 = ___

10. seventy = 70 + 0 = ___

11. eighty = 80 + 0 = ___

12. ninety = 90 + 0 = ___

13. forty-seven = 40 + 7 = ___

14. forty-nine = 40 + 9 = ___

15. fifty-one = 50 + 1 = ___

16. sixty-six = 60 + 6 = ___

17. fifty-seven = 50 + 7 = ___

18. seventy-three = 70 + 3 = ___

19. sixty-two = 60 + 2 = ___

20. fifty-nine = 50 + 9 = ___

21. seventy-five = 70 + 5 = ___

22. eighty-three = 80 + 3 = ___

23. sixty-seven = 60 + 7 = ___

24. seventy-six = 70 + 6 = ___

25. ninety-one = 90 + 1 = ___

26. eighty-five = 80 + 5 = ___

27. ninety-five = 90 + 5 = ___

28. seventy-nine = 70 + 9 = ___

29. eighty-seven = 80 + 7 = ___

30. ninety-nine = 90 + 9 = ___

Who Am I?

1. My digits are 5 and 4.
I come before 50.

2. My digits are 5 and 8.
I come after 60.

3. One of my digits is 0.
I'm between 70 and 90.

4. I come after 88.
My two digits are the same.

Extra Practice—Set B, page 298

Order

Going across (→) shows counting by ones.

Going down (↓) shows counting by tens.

0	1	2	3	4	5	6	7	8	9
10	11	12	13	14	15	16	17	18	19
20	21	22	23	24	25	26	27	28	29
30	31	32	33	34	35	36	37	38	39
40	41	42	43	44	45	46	47	48	49
50	51	52	53	54	55	56	57	58	59
60	61	62	63	64	65	66	67	68	69
70	71	72	73	74	75	76	77	78	79
80	81	82	83	84	85	86	87	88	89
90	91	92	93	94	95	96	97	98	99

32 is **1** less than 33.
33 is **1** more than 32.

61 is **10** less than 71.
71 is **10** more than 61.

Exercises

Find the number that is

1. 1 more than 17

2. 1 more than 44

3. 1 more than 59

4. 1 less than 26

5. 1 less than 79

6. 1 less than 70

7. 10 more than 50   **8.** 10 more than 33   **9.** 10 more than 69

10. 10 less than 41   **11.** 10 less than 99   **12.** 10 less than 76

13. 2 more than 68   **14.** 2 less than 71   **15.** 20 more than 9

Write all numerals from the chart that have

16. 2 in the ones place   **17.** 0 in the ones place

18. 5 in the ones place   **19.** 9 in the ones place

20. 1 in the tens place   **21.** 5 in the tens place

22. 6 in the tens place   **23.** 8 in the tens place

Write < or > for each ⬤.

24. 11 ⬤ 19   **25.** 30 ⬤ 20   **26.** 50 ⬤ 57   **27.** 16 ⬤ 24

28. 31 ⬤ 13   **29.** 70 ⬤ 48   **30.** 44 ⬤ 55   **31.** 39 ⬤ 40

32. 58 ⬤ 62   **33.** 82 ⬤ 91   **34.** 73 ⬤ 69   **35.** 95 ⬤ 86

Complete.

36. 19, 20, 21, ___, ___, ___   **37.** 26, 27, ___, 29, ___, ___

38. 43, 42, 41, ___, ___, ___   **39.** 50, 52, 54, ___, ___, ___

40. 64, 66, ___, ___, 72, ___   **41.** 76, 74, 72, ___, ___, ___

42. 41, 43, ___, 47, ___, ___   **43.** 87, 85, ___, 81, ___, ___

44. 50, 55, 60, ___, ___, ___   **45.** 85, 80, ___, ___, 65, ___

46. 40, 50, ___, ___, 80, ___   **47.** 54, ___, ___, ___, 14, 4

Hundreds, Tens, and Ones

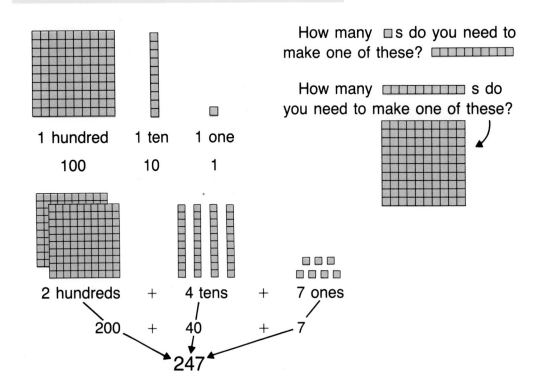

How many ▫s do you need to make one of these? ▭

How many ▭s do you need to make one of these?

1 hundred   1 ten   1 one

100   10   1

2 hundreds   +   4 tens   +   7 ones

200   +   40   +   7

247

Exercises

Write a numeral for each ___.

1. 2 hundreds + 5 tens + 6 ones

      200 + 50 + 6

      ___

2. 3 hundreds + 7 tens + 9 ones

      300 + 70 + 9

      ___

Read each numeral.
Then give the place value of the colored digit.

3. 568

4. 931

5. 807

6. 900

7. 830

8. 777

9. 530

10. 206

Write the numeral.

11. 4 hundreds + 5 tens + 8 ones

12. 400 + 50 + 8

13. 5 hundreds + 6 tens + 3 ones

14. 500 + 60 + 3

15. 5 hundreds + 8 tens + 0 ones

16. 500 + 80 + 0

17. 8 hundreds + 0 tens + 2 ones

18. 800 + 2

19. 200 + 60 + 7

20. 300 + 40 + 1

21. 100 + 90 + 8

22. 800 + 80 + 8

23. 700 + 50 + 1

24. 900 + 20 + 2

25. 900 + 70

26. 500 + 3

27. 600 + 6

28. 300 + 50

29. 400 + 40

30. 800 + 1

31. What number is 10 more than 687?

32. What number is 100 more than 805?

< or >?

1. 123 ● 321

2. 604 ● 406

3. 570 ● 750

4. 299 ● 300

5. 350 ● 349

6. 889 ● 880

Thousands

	9 ones
+	1 one
	10 ones
	or
	1 ten

	T	O
		9
+		1
	1	0

	9 tens
+	1 ten
	10 tens
	or
	1 hundred

	H	T	O
		9	0
+		1	0
	1	0	0

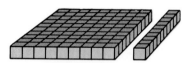

	9 hundreds
+	1 hundred
	10 hundreds
	or
	1 thousand

	Th	H	T	O
		9	0	0
+		1	0	0
	1	0	0	0

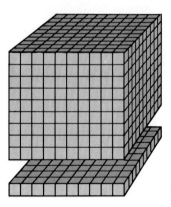

Th	H	T	O	
1	0	0	3	*one thousand three*
1	0	2	0	*one thousand twenty*
1	7	0	0	*one thousand seven hundred*
1	4	5	1	*one thousand four hundred fifty-one*

40

Exercises

Read each numeral.
Then give the place value of the colored digit.

1. 1006
2. 1039
3. 1269
4. 1804

5. 1010
6. 1367
7. 1200
8. 1111

9. 1670
10. 1070
11. 1088
12. 1007

Add.

13.
$$\begin{array}{r} 4 \\ +6 \\ \hline \end{array}$$

14.
$$\begin{array}{r} 4 \text{ tens} \\ +6 \text{ tens} \\ \hline \end{array}$$

15.
$$\begin{array}{r} 40 \\ +60 \\ \hline \end{array}$$

16.
$$\begin{array}{r} 4 \text{ hundreds} \\ +6 \text{ hundreds} \\ \hline \end{array}$$

17.
$$\begin{array}{r} 400 \\ +600 \\ \hline \end{array}$$

18.
$$\begin{array}{r} 3 \\ +7 \\ \hline \end{array}$$

19.
$$\begin{array}{r} 3 \text{ tens} \\ +7 \text{ tens} \\ \hline \end{array}$$

20.
$$\begin{array}{r} 30 \\ +70 \\ \hline \end{array}$$

21.
$$\begin{array}{r} 3 \text{ hundreds} \\ +7 \text{ hundreds} \\ \hline \end{array}$$

22.
$$\begin{array}{r} 300 \\ +700 \\ \hline \end{array}$$

23.
$$\begin{array}{r} 8 \\ +2 \\ \hline \end{array}$$

24.
$$\begin{array}{r} 80 \\ +20 \\ \hline \end{array}$$

25.
$$\begin{array}{r} 800 \\ +200 \\ \hline \end{array}$$

26.
$$\begin{array}{r} 7 \\ +3 \\ \hline \end{array}$$

27.
$$\begin{array}{r} 70 \\ +30 \\ \hline \end{array}$$

28.
$$\begin{array}{r} 700 \\ +300 \\ \hline \end{array}$$

29.
$$\begin{array}{r} 6 \\ +4 \\ \hline \end{array}$$

30.
$$\begin{array}{r} 60 \\ +40 \\ \hline \end{array}$$

31.
$$\begin{array}{r} 600 \\ +400 \\ \hline \end{array}$$

32.
$$\begin{array}{r} 5 \\ +5 \\ \hline \end{array}$$

33.
$$\begin{array}{r} 50 \\ +50 \\ \hline \end{array}$$

34.
$$\begin{array}{r} 500 \\ +500 \\ \hline \end{array}$$

35.
$$\begin{array}{r} 2 \\ +8 \\ \hline \end{array}$$

36.
$$\begin{array}{r} 20 \\ +80 \\ \hline \end{array}$$

37.
$$\begin{array}{r} 200 \\ +800 \\ \hline \end{array}$$

38.
$$\begin{array}{r} 1 \\ +9 \\ \hline \end{array}$$

39.
$$\begin{array}{r} 10 \\ +90 \\ \hline \end{array}$$

40.
$$\begin{array}{r} 100 \\ +900 \\ \hline \end{array}$$

41.
$$\begin{array}{r} 4 \\ +6 \\ \hline \end{array}$$

42.
$$\begin{array}{r} 40 \\ +60 \\ \hline \end{array}$$

43.
$$\begin{array}{r} 400 \\ +600 \\ \hline \end{array}$$

44.
$$\begin{array}{r} 9 \\ +1 \\ \hline \end{array}$$

45.
$$\begin{array}{r} 90 \\ +10 \\ \hline \end{array}$$

46.
$$\begin{array}{r} 900 \\ +100 \\ \hline \end{array}$$

Larger Numbers

This picture was taken at Lake Itasca in Minnesota.

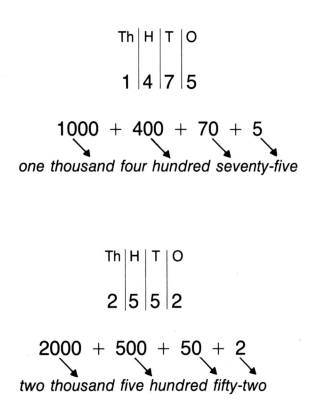

Th	H	T	O
1	4	7	5

1000 + 400 + 70 + 5

one thousand four hundred seventy-five

Th	H	T	O
2	5	5	2

2000 + 500 + 50 + 2

two thousand five hundred fifty-two

Artstreet

Exercises

Read each numeral.
Give the place value of the colored digit.

1. 2834

2. 4570

3. 6300

4. 9876

5. 5027

6. 3050

7. 7003

8. 4444

42

Write the numeral.

9. 2000 + 300 + 40 + 5

10. 3000 + 500 + 60 + 1

11. 4000 + 200 + 70

12. 5000 + 50 + 5

13. 6000 + 700 + 8

14. 8000 + 200 + 30 + 7

15. 7000 + 90

16. 2000 + 80 + 5

17. 4000 + 600

18. 6000 + 6

19. 3000 + 300 + 30

20. 8000 + 10

21. six thousand forty-nine

22. four thousand six hundred fifty

23. nine thousand three

24. five thousand ninety

25. seven thousand eight

26. three thousand two hundred

27. one thousand four hundred twenty-one

28. eight thousand seven hundred five

29. six thousand six hundred sixteen

What number is

30. 1 more than 99

31. 1 more than 999

32. 1 more than 9999

Who Am I?

1. 3▪▪▪

Three of my digits are erased. I am as close to 3000 as I am to 4000.

2. 3▪▪▪

Three of my digits are erased. I am as close to 3000 as I am to 3100.

Dimes and Pennies

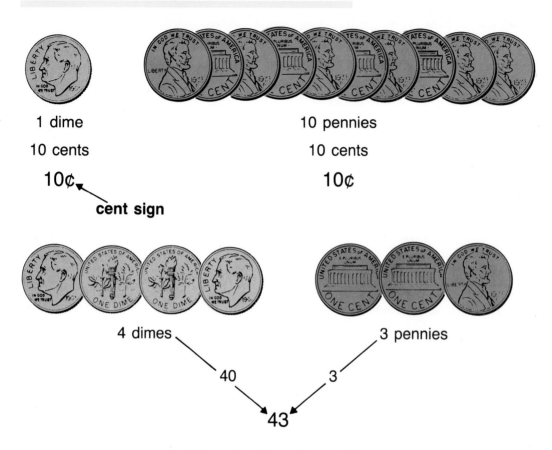

1 dime	10 pennies
10 cents	10 cents
10¢	10¢

cent sign

4 dimes

3 pennies

40

3

43

There is *43 cents* or *43¢.*

Exercises

Complete.

1. 5 dimes and 7 pennies = 50 + 7 or ___¢

2. 7 dimes and 2 pennies = 70 + 2 or ___¢

3. 9 dimes and 6 pennies = 90 + 6 or ___¢

4. 8 dimes and 1 penny = 80 + 1 or ___¢

5. 4 dimes and 9 pennies = 40 + ___ or ___¢

6. 3 dimes and 7 pennies = ___ + 7 or ___¢

7. 8 dimes and 6 pennies = ___ + ___ or ___¢

8. 9 dimes and 9 pennies = ___ + ___ or ___¢

Complete.

	Dimes	Pennies	Total value			Dimes	Pennies	Total value
	3	8	38¢	**12.**	8	1	
9.	2	6		**13.**	7	0	
10.	4	2		**14.**	6	6	
11.	5	8		**15.**	0	9	

Which is worth more,

16. 3 dimes *or*
26 pennies

17. 5 dimes *or*
40 pennies

18. 7 dimes *or*
75 pennies

19. 8 dimes *or*
83 pennies

20. 6 dimes *or*
59 pennies

21. 9 dimes *or*
99 pennies

How to Pay?

You could pay for
a can of corn with
no dimes and 35 pennies.

Find three other ways
to pay for the corn.

Dimes	Pennies
0	35

Dollars, Dimes, and Pennies

1 dollar

100 cents

$1

dollar sign

10 dimes

100 cents

$1

How many dimes can you get for 1 dollar?

How many pennies can you get for 1 dime?

How many pennies can you get for 1 dollar?

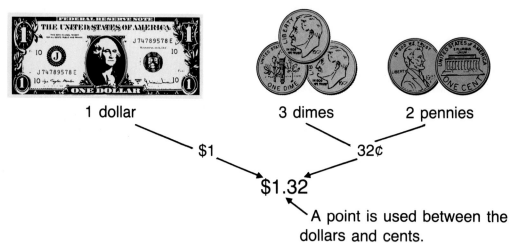

1 dollar   3 dimes   2 pennies

$1   32¢

$1.32

A point is used between the dollars and cents.

$1.32 is read *one dollar and thirty-two cents.*

$2.40 is read *two dollars and forty cents.*

$3.05 is read *three dollars and five cents.*

$0.79 is read *seventy-nine cents.*

Exercises

Use a $ and . to write the value.

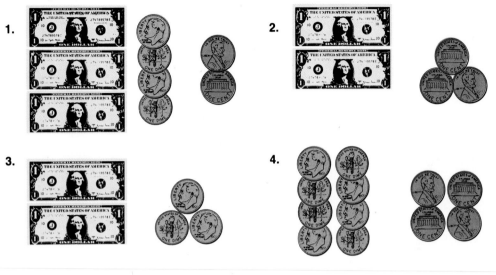

1.

2.

3.

4.

5. 1 dollar, 4 dimes, 8 pennies

6. 1 dollar, 3 dimes

7. 7 dollars, 6 dimes, 9 pennies

8. 2 dollars, 6 pennies

9. 9 dollars, 9 dimes, 9 pennies

10. 4 dimes, 3 pennies

11. 4 dollars, 1 penny

12. 8 dollars, 9 dimes

13. 7 dimes

14. 5 pennies

15. 1 dollar and 43 cents

16. 2 dollars and 59 cents

17. 4 dollars and 60 cents

18. 3 dollars and 7 cents

19. 8 dollars and 2 cents

20. 56 cents

21. 1 dollar, 10 pennies

22. 10 dimes, 5 pennies

23. 1 dollar, 100 pennies

24. 1 dollar, 10 dimes

25. 1 dollar, 10 dimes, 100 pennies

26. 10 dimes, 10 pennies

Counting Money

Kim brought in her penny bank. There were 254 pennies.

Kim wants the most dollars she can get. From what is left, she wants the most dimes. The rest will be pennies.

How many dollars?

How many dimes?

How many pennies?

Pennies	Dollars	Dimes	Pennies
254	2	5	4

Kim changed her mind. Now she wants the most dimes and the rest in pennies.

How many dimes?   How many pennies?

Exercises

Find the most dollars. From what is left, find the most dimes. The rest will be pennies.

	Pennies	Dollars	Dimes	Pennies
1.	371			
2.	160			
3.	208			

Find the most dimes. The rest will be pennies.

	Pennies	Dimes	Pennies
4.	469		
5.	888		
6.	700		

Find the most *hundreds.* From what is left, find the most *tens.* The rest will be *ones.*

	Number	Hundreds	Tens	Ones
7.	316			
8.	209			
9.	140			
10.	72			
11.	521			
12.	600			
13.	444			

Find the most *tens.* The rest will be *ones.*

	Number	Tens	Ones
14.	153		
15.	300		
16.	210		
17.	87		
18.	605		
19.	9		
20.	333		

21. 396 pennies is almost ___ dollars.

22. 88 pennies is almost ___ dimes.

23. You have 689 pennies. Is that enough to buy a toy that sells for 7 dollars?

24. You have 28 dimes. Is that enough to buy a toy that sells for 2 dollars?

25. You have 1 dollar, 8 dimes, and 9 pennies. Do you have enough to buy a toy that costs 1 dollar and 95 cents?

26. You have 64 dimes and 8 pennies. Do you have enough to buy a toy that costs 5 dollars and 99 cents?

27. Who has more money, Jack or Mary?

28. Who has more money, Jack or Don?

Pupil	Money
Jack	3 dollars, 5 dimes, 7 pennies
Mary	34 dimes, 9 pennies
Don	356 pennies

Solving Problems

Use only dimes and pennies in problems 1–8.

1. You have 60 pennies.
   Trade them for dimes.
   How many dimes will you get?

2. You have 8 dimes.
   Trade them for pennies.
   How many pennies will you get?

3. You have 56¢.
   There are 6 pennies.
   How many dimes do you have?

4. You have 77¢.
   There are 17 pennies.
   How many dimes do you have?

5. You have 68¢.
   There are 6 dimes.
   How many pennies do you have?

6. You have 93¢.
   There are 7 dimes.
   How many pennies do you have?

7. Max has 8 coins. He has as many dimes as pennies. How much money does he have?

8. You have 5 coins. There is 1 more dime than pennies. How much money do you have?

9. Kevin has $1.49. Gene has 15 dimes. Who has more money? How much more?

10. Emily has 10 dimes. Sherry has 110 pennies. Who has more money? How much more?

11. You could buy the puppet with *no* dollars and *23* dimes. Find two other ways to buy it using only dollars and dimes.

12. You could buy the puppet with *no* dollars and *230* pennies. Find two other ways to buy it using only dollars and pennies.

$2.30

50

Add.

1. 4 +4	**2.** 8 +0	**3.** 1 +7	**4.** 5 +5	**5.** 4 +7	**6.** 6 +6
7. 8 +7	**8.** 5 +9	**9.** 4 +8	**10.** 9 +9	**11.** 7 +6	**12.** 9 +8
13. 3 3 +3	**14.** 5 2 +3	**15.** 6 4 +5	**16.** 4 5 +5	**17.** 6 3 +6	**18.** 5 1 +8

Subtract.

19. 9 −6	**20.** 10 − 7	**21.** 8 −0	**22.** 9 −1	**23.** 13 − 9	**24.** 15 − 8
25. 14 − 7	**26.** 17 − 8	**27.** 16 − 9	**28.** 19 − 9	**29.** 15 − 6	**30.** 13 − 6

31. Find the cost of both toy horses.

32. How much more does the brown horse cost than the other horse?

Write < or > for each ●.

33. 9 ● 6   **34.** 14 ● 4   **35.** 0 ● 5   **36.** 1 ● 0

51

CHAPTER REVIEW

1. Name the sixth letter in this word.   AMERICA

Write the numeral.

2. 30 + 8

3. 800 + 90 + 1

4. 500 + 5

5. 1000 + 100 + 20 + 6

6. 3000 + 800 + 90

7. 4000 + 50 + 8

8. 8000 + 900

9. 6000 + 6

Complete.

10. 26, 27, 28, ___, ___, ___

11. 35, 33, 31, ___, ___, ___

Use a ¢ to write the value.

12. 8 dimes and 4 pennies

13. 6 dimes and 5 pennies

Use a $ and . to write the value.

14. 3 dollars, 5 dimes, 2 pennies

15. 5 dollars, 6 dimes

16. 1 dollar and 59 cents

17. 6 dollars and 9 cents

Find the most dollars. From what is left, find the most dimes. The rest will be pennies.

Find the most dimes. The rest will be pennies.

Pennies	Dollars	Dimes	Pennies
18. 199			
19. 803			

Pennies	Dimes	Pennies
20. 86		
21. 720		

3 Addition and Subtraction

E. Johnson/Photri

Adding 10's

Mary Elenz Tranter

Exercises

1. $\begin{array}{r} 1 \text{ ten} \\ +2 \text{ tens} \\ \hline \text{tens} \end{array}$ $\begin{array}{r} 1\,0 \\ +2\,0 \\ \hline 0 \end{array}$

2. $\begin{array}{r} 2 \text{ tens} \\ +6 \text{ tens} \\ \hline \end{array}$ $\begin{array}{r} 20 \\ +60 \\ \hline \end{array}$

3. $\begin{array}{r} 6 \text{ tens} \\ +4 \text{ tens} \\ \hline \end{array}$ $\begin{array}{r} 60 \\ +40 \\ \hline \end{array}$

4. $\begin{array}{r} 10 \\ +10 \\ \hline \end{array}$

5. $\begin{array}{r} 20 \\ +40 \\ \hline \end{array}$

6. $\begin{array}{r} 30 \\ +50 \\ \hline \end{array}$

7. $\begin{array}{r} 20 \\ +20 \\ \hline \end{array}$

8. $\begin{array}{r} 10 \\ +40 \\ \hline \end{array}$

9. $\begin{array}{r} 30 \\ +30 \\ \hline \end{array}$

10. $\begin{array}{r} 20 \\ +50 \\ \hline \end{array}$

11. $\begin{array}{r} 30 \\ +10 \\ \hline \end{array}$

12. $\begin{array}{r} 60 \\ +30 \\ \hline \end{array}$

13. $\begin{array}{r} 20 \\ +70 \\ \hline \end{array}$

14. $\begin{array}{r} 50 \\ +10 \\ \hline \end{array}$

15. $\begin{array}{r} 60 \\ +10 \\ \hline \end{array}$

16. $\begin{array}{r} 10 \\ +30 \\ \hline \end{array}$

17. $\begin{array}{r} 20 \\ +10 \\ \hline \end{array}$

18. $\begin{array}{r} 10 \\ +70 \\ \hline \end{array}$

19. $\begin{array}{r} 40 \\ +30 \\ \hline \end{array}$

20. $\begin{array}{r} 40 \\ +10 \\ \hline \end{array}$

21. $\begin{array}{r} 50 \\ +20 \\ \hline \end{array}$

22. $\begin{array}{r} 40 \\ +60 \\ \hline \end{array}$

23. $\begin{array}{r} 20 \\ +30 \\ \hline \end{array}$

24. $\begin{array}{r} 80 \\ +20 \\ \hline \end{array}$

25. $\begin{array}{r} 70 \\ +20 \\ \hline \end{array}$

26. $\begin{array}{r} 30 \\ +40 \\ \hline \end{array}$

27. $\begin{array}{r} 10 \\ +50 \\ \hline \end{array}$

28. 60 +20	29. 10 +80	30. 30 +20	31. 40 +50	32. 10 +90	33. 40 +20
34. 70 +10	35. 30 +70	36. 70 +30	37. 30 +60	38. 50 +30	39. 50 +40
40. 40 +40	41. 50 +50	42. 80 +10	43. 90 +10	44. 10 +60	45. 20 +80

46. April has 30 days. June has 30 days. How many days are in both months?

47. Eli scored 50 points. Sid scored 40 points more than that. How many points did Sid score?

48. 20 50 +20	49. 30 30 +30	50. 60 30 +10	51. 50 10 +40	52. 20 30 +40	53. 80 10 +10

What Animal?

Add. Use the code to name the animal.

1. 30 +30	2. 60 +20	3. 70 +10
4. 20 +20	5. 50 +50	6. 40 +20
7. 10 +40	8. 60 +30	9. 30 +40

40	50	60	70	80	90	100
I	T	A	R	L	O	G

Addition

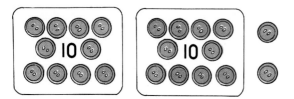 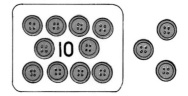

How many purple buttons?   How many orange buttons?

To find how many in all, you could do this.

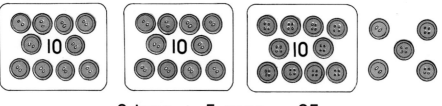

3 tens + 5 ones = 35

To find how many in all, you could add the numbers.

Add the ones.

```
  T | O
  2 | 2
+ 1 | 3
  ‾‾‾|‾5
```

Add the tens.

```
  T | O
  2 | 2
+ 1 | 3
  3 | 5
```

How would you find each sum?

82	60	56	24	91
+17	+28	+30	+ 5	+ 8

56

Exercises

1. 18 +31	2. 22 +24	3. 27 +52	4. 21 +11	5. 44 +14	6. 12 + 6
7. 61 +36	8. 70 +18	9. 17 + 2	10. 36 +42	11. 23 + 6	12. 33 +35
13. 42 + 3	14. 76 +23	15. 89 +10	16. 51 + 8	17. 41 +25	18. 61 + 1
19. 47 +30	20. 44 + 4	21. 82 +17	22. 53 +36	23. 61 + 7	24. 30 + 9
25. 41 +27	26. 40 +55	27. 83 + 6	28. 45 +54	29. 61 + 8	30. 90 + 0

31. There are 15 boys in class.
There are 14 girls.
How many pupils are in class?

32. We went 52 miles Saturday.
We went 36 miles Sunday.
How many miles did we go?

33. How far is it from Roscoe to Belden to Condo?

Condo

Roscoe

Belden

40 miles

49 miles

What Is Missing?

1. 1 3 + ▓ 1 7	2. 1 2 + ▓ 2 6 4	3. ▓ 3 + 2 6 4 ▓	4. 2 ▓ + 1 1 ▓ 3	5. 7 ▓ + ▓ 3 8 5

Extra Practice—Set A, page 300

Addition (with renaming)

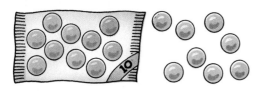

How many green marbles?　　　How many orange marbles?

To find how many in all, you could do this.

Make another bag of 10.

3 tens and 2

32

To find how many in all, you could add the numbers.

Add the ones.　　　　　**Add the tens.**

	T	O
	1	
	1	8
+	1	4
		2

+	8
+	4
1	2

	T	O
	1	
	1	8
+	1	4
	3	2

Exercises

1.　　26
　　+38

2.　　18
　　+55

3.　　76
　　+16

4.　　37
　　+46

5.　　59
　　+28

6.　　35
　　+ 5

7.　　35
　　+38

8.　　15
　　+66

9.　　62
　　+ 9

10.　27
　　+57

11.　21
　　+ 9

12.　38
　　+16

58

13. 42 +38	14. 39 +29	15. 49 + 6	16. 28 + 8	17. 47 +49	18. 19 + 1
19. 68 + 2	20. 38 +54	21. 27 + 4	22. 45 +49	23. 56 + 7	24. 36 + 5
25. 47 + 5	26. 79 +15	27. 74 + 9	28. 58 + 7	29. 27 +48	30. 83 + 8
31. 56 +39	32. 35 + 7	33. 53 + 9	34. 19 +77	35. 44 + 8	36. 88 + 9

37. Jose had 46 balloons.
Maria gave him 7 more.
How many does he have now?

38. Sadie picked 38 apples.
Sam picked 24 more than that.
How many apples did Sam pick?

Find the cost.

39.

40.

41.

42.

43.

44.

45.

46.

Subtracting 10's

You have this much money.

You spend this much. ─────▶

How many cents do you have left?

$$
\begin{array}{r}
6\ \text{tens} \\
-4\ \text{tens} \\
\hline
2\ \text{tens}
\end{array}
\qquad
\begin{array}{r}
6\ 0 \\
-4\ 0 \\
\hline
2\ 0
\end{array}
$$
You have 20¢ left.

Exercises

1.
$$
\begin{array}{r}
8\ \text{tens} \\
-4\ \text{tens} \\
\hline
\ \text{tens}
\end{array}
\quad
\begin{array}{r}
8\ 0 \\
-4\ 0 \\
\hline
\ 0
\end{array}
$$

2.
$$
\begin{array}{r}
7\ \text{tens} \\
-6\ \text{tens} \\
\hline
\end{array}
\quad
\begin{array}{r}
70 \\
-60 \\
\hline
\end{array}
$$

3.
$$
\begin{array}{r}
6\ \text{tens} \\
-3\ \text{tens} \\
\hline
\end{array}
\quad
\begin{array}{r}
60 \\
-30 \\
\hline
\end{array}
$$

4.
$$
\begin{array}{r}
50 \\
-20 \\
\hline
\end{array}
$$

5.
$$
\begin{array}{r}
40 \\
-20 \\
\hline
\end{array}
$$

6.
$$
\begin{array}{r}
50 \\
-10 \\
\hline
\end{array}
$$

7.
$$
\begin{array}{r}
40 \\
-10 \\
\hline
\end{array}
$$

8.
$$
\begin{array}{r}
70 \\
-50 \\
\hline
\end{array}
$$

9.
$$
\begin{array}{r}
10 \\
-10 \\
\hline
\end{array}
$$

10.
$$
\begin{array}{r}
90 \\
-10 \\
\hline
\end{array}
$$

11.
$$
\begin{array}{r}
60 \\
-40 \\
\hline
\end{array}
$$

12.
$$
\begin{array}{r}
50 \\
-30 \\
\hline
\end{array}
$$

13.
$$
\begin{array}{r}
40 \\
-30 \\
\hline
\end{array}
$$

14.
$$
\begin{array}{r}
30 \\
-10 \\
\hline
\end{array}
$$

15.
$$
\begin{array}{r}
60 \\
-10 \\
\hline
\end{array}
$$

16.
$$
\begin{array}{r}
80 \\
-20 \\
\hline
\end{array}
$$

17.
$$
\begin{array}{r}
90 \\
-70 \\
\hline
\end{array}
$$

18.
$$
\begin{array}{r}
30 \\
-20 \\
\hline
\end{array}
$$

19.
$$
\begin{array}{r}
20 \\
-10 \\
\hline
\end{array}
$$

20.
$$
\begin{array}{r}
70 \\
-30 \\
\hline
\end{array}
$$

21.
$$
\begin{array}{r}
90 \\
-50 \\
\hline
\end{array}
$$

22.
$$
\begin{array}{r}
90 \\
-60 \\
\hline
\end{array}
$$

23.
$$
\begin{array}{r}
80 \\
-50 \\
\hline
\end{array}
$$

24.
$$
\begin{array}{r}
60 \\
-20 \\
\hline
\end{array}
$$

25.
$$
\begin{array}{r}
80 \\
-30 \\
\hline
\end{array}
$$

26.
$$
\begin{array}{r}
50 \\
-40 \\
\hline
\end{array}
$$

27.
$$
\begin{array}{r}
70 \\
-70 \\
\hline
\end{array}
$$

28. 90	29. 70	30. 60	31. 90	32. 80	33. 70
−30	−40	−50	−20	−10	−10

34. 90	35. 80	36. 90	37. 80	38. 70	39. 90
−40	−60	−80	−70	−20	−90

Speed of Animals in Miles per Hour

70   40   50   30   10

How much faster can

40. a bear run than a chicken

41. a lion run than a zebra

42. a zebra run than a bear

How much slower does

43. a chicken run than a lion

44. a chicken run than a cheetah

45. a lion run than a cheetah

---

46. François had 60 newspapers. He sold 20. How many did he have left?

47. 80 scouts were on a hike. 10 went home. How many were still hiking?

48. Carol wants to save $80. She has saved $30 so far. How much more does she need?

49. A teacher graded 40 papers. There are 70 papers in all. How many more papers must be graded?

50. You buy the two items. You give the clerk 50¢. How much change should you get?

61

Subtraction

You have this much money.

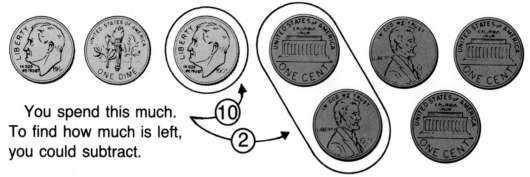

You spend this much.
To find how much is left,
you could subtract.

Subtract the ones.			Subtract the tens.	
T	O		T	O
3	5		**3**	5
−1	2		**−1**	2
	3		**2**	3

23¢ is left.

How would you do each subtraction?

58	82	75	85	66
−31	−80	−25	− 1	− 6

Exercises

1. 69	2. 39	3. 78	4. 46	5. 36	6. 64
−32	−23	−54	−16	− 5	−53

7. 87	8. 47	9. 15	10. 35	11. 43	12. 74
−44	− 3	−14	− 5	−22	−52

13. 18	14. 57	15. 43	16. 56	17. 16	18. 73
$\underline{-\ 6}$	$\underline{-45}$	$\underline{-20}$	$\underline{-\ 4}$	$\underline{-\ 5}$	$\underline{-41}$

19. 26	20. 69	21. 88	22. 29	23. 95	24. 48
$\underline{-23}$	$\underline{-\ 1}$	$\underline{-\ 2}$	$\underline{-15}$	$\underline{-42}$	$\underline{-\ 7}$

25. 81	26. 49	27. 46	28. 57	29. 98	30. 97
$\underline{-81}$	$\underline{-\ 6}$	$\underline{-42}$	$\underline{-\ 2}$	$\underline{-\ 7}$	$\underline{-76}$

31. 93	32. 75	33. 96	34. 97	35. 78	36. 64
$\underline{-\ 3}$	$\underline{-15}$	$\underline{-\ 4}$	$\underline{-50}$	$\underline{-33}$	$\underline{-\ 1}$

37. 89	38. 76	39. 59	40. 37	41. 97	42. 79
$\underline{-53}$	$\underline{-61}$	$\underline{-\ 6}$	$\underline{-\ 7}$	$\underline{-97}$	$\underline{-\ 8}$

43. 35 pupils were in a class. 2 pupils moved away. How many are in the class now?

44. 48 apples came in a box. 26 have been eaten. How many are left?

45. You are 8 years old. Your sister is 19. How much younger are you?

46. You gave the clerk 75¢. You got back 13¢ change. How much did you spend?

Subtraction Check

Do $\quad$ 27
$\quad\quad \underline{-\ 3}$
$\quad\quad$ 24 $\quad$ Same
Undo $\quad \underline{+\ 3}$
$\quad\quad$ 27

1. 8 6	2. 5 4	3. 6 9	4. 7 5
$\underline{-\ \ \ 1}$	$\underline{-\ \ \ 2}$	$\underline{-\ 3\ 2}$	$\underline{-\ 5\ 4}$
■ ■	■ ■	■ ■	■ ■
$\underline{+\ \ \ 1}$	$\underline{+\ \ \ 2}$	$\underline{+\ 3\ 2}$	$\underline{+\ 5\ 4}$
■ ■	■ ■	■ ■	■ ■

SKILLS REVIEW

Subtract.

1. 10
  − 8
	2. 12
	  − 6
		3. 11
		  − 5
			4. 17
			  − 7
				5. 14
				  − 6
					6. 15
					  − 7

7. 13
  − 5
	8. 11
	  − 7
		9. 14
		  − 8
			10. 16
			  − 8
				11. 15
				  − 9
					12. 18
					  − 9

Write the following in this word: PRESIDENT

13. fourth letter   14. sixth letter   15. ninth letter

Write the numeral.

16. 20 + 6   17. 40 + 5

18. 200 + 10 + 7   19. 300 + 50 + 1

20. 100 + 30 + 2   21. 500 + 30 + 8

22. 400 + 70   23. 700 + 9

24. 1000 + 800 + 60 + 3   25. 3000 + 600 + 90 + 4

26. 2000 + 80 + 1   27. 5000 + 100 + 20

Complete.

28. 36, 37, 38, ___, ___, ___   29. 46, 44, 42, ___, ___, ___

30. 15, 20, ___, 30, ___, ___   31. 80, 70, ___, ___, 40, ___

32. 71, ___, ___, 65, ___, 61   33. ___, 34, 44, ___, ___, 74

64

Renaming

Study how you can rename 4 tens and 2 ones as 3 tens and 12 ones.

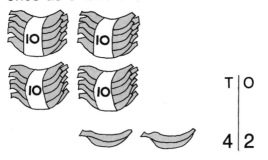

$$\begin{array}{c|c} T & O \\ \hline 4 & 2 \end{array}$$

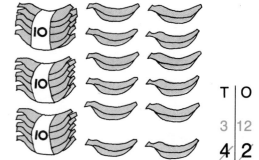

$$\begin{array}{c|c} T & O \\ \hline 3 & 12 \\ \cancel{4} & 2 \end{array}$$

Exercises

Complete.

1. 2 tens, 3 ones = 1 ten, ▨ ones

2. 4 tens, 0 ones = 3 tens, ▨ ones

3. 1 ten, 7 ones = 0 tens, ▨ ones

4. 5 tens, 5 ones = ▨ tens, 15 ones

5. 3 tens, 7 ones = ▨ tens, 17 ones

Rename each number to show 10 more ones.

6. $\begin{array}{c|c} T & O \\ \hline 3 & 0 \end{array}$
7. $\begin{array}{c|c} T & O \\ \hline 5 & 0 \end{array}$
8. $\begin{array}{c|c} T & O \\ \hline 3 & 4 \end{array}$
9. $\begin{array}{c|c} T & O \\ \hline 5 & 6 \end{array}$
10. $\begin{array}{c|c} T & O \\ \hline 6 & 5 \end{array}$

11. $\begin{array}{c|c} T & O \\ \hline 4 & 8 \end{array}$
12. $\begin{array}{c|c} T & O \\ \hline 7 & 7 \end{array}$
13. $\begin{array}{c|c} T & O \\ \hline 8 & 1 \end{array}$
14. $\begin{array}{c|c} T & O \\ \hline 1 & 2 \end{array}$
15. $\begin{array}{c|c} T & O \\ \hline 9 & 3 \end{array}$

65

Subtraction (with renaming)

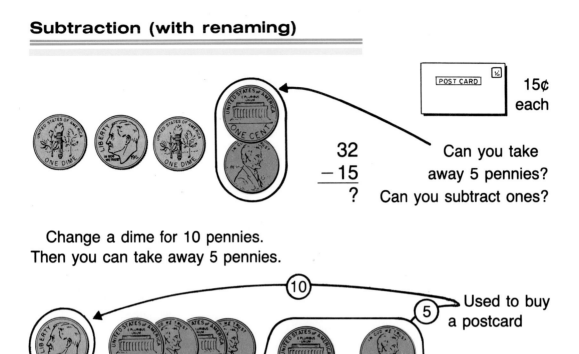

POST CARD

15¢ each

```
  32
- 15
   ?
```

Can you take
away 5 pennies?
Can you subtract ones?

Change a dime for 10 pennies.
Then you can take away 5 pennies.

⑩

⑤ Used to buy
a postcard

How much is left?

In order to subtract ones, rename
3 tens and 2 as **2 tens and 12.**

Rename.	Subtract the ones.	Subtract the tens.

	T	O		T	O		T	O
	2	12		2	12		2	12
	3	2		3	2		3	2
−	1	5	−	1	5	−	1	5
					7		1	7

Exercises

1. 81 −45	2. 37 −19	3. 98 −69	4. 22 − 4	5. 44 −28	6. 23 − 6
7. 76 −37	8. 40 − 5	9. 91 − 9	10. 61 −37	11. 35 −16	12. 42 −18
13. 36 − 9	14. 73 −49	15. 95 −47	16. 22 − 5	17. 61 − 4	18. 50 −23
19. 80 −29	20. 67 −28	21. 70 − 2	22. 94 −39	23. 54 − 7	24. 66 −58

25. In 1777 the United States flag had 13 stars. Today the flag has 50 stars. How many more stars are on the flag today?

26. A toy is marked 82¢. You have only 69¢. How much more do you need?

Whose Flag?

Use the code to name the country.

7	9	15	26	37	48
C	E	I	M	O	X

62	41	80	60	54	93
−36	−32	−32	−45	−47	−56
26					
M					

Artstreet

Extra Practice—Set B, page 301

Problems Without Computation

Dora   Kurt   Dan

Mary Elenz Tranter

1. I am a boy.
   I don't wear glasses.
   Who am I?

2. I am taller than Dan.
   Dora is taller than I.
   Who am I?

3. My name begins with the
   letter *D*. I am not the
   shortest. Who am I?

4. I am not wearing a red shirt.
   I am not the tallest.
   Who am I?

5. My name has four letters.
   I am not the tallest.
   Who am I?

6. Dora is older than Kurt.
   Kurt is older than Dan.
   Who is the oldest?

7. Kurt and Dan go to different schools.
   Dora and Dan go to different schools.
   We go to the same school. Who are we?

68

Answer each question by writing *A, B, C,* or *D.*

8. Help Debbie find her present.
   There is a bow on the box.
   There is ribbon around the box.
   Which present is hers?

9. Help Rich find his present.
   It is not in the largest box.
   The paper is yellow.
   There is ribbon around the box.
   Which present is his?

Some blocks are in each bag.
(Nothing else is in the bags.)

Both sides weigh the same.

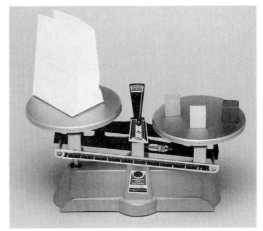

This side weighs more.⬆

10. How many blocks are in the
    bag?

11. How many blocks *could be* in
    the bag?

Solving Problems

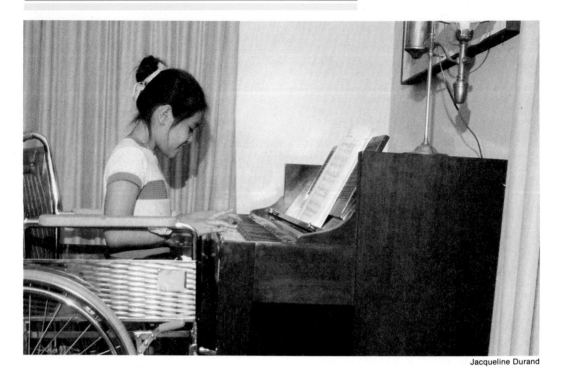

Jacqueline Durand

A piano has 52 white keys and 36 black keys.

How many more white keys are there than black keys?

What numbers?	+ or −?	4 12
		5̶ 2̶
52 and 36	−	−3 6
There are 16 more white keys.		1 6

Exercises

1. How many keys does a piano have in all?

2. Raul practiced 45 minutes and Mae practiced 25 minutes. How much longer did Raul practice?

70

3. Diane found 24 pinecones. Ben found 17. How many were found in all?

4. Len had 75¢. He spent 50¢ for lunch. How much did he have left?

5. 36 pictures can be taken with a roll of film. So far we have taken 18. How many more can we take?

6. The Bulls scored 79 points. The Bucks scored 18 points more than that. How many points did the Bucks score?

7. Gertrude saw 34 red flowers. She saw 19 other flowers. How many did she see in all?

8. We brought 24 hot dogs. We ate 19 of them. How many were left?

9. Rena was 19 inches long when she was born. Since then she has grown 33 inches. How tall is she now?

10. Lois was 18 inches long when she was born. Now she is 55 inches tall. How much has she grown?

Make up a problem for each picture.

11.

12. 54¢ 36¢

13. 9 TOYS 38 TOYS

71

Addition-Subtraction Practice

Add.

1.	36 +23	2.	44 + 5	3.	11 +29	4.	37 +61	5.	14 +78	6.	88 +11
7.	54 +45	8.	60 +20	9.	49 + 8	10.	16 +36	11.	71 +25	12.	39 +39

Subtract.

13.	68 −35	14.	87 − 6	15.	60 −20	16.	51 −23	17.	87 − 8	18.	92 −48
19.	48 −46	20.	55 − 5	21.	73 −37	22.	57 −24	23.	78 −59	24.	45 −37

Add or subtract. Watch the signs!

25.	50 +30	26.	23 +47	27.	32 − 6	28.	42 +16	29.	96 −70	30.	55 + 5
31.	44 −28	32.	60 −38	33.	10 +90	34.	49 − 8	35.	52 + 6	36.	70 −10
37.	80 −80	38.	64 + 7	39.	16 +78	40.	76 −19	41.	84 − 5	42.	32 +29
43.	26 + 3	44.	60 −51	45.	37 +48	46.	77 −53	47.	65 − 9	48.	65 +29

Treasure Hunt

Follow the directions to find the treasure.

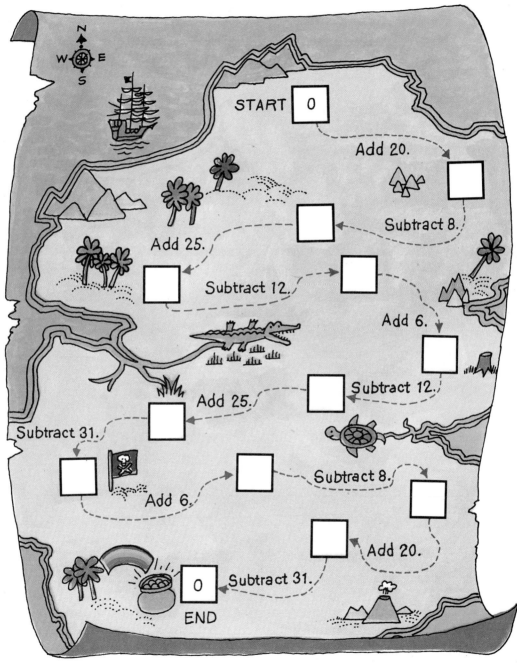

CHAPTER REVIEW

Add.

1. $\begin{array}{r} 30 \\ +40 \\ \hline \end{array}$	2. $\begin{array}{r} 70 \\ +20 \\ \hline \end{array}$	3. $\begin{array}{r} 50 \\ +50 \\ \hline \end{array}$	4. $\begin{array}{r} 60 \\ +39 \\ \hline \end{array}$	5. $\begin{array}{r} 32 \\ +\ 5 \\ \hline \end{array}$	6. $\begin{array}{r} 12 \\ +85 \\ \hline \end{array}$
7. $\begin{array}{r} 46 \\ +\ 3 \\ \hline \end{array}$	8. $\begin{array}{r} 34 \\ +55 \\ \hline \end{array}$	9. $\begin{array}{r} 81 \\ +\ 8 \\ \hline \end{array}$	10. $\begin{array}{r} 25 \\ +15 \\ \hline \end{array}$	11. $\begin{array}{r} 34 \\ +27 \\ \hline \end{array}$	12. $\begin{array}{r} 31 \\ +\ 9 \\ \hline \end{array}$
13. $\begin{array}{r} 47 \\ +47 \\ \hline \end{array}$	14. $\begin{array}{r} 36 \\ +45 \\ \hline \end{array}$	15. $\begin{array}{r} 72 \\ +\ 9 \\ \hline \end{array}$	16. $\begin{array}{r} 53 \\ +27 \\ \hline \end{array}$	17. $\begin{array}{r} 49 \\ +29 \\ \hline \end{array}$	18. $\begin{array}{r} 86 \\ +\ 7 \\ \hline \end{array}$

Subtract.

19. $\begin{array}{r} 50 \\ -30 \\ \hline \end{array}$	20. $\begin{array}{r} 60 \\ -50 \\ \hline \end{array}$	21. $\begin{array}{r} 90 \\ -30 \\ \hline \end{array}$	22. $\begin{array}{r} 64 \\ -23 \\ \hline \end{array}$	23. $\begin{array}{r} 96 \\ -\ 6 \\ \hline \end{array}$	24. $\begin{array}{r} 87 \\ -\ 5 \\ \hline \end{array}$
25. $\begin{array}{r} 59 \\ -30 \\ \hline \end{array}$	26. $\begin{array}{r} 99 \\ -74 \\ \hline \end{array}$	27. $\begin{array}{r} 48 \\ -\ 2 \\ \hline \end{array}$	28. $\begin{array}{r} 43 \\ -16 \\ \hline \end{array}$	29. $\begin{array}{r} 75 \\ -\ 8 \\ \hline \end{array}$	30. $\begin{array}{r} 88 \\ -39 \\ \hline \end{array}$
31. $\begin{array}{r} 91 \\ -12 \\ \hline \end{array}$	32. $\begin{array}{r} 51 \\ -44 \\ \hline \end{array}$	33. $\begin{array}{r} 70 \\ -\ 7 \\ \hline \end{array}$	34. $\begin{array}{r} 62 \\ -33 \\ \hline \end{array}$	35. $\begin{array}{r} 92 \\ -\ 7 \\ \hline \end{array}$	36. $\begin{array}{r} 95 \\ -59 \\ \hline \end{array}$

37. How many points were scored by both teams?

38. How many more points did the Stars score than the Dribbles?

Final Score	
Stars	56
Dribbles	39

4 Multiplication Facts

Grant Heilman

Multiplication

The table is set with 4 items for each doll.

Here are some ways to find the number of items on the table.

Counting   4, 8, 12

Addition $4 + 4 + 4 = 12$

3 fours are 12.

Multiplication $3 \times 4 = 12$

Three times four is equal to twelve.

Exercises

1.

$$2 \quad + \quad 2 \quad + \quad 2 \quad + \quad 2 \quad + \quad 2 \quad = \square$$

$$5 \times 2 = \square$$

76

2.

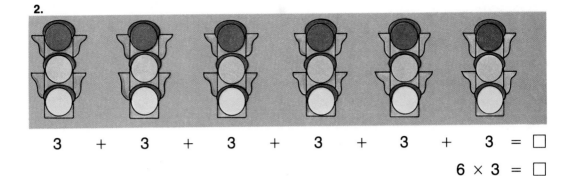

$$3 \; + \; 3 \; + \; 3 \; + \; 3 \; + \; 3 \; + \; 3 \; = \; \square$$

$$6 \times 3 = \square$$

3.

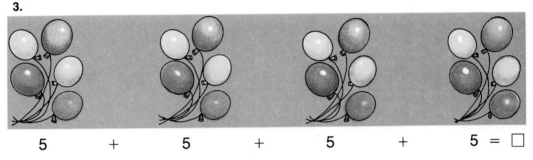

$$5 \; + \; 5 \; + \; 5 \; + \; 5 \; = \; \square$$

$$4 \times 5 = \square$$

4.

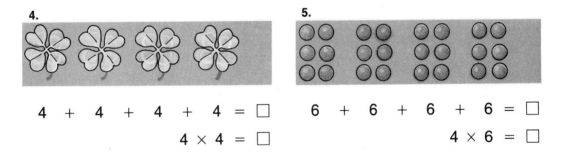

$$4 + 4 + 4 + 4 = \square$$

$$4 \times 4 = \square$$

5.

$$6 + 6 + 6 + 6 = \square$$

$$4 \times 6 = \square$$

6. $2 + 2 + 2 + 2 = \square$

$$4 \times 2 = \square$$

7. $3 + 3 + 3 + 3 = \square$

$$4 \times 3 = \square$$

8. $2 + 2 + 2 + 2 + 2 + 2 = \square$

$$6 \times 2 = \square$$

9. $5 + 5 + 5 = \square$

$$3 \times 5 = \square$$

10. $5 + 5 + 5 + 5 + 5 = \square$

$$5 \times 5 = \square$$

11. $7 + 7 + 7 = \square$

$$3 \times 7 = \square$$

77

Groups of 2 and 3

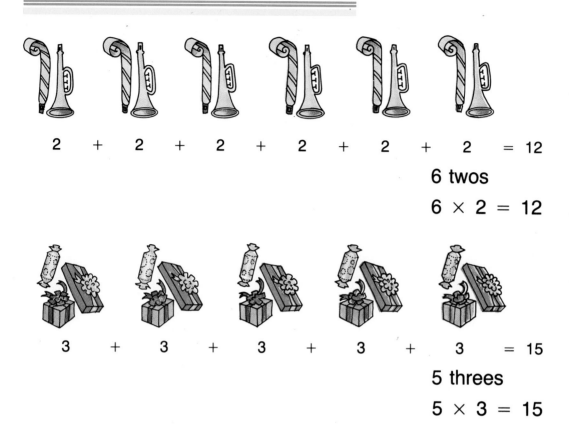

$$2 + 2 + 2 + 2 + 2 + 2 = 12$$

6 twos

$$6 \times 2 = 12$$

$$3 + 3 + 3 + 3 + 3 = 15$$

5 threes

$$5 \times 3 = 15$$

Exercises

1. Count by 2's to 18.

   2, 4, 6, ___, ___, ___, ___, ___, ___

2. Count by 3's to 27.

   3, 6, 9, ___, ___, ___, ___, ___, ___

3. $2 + 2 + 2 + 2 = \square$

4. $4 \times 2 = \square$

5. $2 + 2 + 2 + 2 + 2 = \square$

6. $5 \times 2 = \square$

7. $3 + 3 + 3 + 3 + 3 + 3 = \square$

8. $6 \times 3 = \square$

78

9. 1 × 2 = ☐
10. 2 × 2 = ☐
11. 3 × 2 = ☐
12. 4 × 2 = ☐
13. 5 × 2 = ☐
14. 6 × 2 = ☐
15. 7 × 2 = ☐
16. 8 × 2 = ☐
17. 9 × 2 = ☐

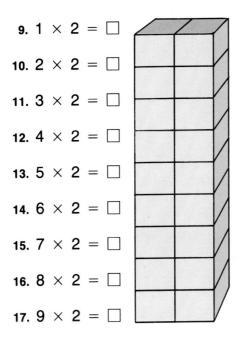

18. 1 × 3 = ☐
19. 2 × 3 = ☐
20. 3 × 3 = ☐
21. 4 × 3 = ☐
22. 5 × 3 = ☐
23. 6 × 3 = ☐
24. 7 × 3 = ☐
25. 8 × 3 = ☐
26. 9 × 3 = ☐

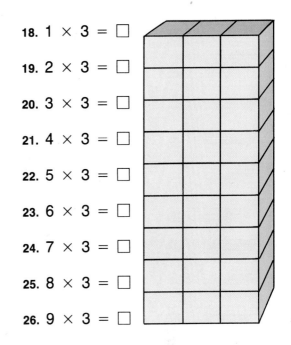

27. There are 2 horses, 2 lions, 2 elephants, 2 monkeys, and 2 ducks in the show. How many animals are there in all?

28. 5 kinds of animals are in the show. There are 2 animals of each kind. How many animals are there in all?

29. There are 8 pairs of shoes. 2 shoes are in each pair. How many shoes are there in all?

30. There are 9 flowers. Each has 3 petals. How many petals are there in all?

31. Find the cost of 6 bows.

32. Find the cost of 7 balloons.

33. Find the cost of 6 bows and 7 balloons.

Groups of 4

5 groups of 4

5 fours

5 × 4 = 20   can be written

$$\begin{array}{r} 4 \\ \times 5 \\ \hline 20 \end{array}$$

Exercises

1. Count by 4's to 36.

    4,   8,   12,   ___,   ___,   ___,   ___,   ___,   ___

   1 × 4   2 × 4   3 × 4   4 × 4   5 × 4   6 × 4   7 × 4   8 × 4   9 × 4

2. 4 + 4 = ☐   3. 4 + 4 + 4 = ☐   4. 4 + 4 + 4 + 4 = ☐

5. 2 × 4 = ☐   6. 3 × 4 = ☐   7. 4 × 4 = ☐

8. 6 × 4 = ☐   9. 7 × 4 = ☐   10. 8 × 4 = ☐

11. 9 × 4 = ☐   12. 1 × 4 = ☐   13. 5 × 4 = ☐

14. 4×1	15. 4×5	16. 4×4	17. 4×9	18. 4×7	19. 4×3

20. 4×2	21. 4×6	22. 4×8	23. 2×6	24. 3×7	25. 3×9

26. Sara, Jane, Al, Judy, and Bob each have 4 cards. How many cards do they have in all?

27. There are 3 players. Each has 4 cards. How many cards do they have in all?

28. There are 8 wagons. Each has 4 wheels. How many wheels are there?

29. Molly scored 7 points. Bill scored 4 times as many points. How many points did Bill score?

30. You walk to school and back twice. How far do you walk?

31. You walk to school and back 5 times. How far do you walk?

Home   2 blocks   School

Odds and Evens

Even numbers

0   2   4   6   8   10   12   14   16   18

1   3   5   7   9   11   13   15   17

Odd numbers

2×1	2×2	2×3	2×4	2×5	2×6	2×7	2×8	2×9

In the multiplication facts for 2, is the answer always an *even number* or an *odd number?*

Groups of 5

3 groups of 5

3 fives

3 × 5 = 15

Exercises

1. Count by 5's to 45.

5,	10,	15,	——,	——,	——,	——,	——,	——
1 × 5	2 × 5	3 × 5	4 × 5	5 × 5	6 × 5	7 × 5	8 × 5	9 × 5

2. 5 + 5 = ☐   3. 5 + 5 + 5 = ☐   4. 5 + 5 + 5 + 5 = ☐

5. 2 × 5 = ☐   6. 3 × 5 = ☐   7. 4 × 5 = ☐

8. 6 × 5 = ☐   9. 7 × 5 = ☐   10. 8 × 5 = ☐

11. 9 × 5 = ☐   12. 5 × 5 = ☐   13. 1 × 5 = ☐

14. 5   15. 5   16. 5   17. 5   18. 5   19. 5
    ×1   ×3   ×2   ×5   ×4   ×7

20. 5   21. 5   22. 5   23. 3   24. 4   25. 4
    ×6   ×9   ×8   ×8   ×9   ×8

26. You bought 8 pencils.
Each cost 5¢.
How much did you spend?

27. 7 boys got tickets.
Each boy got 5 tickets.
How many tickets did they get?

28. 4 girls went to the beach.
Each found 5 shells.
How many shells were found?

29. You trade 5 nickels for
pennies. How many pennies
will you get?

30. Mom made 2 dresses.
She put 5 buttons on each.
How many buttons were used?

31. Jim walked 3 blocks. Beth
walked 5 times that far.
How far did Beth walk?

32. $5 \times 3 = \square$

33. $3 \times 5 = \square$

Are the answers
the same?

34. $4 \times 2 = \square$

35. $2 \times 4 = \square$

Are the answers
the same?

36. $3 \times 4 = \square$

37. $4 \times 3 = \square$

Are the answers
the same?

38. Which way would you multiply 5 and 2?

$5 \times 2 = \square$ or $2 \times 5 = \square$

Are both ways correct?

39. Cards **A** and **F** have the same answer.
Which other pairs of cards have the same answer?

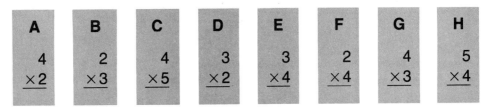

A	B	C	D	E	F	G	H
4 ×2	2 ×3	4 ×5	3 ×2	3 ×4	2 ×4	4 ×3	5 ×4

Groups of 6

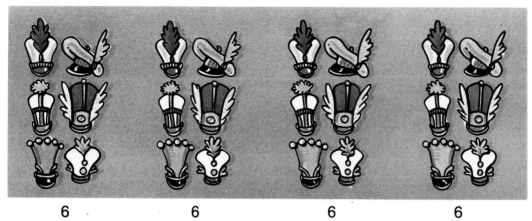

6   6   6   6

$$4 \text{ sixes} \quad \begin{array}{r} 6 \\ \times 4 \\ \hline 24 \end{array}$$

Exercises

1. Count by 6's to 54.

6,   12,   18,   ——,   ——,   ——,   ——,   ——,   ——

1×6 2×6 3×6 4×6 5×6 6×6 7×6 8×6 9×6

2. $2 \times 6 = \square$ **3.** $4 \times 6 = \square$ **4.** $1 \times 6 = \square$

5. $3 \times 6 = \square$ **6.** $6 \times 6 = \square$ **7.** $5 \times 6 = \square$

8. $8 \times 6 = \square$ **9.** $7 \times 6 = \square$ **10.** $9 \times 6 = \square$

11. $\begin{array}{r} 6 \\ \times 1 \\ \hline \end{array}$ **12.** $\begin{array}{r} 6 \\ \times 2 \\ \hline \end{array}$ **13.** $\begin{array}{r} 6 \\ \times 5 \\ \hline \end{array}$ **14.** $\begin{array}{r} 6 \\ \times 6 \\ \hline \end{array}$ **15.** $\begin{array}{r} 6 \\ \times 3 \\ \hline \end{array}$ **16.** $\begin{array}{r} 6 \\ \times 4 \\ \hline \end{array}$

17. $\begin{array}{r} 6 \\ \times 7 \\ \hline \end{array}$ **18.** $\begin{array}{r} 6 \\ \times 9 \\ \hline \end{array}$ **19.** $\begin{array}{r} 6 \\ \times 8 \\ \hline \end{array}$ **20.** $\begin{array}{r} 4 \\ \times 7 \\ \hline \end{array}$ **21.** $\begin{array}{r} 5 \\ \times 8 \\ \hline \end{array}$ **22.** $\begin{array}{r} 5 \\ \times 9 \\ \hline \end{array}$

84

23. Cards **A** and **H** have the same answer.
Which other pairs of cards have the same answer?

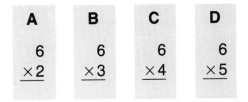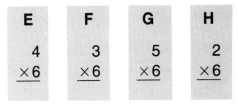

A	B	C	D	E	F	G	H
6	6	6	6	4	3	5	2
×2	×3	×4	×5	×6	×6	×6	×6

24. We have 3 tanks. Each has 6 fish. How many fish are there?

25. She works 6 hours each day. How many hours does she work in 5 days?

26. There are 6 rows of desks. Each row has 6 desks. How many desks are there?

27. There are 9 cartons of eggs. Each has 6 eggs. How many eggs are there?

28. You buy 7 magic rings. Find the total cost.

29. You give the clerk 50¢ for the 7 rings. How much money should you get back?

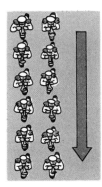

You Lead the Band

Here are two ways a band could march.

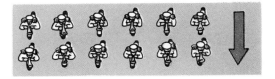

2 × 6 = 12   or   6 × 2 = 12

Draw other ways to march. Use full rows.

Write a multiplication sentence for each.

Groups of 7

There are 7 days in a week.

February						
S	**M**	**T**	**W**	**Th**	**F**	**S**
1	2	3	4	5	6	7
8	9	10	11	12	13	14
15	16	17	18	19	20	21
22	23	24	25	26	27	28

$$\left.\begin{array}{r} 7 \\ 7 \\ 7 \\ 7 \end{array}\right\} \text{4 sevens}$$

$$\begin{array}{r} 7 \\ \times 4 \\ \hline 28 \end{array}$$

Exercises

1. Count by 7's to 63.

   7,   14,   21,   ——,   ——,   ——,   ——,   ——,   ——

   1×7 2×7 3×7 4×7 5×7 6×7 7×7 8×7 9×7

2. $1 \times 7 = \square$ 3. $3 \times 7 = \square$ 4. $2 \times 7 = \square$

5. $4 \times 7 = \square$ 6. $5 \times 7 = \square$ 7. $7 \times 7 = \square$

8. $6 \times 7 = \square$ 9. $9 \times 7 = \square$ 10. $8 \times 7 = \square$

11. $\begin{array}{r} 7 \\ \times 2 \\ \hline \end{array}$ 12. $\begin{array}{r} 7 \\ \times 3 \\ \hline \end{array}$ 13. $\begin{array}{r} 7 \\ \times 1 \\ \hline \end{array}$ 14. $\begin{array}{r} 7 \\ \times 4 \\ \hline \end{array}$ 15. $\begin{array}{r} 7 \\ \times 6 \\ \hline \end{array}$ 16. $\begin{array}{r} 7 \\ \times 8 \\ \hline \end{array}$

17. $\begin{array}{r} 7 \\ \times 5 \\ \hline \end{array}$ 18. $\begin{array}{r} 7 \\ \times 7 \\ \hline \end{array}$ 19. $\begin{array}{r} 7 \\ \times 9 \\ \hline \end{array}$ 20. $\begin{array}{r} 5 \\ \times 7 \\ \hline \end{array}$ 21. $\begin{array}{r} 6 \\ \times 8 \\ \hline \end{array}$ 22. $\begin{array}{r} 6 \\ \times 9 \\ \hline \end{array}$

23. Which pairs of cards have the same answer?

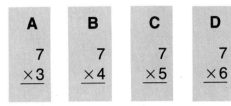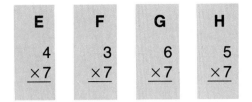

A	B	C	D	E	F	G	H
7 ×3	7 ×4	7 ×5	7 ×6	4 ×7	3 ×7	6 ×7	5 ×7

24. There are 3 pupils.
Each brought 7¢.
How much did they bring?

25. There are 8 pupils.
Each brought 7¢.
How much did they bring?

26. How many days are in 5
weeks?

27. How many days are in 6
weeks?

28. Anne will have her birthday in 7
weeks. How many days is that?

29. Stan will have his birthday in 9
weeks. How many days is that?

30. How many hours did
Mrs. Buff work?

31. How many hours did
Mr. Frost work?

32. How many hours did
Mr. Doe work?

33. How many hours did
Mrs. Buff and Mr.
Frost work?

Work Log

Mrs. Buff	7 hours each day for 4 days
Mr. Frost	7 hours each day for 8 days
Mr. Doe	7 hours each day for 3 days *and* 6 hours each day for 3 days

Who Am I?

1. I am less than 10. Multiply any
whole number and me. The
answer always ends in 5 or 0.

2. Multiply me by myself.
The answer is 1 less
than 50.

Groups of 8

An octopus has 8 arms. How many arms are on 5 octopuses?

5 eights
$$\begin{array}{r} 8 \\ \times\,5 \\ \hline 40 \end{array}$$

There are 40 arms.

Exercises

1. Count by 8's to 72.

8,	16,	24,	——,	——,	——,	——,	——,	——
1 × 8	2 × 8	3 × 8	4 × 8	5 × 8	6 × 8	7 × 8	8 × 8	9 × 8

2. 2 × 8 = ☐   3. 1 × 8 = ☐   4. 5 × 8 = ☐

5. 4 × 8 = ☐   6. 3 × 8 = ☐   7. 6 × 8 = ☐

8. 7 × 8 = ☐   9. 9 × 8 = ☐   10. 8 × 8 = ☐

11. $\begin{array}{r} 8 \\ \times 1 \\ \hline \end{array}$ 12. $\begin{array}{r} 8 \\ \times 2 \\ \hline \end{array}$ 13. $\begin{array}{r} 8 \\ \times 4 \\ \hline \end{array}$ 14. $\begin{array}{r} 8 \\ \times 6 \\ \hline \end{array}$ 15. $\begin{array}{r} 8 \\ \times 3 \\ \hline \end{array}$ 16. $\begin{array}{r} 8 \\ \times 5 \\ \hline \end{array}$

17. $\begin{array}{r} 8 \\ \times 9 \\ \hline \end{array}$ 18. $\begin{array}{r} 8 \\ \times 7 \\ \hline \end{array}$ 19. $\begin{array}{r} 8 \\ \times 8 \\ \hline \end{array}$ 20. $\begin{array}{r} 6 \\ \times 7 \\ \hline \end{array}$ 21. $\begin{array}{r} 7 \\ \times 8 \\ \hline \end{array}$ 22. $\begin{array}{r} 7 \\ \times 9 \\ \hline \end{array}$

23. Which pairs of cards have the same answer?

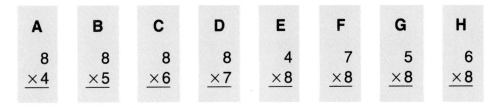

A	B	C	D	E	F	G	H
8 ×4	8 ×5	8 ×6	8 ×7	4 ×8	7 ×8	5 ×8	6 ×8

24. There are 9 octopuses. Each has 8 arms. How many arms are there in all?

25. Joy has $8. Ed has 3 times that much money. How much money does Ed have?

Multiply as shown below.

$4 \times 2 \times 8$

8×8

64

26. $2 \times 2 \times 8$

27. $3 \times 3 \times 8$

28. $2 \times 4 \times 8$

Pairings

Allene has 4 blouses and 3 pairs of jeans. Three possible outfits are shown. (An outfit is a blouse and a pair of jeans.)

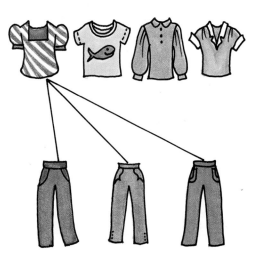

1. How many possible outfits can she make?

2. Allene bought 2 more blouses and 1 more pair of jeans. Now how many possible outfits can she make?

Groups of 9

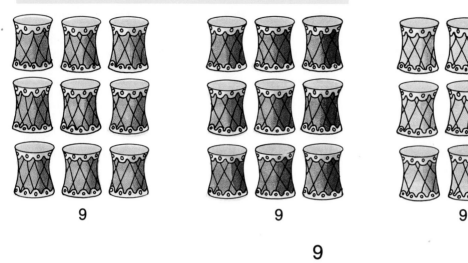

9   9   9

3 nines $\begin{array}{r} 9 \\ \times 3 \\ \hline 27 \end{array}$

Exercises

1. Count by 9's to 81.

9,   18,   27,   ——,   ——,   ——,   ——,   ——,   ——

1×9 2×9 3×9 4×9 5×9 6×9 7×9 8×9 9×9

2. $1 \times 9 = \square$ 3. $2 \times 9 = \square$ 4. $4 \times 9 = \square$

5. $6 \times 9 = \square$ 6. $3 \times 9 = \square$ 7. $5 \times 9 = \square$

8. $9 \times 9 = \square$ 9. $8 \times 9 = \square$ 10. $7 \times 9 = \square$

11. $\begin{array}{r} 9 \\ \times 3 \\ \hline \end{array}$
12. $\begin{array}{r} 9 \\ \times 4 \\ \hline \end{array}$
13. $\begin{array}{r} 9 \\ \times 1 \\ \hline \end{array}$
14. $\begin{array}{r} 9 \\ \times 2 \\ \hline \end{array}$
15. $\begin{array}{r} 9 \\ \times 6 \\ \hline \end{array}$
16. $\begin{array}{r} 9 \\ \times 5 \\ \hline \end{array}$

17. $\begin{array}{r} 9 \\ \times 7 \\ \hline \end{array}$
18. $\begin{array}{r} 9 \\ \times 9 \\ \hline \end{array}$
19. $\begin{array}{r} 9 \\ \times 8 \\ \hline \end{array}$
20. $\begin{array}{r} 7 \\ \times 7 \\ \hline \end{array}$
21. $\begin{array}{r} 8 \\ \times 8 \\ \hline \end{array}$
22. $\begin{array}{r} 8 \\ \times 9 \\ \hline \end{array}$

90

23. Which pairs of cards have the same answer?

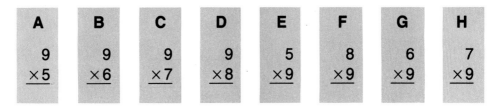

A	B	C	D	E	F	G	H
9	9	9	9	5	8	6	7
×5	×6	×7	×8	×9	×9	×9	×9

Mr. Benny gives 9 violin lessons each day.

24. How many lessons does he give in 2 days?

25. How many lessons does he give in 5 days?

26. How many lessons does he give in 6 days?

Multiply as shown below.

27. $2 \times 2 \times 9$

28. $3 \times 3 \times 9$

29. $4 \times 2 \times 9$

Magic Nine

Multiply. Add the digits of each answer.
What did you discover?

1. $2 \times 9 = 18$ | $1 + 8 = \underline{}$ **5.** $6 \times 9 = \underline{}$ | $\underline{} + \underline{} = \underline{}$

2. $3 \times 9 = \underline{}$ | $2 + \underline{} = 9$ **6.** $7 \times 9 = \underline{}$ | $\underline{} + \underline{} = \underline{}$

3. $4 \times 9 = \underline{}$ | $\underline{} + \underline{} = \underline{}$ **7.** $8 \times 9 = \underline{}$ | $\underline{} + \underline{} = \underline{}$

4. $5 \times 9 = \underline{}$ | $\underline{} + \underline{} = \underline{}$ **8.** $9 \times 9 = \underline{}$ | $\underline{} + \underline{} = \underline{}$

0 and 1 in Multiplication

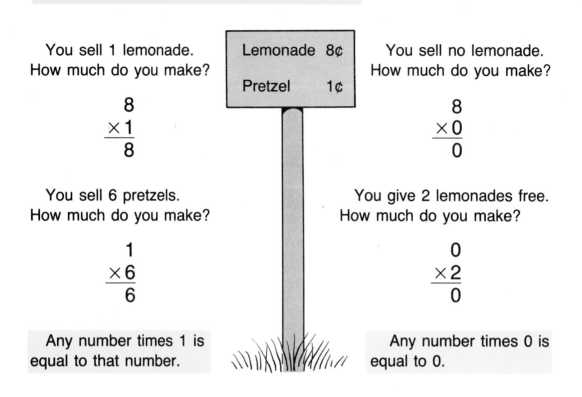

You sell 1 lemonade.
How much do you make?

$$\begin{array}{r} 8 \\ \times 1 \\ \hline 8 \end{array}$$

Lemonade 8¢

Pretzel 1¢

You sell no lemonade.
How much do you make?

$$\begin{array}{r} 8 \\ \times 0 \\ \hline 0 \end{array}$$

You sell 6 pretzels.
How much do you make?

$$\begin{array}{r} 1 \\ \times 6 \\ \hline 6 \end{array}$$

You give 2 lemonades free.
How much do you make?

$$\begin{array}{r} 0 \\ \times 2 \\ \hline 0 \end{array}$$

Any number times 1 is equal to that number.

Any number times 0 is equal to 0.

Exercises

1. $\begin{array}{r} 0 \\ \times 3 \\ \hline \end{array}$
2. $\begin{array}{r} 0 \\ \times 8 \\ \hline \end{array}$
3. $\begin{array}{r} 6 \\ \times 0 \\ \hline \end{array}$
4. $\begin{array}{r} 1 \\ \times 2 \\ \hline \end{array}$
5. $\begin{array}{r} 1 \\ \times 7 \\ \hline \end{array}$
6. $\begin{array}{r} 8 \\ \times 1 \\ \hline \end{array}$

7. $\begin{array}{r} 1 \\ \times 8 \\ \hline \end{array}$
8. $\begin{array}{r} 0 \\ \times 7 \\ \hline \end{array}$
9. $\begin{array}{r} 4 \\ \times 1 \\ \hline \end{array}$
10. $\begin{array}{r} 9 \\ \times 0 \\ \hline \end{array}$
11. $\begin{array}{r} 6 \\ \times 3 \\ \hline \end{array}$
12. $\begin{array}{r} 0 \\ \times 1 \\ \hline \end{array}$

13. $\begin{array}{r} 9 \\ \times 1 \\ \hline \end{array}$
14. $\begin{array}{r} 4 \\ \times 5 \\ \hline \end{array}$
15. $\begin{array}{r} 3 \\ \times 1 \\ \hline \end{array}$
16. $\begin{array}{r} 1 \\ \times 1 \\ \hline \end{array}$
17. $\begin{array}{r} 0 \\ \times 0 \\ \hline \end{array}$
18. $\begin{array}{r} 4 \\ \times 0 \\ \hline \end{array}$

19. $4 \times 2 \times 0 = \square$
20. $5 \times 6 \times 0 = \square$
21. $7 \times 8 \times 1 = \square$

92

Multiplication Practice

×	0	1	2	3	4	5	6	7	8	9
0	0	0	0	0	0	0	0	0	0	0
1	0	1	2	3	4	5	6	7	8	9
2	0	2	4	6	8	10	12	14	16	18
3	0	3	6	9	12	15	18	21	24	27
4	0	4	8	12	16	20	24	28	32	36
5	0	5	10	15	20	25	30	35	40	45
6	0	6	12	18	24	30	36	42	48	54
7	0	7	14	21	28	35	42	49	56	63
8	0	8	16	24	32	40	48	56	64	72
9	0	9	18	27	36	45	54	63	72	81

1. 6
   ×5

2. 6
   ×1

3. 9
   ×5

4. 5
   ×7

5. 5
   ×4

6. 8
   ×6

7. 7
   ×3

8. 9
   ×3

9. 5
   ×5

10. 8
    ×9

11. 7
    ×7

12. 9
    ×6

13. 5
    ×0

14. 6
    ×6

15. 1
    ×8

16. 8
    ×8

17. 4
    ×9

18. 7
    ×8

19. 0
    ×7

20. 4
    ×7

21. 5
    ×9

22. 2
    ×9

23. 8
    ×4

24. 7
    ×6

25. 9
    ×7

26. 9
    ×9

27. There are 4 bags.
    8 oranges are in each.
    How many oranges are there?

28. There are 8 cartons of soap.
    5 boxes are in each.
    How many boxes are there?

Using a Calculator

When you push a key, you tell the calculator what to do.

 ×   = 32

8	×	4	=	32
Start with this number.	Multiply by	this number.	Show the answer.	Answer

What other number key was pushed?

1. 7 × ? = 14

2. 8 × ? = 24

3. 9 × ? = 36

4. 4 × ? = 20

5. 6 × ? = 18

6. 3 × ? = 12

Was ＋ , － , or × pushed?

7. 7 ? 2 = 5

8. 8 ? 6 = 48

9. 9 ? 9 = 18

10. 3 6 ? 3 6 = 0

11. 7 ? 1 = 7

12. 4 5 ? 5 = 50

13. 9 ? 0 = 9

14. 0 ? 0 = 0

94

SKILLS REVIEW

Add.

1. 20 + 6	2. 43 + 5	3. 14 +74	4. 75 +23	5. 81 +12
6. 19 + 5	7. 58 + 6	8. 31 + 9	9. 43 + 8	10. 54 + 9
11. 67 +27	12. 36 +39	13. 22 +48	14. 62 +19	15. 75 +17

16. You had 28 stamps.
You got 3 more.
How many do you have now?

17. You spent 37¢.
You spent 9¢ more.
How much did you spend?

Subtract.

18. 53 − 3	19. 44 − 2	20. 29 −14	21. 36 −25	22. 56 −30
23. 68 − 9	24. 47 − 8	25. 20 − 5	26. 61 − 6	27. 74 − 7
28. 75 −27	29. 81 −68	30. 32 −13	31. 83 −38	32. 92 −49

33. Rosa is 8 years old.
Her father is 36 years old.
How much older is her father?

34. You had 50 cards.
You gave away 37.
How many were left?

CHAPTER REVIEW

1. $3 + 3 + 3 + 3 + 3 = \square$, so $5 \times 3 = \square$.

2. $\begin{array}{r} 2 \\ \times 4 \\ \hline \end{array}$ 3. $\begin{array}{r} 2 \\ \times 8 \\ \hline \end{array}$ 4. $\begin{array}{r} 2 \\ \times 6 \\ \hline \end{array}$ 5. $\begin{array}{r} 3 \\ \times 3 \\ \hline \end{array}$ 6. $\begin{array}{r} 3 \\ \times 9 \\ \hline \end{array}$ 7. $\begin{array}{r} 3 \\ \times 8 \\ \hline \end{array}$

8. $\begin{array}{r} 4 \\ \times 3 \\ \hline \end{array}$ 9. $\begin{array}{r} 4 \\ \times 5 \\ \hline \end{array}$ 10. $\begin{array}{r} 4 \\ \times 8 \\ \hline \end{array}$ 11. $\begin{array}{r} 5 \\ \times 2 \\ \hline \end{array}$ 12. $\begin{array}{r} 5 \\ \times 6 \\ \hline \end{array}$ 13. $\begin{array}{r} 5 \\ \times 8 \\ \hline \end{array}$

14. Mom has 6 boxes. There are 4 tacos in each. How many tacos are there?

15. You trade 9 nickels for pennies. How many pennies will you get?

16. $\begin{array}{r} 6 \\ \times 3 \\ \hline \end{array}$ 17. $\begin{array}{r} 6 \\ \times 8 \\ \hline \end{array}$ 18. $\begin{array}{r} 6 \\ \times 7 \\ \hline \end{array}$ 19. $\begin{array}{r} 7 \\ \times 5 \\ \hline \end{array}$ 20. $\begin{array}{r} 7 \\ \times 7 \\ \hline \end{array}$ 21. $\begin{array}{r} 7 \\ \times 9 \\ \hline \end{array}$

22. $9 \times 6 = \square$ 23. $4 \times 7 = \square$ 24. $8 \times 7 = \square$

25. $\begin{array}{r} 8 \\ \times 2 \\ \hline \end{array}$ 26. $\begin{array}{r} 8 \\ \times 5 \\ \hline \end{array}$ 27. $\begin{array}{r} 8 \\ \times 3 \\ \hline \end{array}$ 28. $\begin{array}{r} 8 \\ \times 8 \\ \hline \end{array}$ 29. $\begin{array}{r} 8 \\ \times 6 \\ \hline \end{array}$ 30. $\begin{array}{r} 8 \\ \times 9 \\ \hline \end{array}$

31. $\begin{array}{r} 9 \\ \times 2 \\ \hline \end{array}$ 32. $\begin{array}{r} 9 \\ \times 4 \\ \hline \end{array}$ 33. $\begin{array}{r} 9 \\ \times 6 \\ \hline \end{array}$ 34. $\begin{array}{r} 9 \\ \times 5 \\ \hline \end{array}$ 35. $\begin{array}{r} 9 \\ \times 8 \\ \hline \end{array}$ 36. $\begin{array}{r} 9 \\ \times 9 \\ \hline \end{array}$

37. A store is open 8 hours a day. How many hours is it open in 7 days?

38. Beth is 9 years old. Mr. Long is 7 times older than Beth. How old is Mr. Long?

39. $\begin{array}{r} 0 \\ \times 2 \\ \hline \end{array}$ 40. $\begin{array}{r} 6 \\ \times 1 \\ \hline \end{array}$ 41. $\begin{array}{r} 0 \\ \times 9 \\ \hline \end{array}$ 42. $\begin{array}{r} 1 \\ \times 3 \\ \hline \end{array}$ 43. $\begin{array}{r} 1 \\ \times 7 \\ \hline \end{array}$ 44. $\begin{array}{r} 8 \\ \times 0 \\ \hline \end{array}$

5 Geometry

Angles

Open a scissors as shown. Trace along the edges. You have drawn an **angle.**

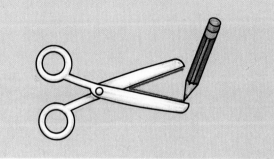

Open the scissors a little more. Trace along the edges again. You have drawn a larger angle.

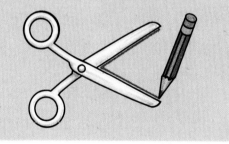

Open the scissors all the way. Trace again. This is a still larger angle.

Tear off the square corner of a card.

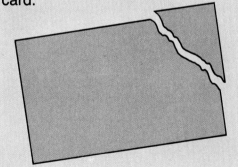

Trace the square corner. You have drawn a **right angle.**

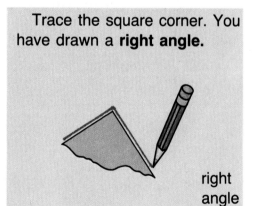

right
angle

Exercises

Use a square corner to check the angle shown
in blue.

Write *R* if it is a right angle.
Write *S* if it is smaller than a right angle.
Write *L* if it is larger than a right angle.

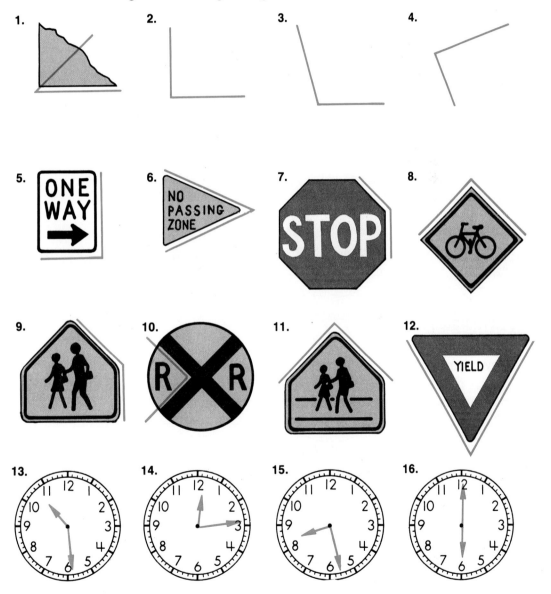

1.

2.

3.

4.

5. ONE WAY

6. NO PASSING ZONE

7. STOP

8.

9.

10. R R

11.

12. YIELD

13.

14.

15.

16.

99

Rectangles

Trace along 1 edge of a box. You have drawn a **line segment.**

Trace along 2 edges that meet at a corner. This is a **right angle.**

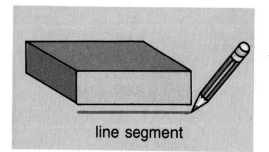

line segment

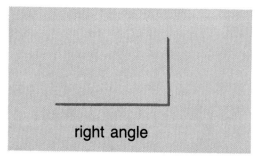

right angle

Trace completely around the bottom. You have drawn a **rectangle.**

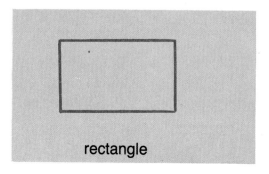

rectangle

Exercises

1. How many sides does a rectangle have?

2. How many right angles does a rectangle have?

Tell why each figure is not a rectangle.

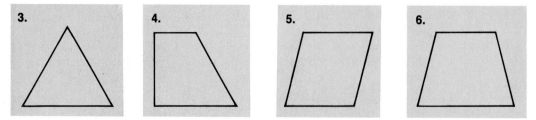

3. 4. 5. 6.

100

Write *Yes* if the picture shows a rectangle.
Write *No* if it does not.

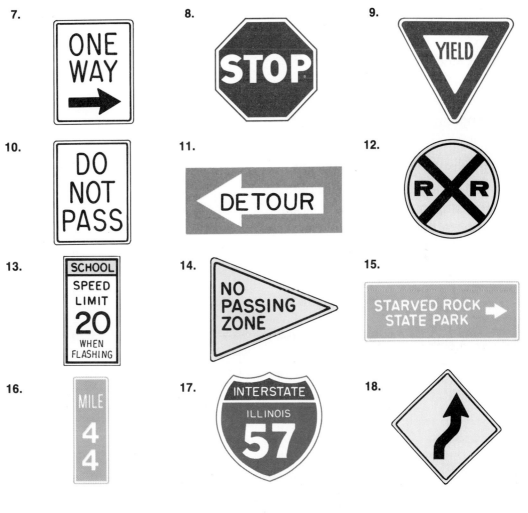

7.

8.

9.

10.

11.

12.

13.

14.

15.

16.

17.

18.

19. How many rectangles are shown in the last figure below?

1 rectangle

3 rectangles

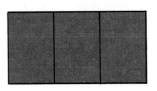

Rectangles and Squares

Use your square corner to check the angles of this rectangle.

What kind of angles are they?

A rectangle has 4 sides and 4 right angles.

Mark the length of one side of this rectangle on a strip of paper. Lay the strip along the other sides to compare their lengths.

What did you discover?

We call this rectangle a **square**.

If all 4 sides of a rectangle have the same length, the rectangle is called a square.

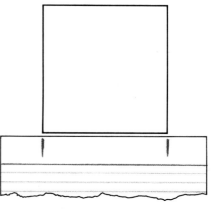

Exercises

Four children were asked to draw rectangles. Check their work. If the figure is not a rectangle, tell why not.

1. Maria drew this.

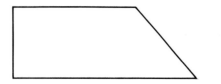

2. Juanita drew this.

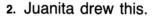

3. Chang drew this.

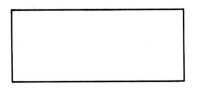

4. Yoko drew this.

5. Which child drew a square?

Write *R* for each rectangle.
Write *S* for each square.
Both letters will be written for some figures.

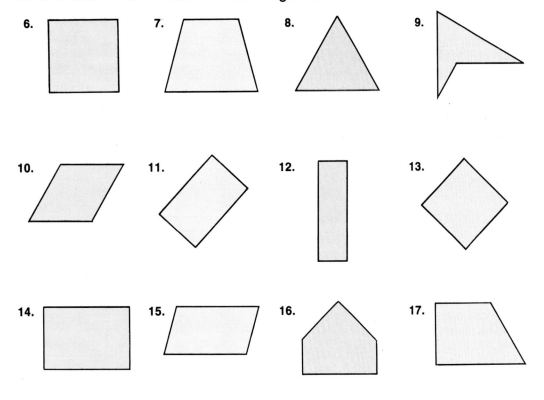

18. Is every square a rectangle?   **19.** Is every rectangle a square?

Circles

Trace around the bottom of a can. You have drawn a **circle.**

Use a strip of paper to mark the distance from the center of the circle to point A.

Compare that with the distance from the center to points B and C.

What did you discover?

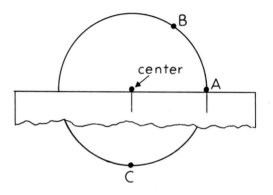

Exercises

Three points are named on each circle.
Compare the distances of these points from the center.

What did you discover?

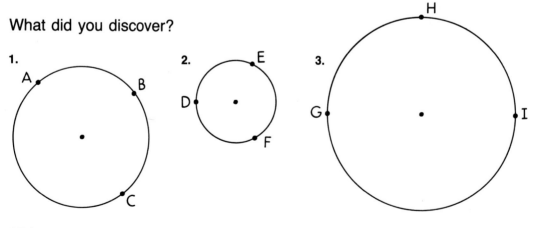

1.

2.

3.

Write *Yes* if the picture shows a circle.
Write *No* if it does not.

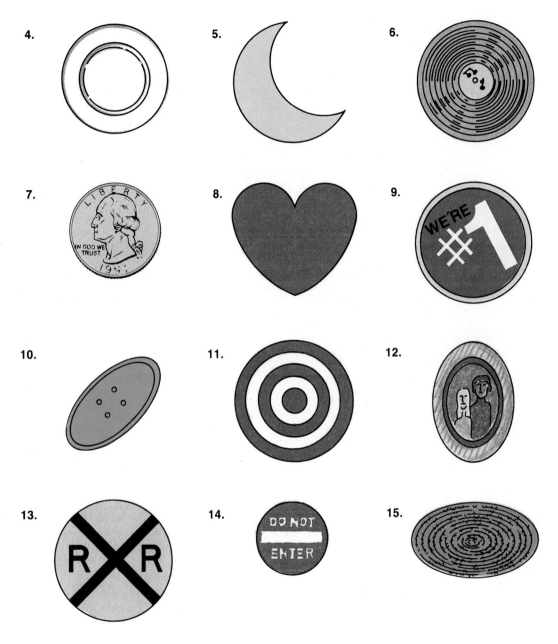

4.

5.

6.

7.

8.

9.

10.

11.

12.

13.

14.

15.

16. How many circles are shown in exercise 11?

Triangles

rectangles	circles	triangles

Exercises

1. How many sides does a triangle have?

2. How many angles does a triangle have?

Tell why each figure is not a triangle.

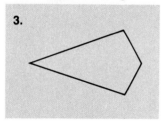

3.

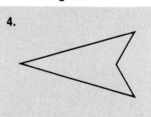

4.

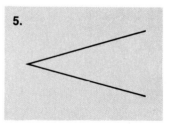

5.

106

Write *Yes* if the picture shows a triangle.
Write *No* if it does not.

6.

7.

8.

9.

10.

11.

12.

13.

14.

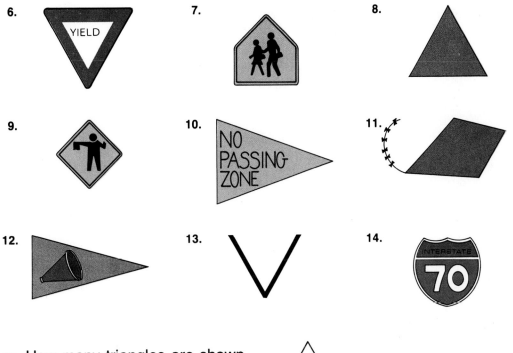

15. How many triangles are shown
    in the figure?

Find the Letters

Tell which letters are

1. inside the rectangle

2. inside the circle

3. inside the triangle

4. inside the rectangle and also inside the circle

5. inside the rectangle and also inside the triangle

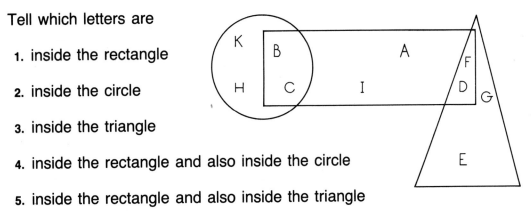

Geometric Shapes

Here are some shapes we see and use.

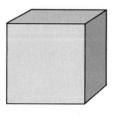   

cube   **cylinder**   **cone**   **sphere**

Exercises

Write the name of each shape.

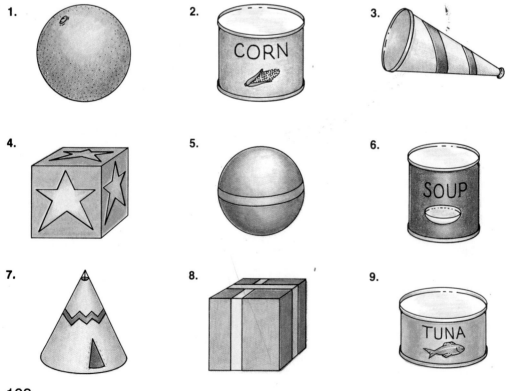

1.

2.

3.

4.

5.

6.

7.

8.

9.

108

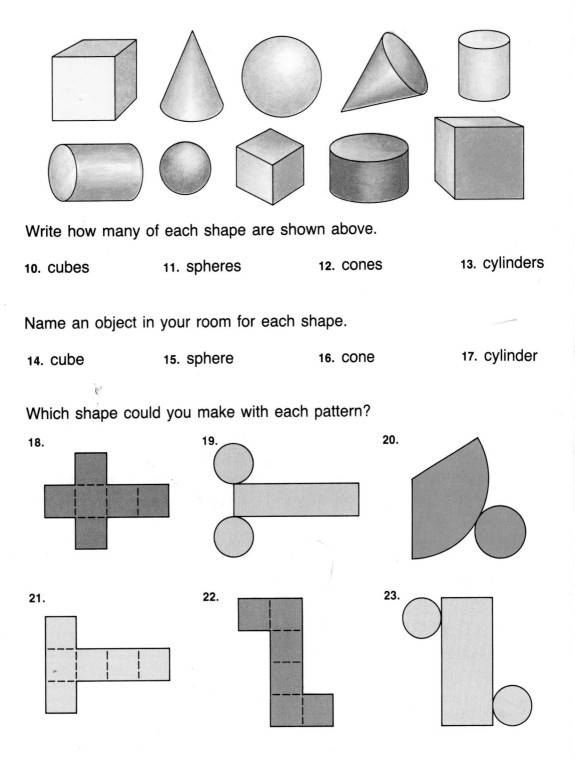

Write how many of each shape are shown above.

10. cubes   **11.** spheres   **12.** cones   **13.** cylinders

Name an object in your room for each shape.

14. cube   **15.** sphere   **16.** cone   **17.** cylinder

Which shape could you make with each pattern?

18.

19.

20.

21.

22.

23.

SKILLS REVIEW

Add.

1.	14 $+\ 0$	**2.**	92 $+\ 7$	**3.**	73 $+24$	**4.**	85 $+13$	**5.**	66 $+23$	**6.**	57 $+32$

7.	25 $+\ 7$	**8.**	34 $+\ 8$	**9.**	53 $+19$	**10.**	42 $+29$	**11.**	16 $+34$	**12.**	18 $+49$

Subtract.

13.	35 $-\ 0$	**14.**	89 $-\ 7$	**15.**	46 -12	**16.**	77 -53	**17.**	98 -65	**18.**	64 -24

19.	56 -38	**20.**	65 -39	**21.**	84 -26	**22.**	92 -45	**23.**	73 -47	**24.**	77 -68

25. There are 86 pages in a book. Bonnie read 68 pages. How many more pages does she have to read?

26. David played the piano 15 minutes before dinner and 25 minutes after dinner. How long did he play in all?

Multiply.

27.	3 $\times 8$	**28.**	2 $\times 9$	**29.**	6 $\times 6$	**30.**	7 $\times 1$	**31.**	5 $\times 4$	**32.**	8 $\times 4$

33.	0 $\times 9$	**34.**	7 $\times 5$	**35.**	6 $\times 8$	**36.**	9 $\times 7$	**37.**	8 $\times 8$	**38.**	9 $\times 9$

Rectangular Box

Look at a box like the one shown below.

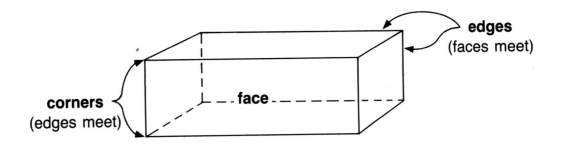

How many of each of the following does a box have?

1. faces

2. edges

3. corners

Hold a box so it looks like each figure below.
Tell how many faces, edges, and corners you can see.

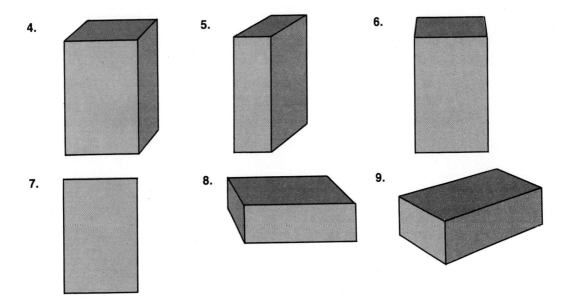

4.

5.

6.

7.

8.

9.

CHAPTER REVIEW

Write *R* if the angle is a right angle.
Write *S* if it is smaller than a right angle.
Write *L* if it is larger than a right angle.

1.   2.   3.

Write the letter of each figure that is

4. a rectangle   **5.** a triangle   **6.** a square   **7.** a circle

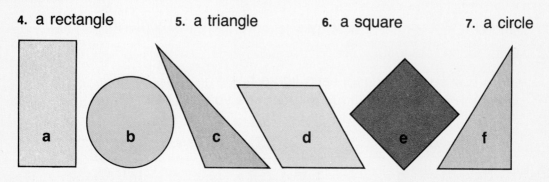

a   b   c   d   e   f

Write the letter of the figure for each of the
following shapes:

8. cube   **9.** cylinder   **10.** cone   **11.** sphere

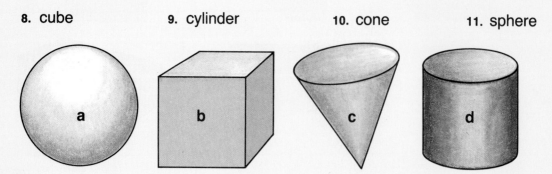

a   b   c   d

6 Measurement

Jacqueline Durand

Centimeter

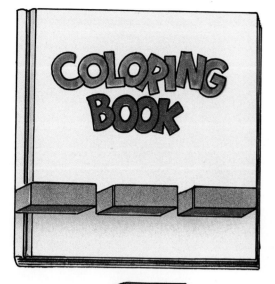

Dan used as a unit of length.

He said the length was about 3 erasers.

Peggy used as a unit of length.

She said the length was about 4 nails.

Why did they get different answers?

Could they both be right?

Would it help if everyone used the same unit?

One unit of length people use is **centimeter.**

$$\vdash\!\!\!-\!\!\!\dashv$$

1 centimeter

You can write *1 centimeter* as **1 cm.**

Exercises

Give the length in centimeters.

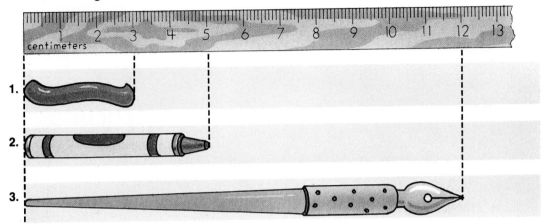

1.
2.
3.

Use a ruler to find the length of each object in centimeters.

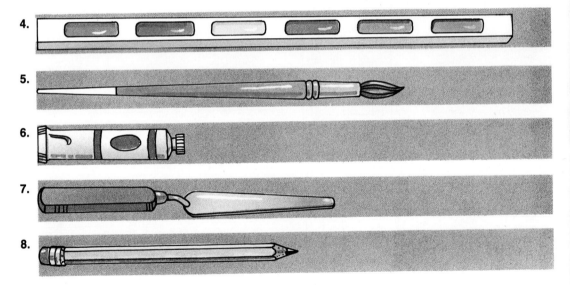

4.
5.
6.
7.
8.

Use a ruler to draw line segments with these lengths.

9. 3 cm　　　10. 6 cm　　　11. 10 cm　　　12. 14 cm

Meter

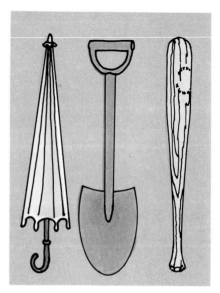

Each object shown is about **1 meter** long.

100 centimeters = 1 meter

You can write *1 meter* as **1 m.**

Exercises

Choose the best answer.

1. a. 1 meter
   b. 2 meters
   c. 3 meters

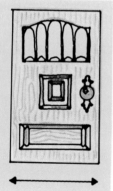

2. a. 1 meter
   b. 2 meters
   c. 4 meters

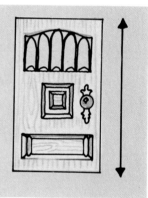

3. a. 1 meter
   b. 2 meters
   c. 4 meters

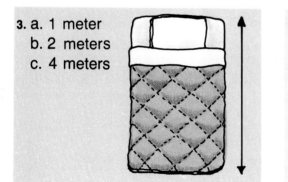

4. a. 1 meter
   b. more than 1 meter, but less than 2 meters
   c. 2 meters

To find the length of the real objects, would you use *centimeters* or *meters?*

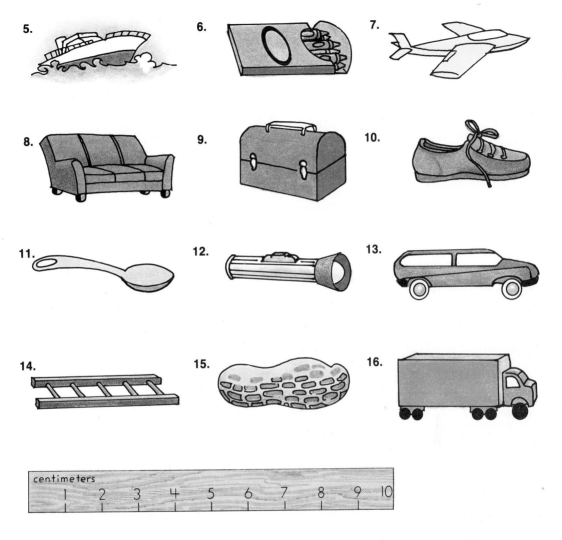

5.

6.

7.

8.

9.

10.

11.

12.

13.

14.

15.

16.

17. If you made a ruler twice this long, how many centimeters long would it be?

18. If you made a ruler 3 times as long, how many centimeters long would it be?

19. If you made a ruler 10 times as long, how many centimeters long would it be?

20. Complete this sentence. A ruler 100 centimeters long is ___ meter long.

Inch

Another unit of length is **inch.**

You can write *1 inch* as **1 in.**

Give each length in inches.

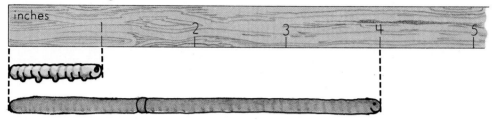

Exercises

Use a ruler to find the length of each picture in inches.

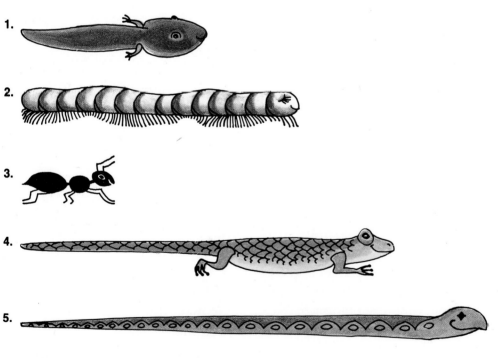

1.

2.

3.

4.

5.

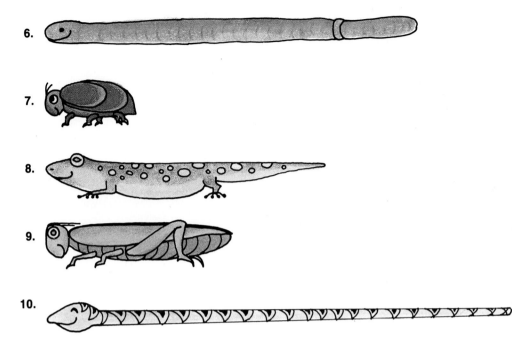

6.

7.

8.

9.

10.

Use a ruler to draw line segments with these lengths.

11. 3 inches   **12.** 5 inches   **13.** 8 inches   **14.** 10 inches

Distance Around

An ant starts at point A and goes all the way around. How many inches does it go?

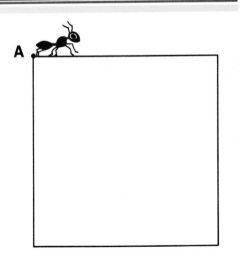

119

Half Inch

This ruler has a mark at each **half inch**.
Each length is given to the *nearest $\frac{1}{2}$ inch.*

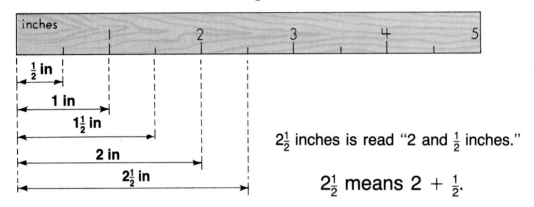

$2\frac{1}{2}$ inches is read "2 and $\frac{1}{2}$ inches."

$2\frac{1}{2}$ means $2 + \frac{1}{2}$.

Exercises

Read.

1. $1\frac{1}{2}$ inches

2. $3\frac{1}{2}$ inches

3. $4\frac{1}{2}$ inches

4. $5\frac{1}{2}$ inches

Find each length to the nearest $\frac{1}{2}$ inch.

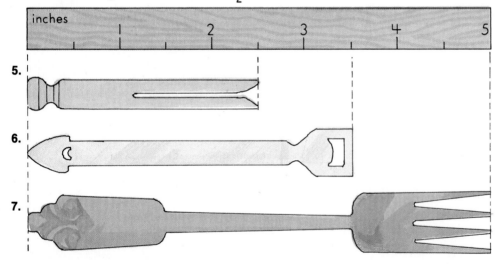

5.

6.

7.

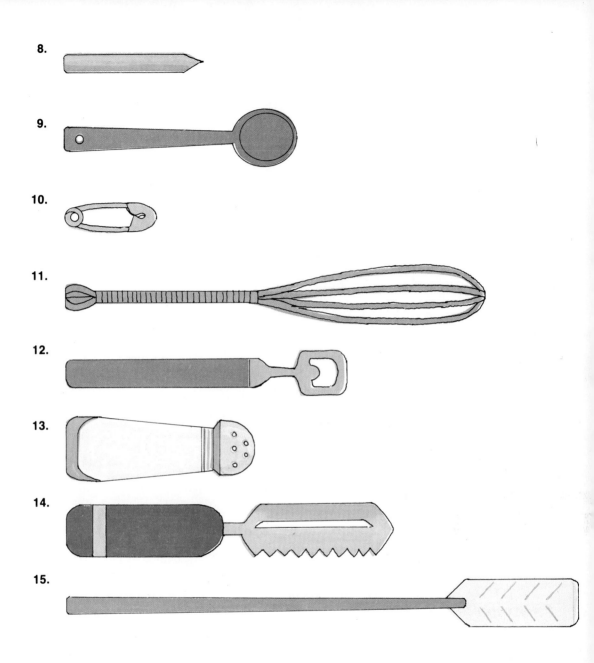

8.

9.

10.

11.

12.

13.

14.

15.

Use a ruler to draw line segments with these lengths.

16. $\frac{1}{2}$ inch   **17.** $2\frac{1}{2}$ inches   **18.** $4\frac{1}{2}$ inches   **19.** $7\frac{1}{2}$ inches

Foot

If you made a ruler twice this long, how many inches long would it be?

inches						
	1	2	3	4	5	6

Something that is 12 inches long is **1 foot** long.

$$12 \text{ inches} = 1 \text{ foot}$$

You can write *1 foot* as **1 ft.**

These real objects are about 1 foot long.

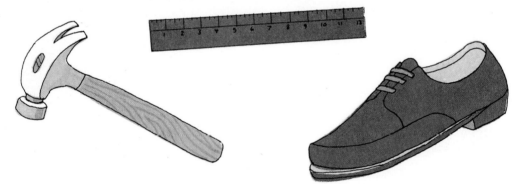

Exercises

Which is longer?

1. 1 ft or 10 in   2. 1 ft or 1 in   3. 1 ft or 18 in

4. 1 ft or 15 in   5. 1 ft or 11 in   6. 1 ft or 9 in

7. 2 ft or 12 in   8. 2 ft or 20 in   9. 2 ft or 25 in

To find the length of the real objects, would you use *inches* or *feet*?

10.

11.

12.

13.

14.

15.

16.

17.

18.

19. Mr. Finder's shoe is 1 foot long. How many inches is that?

20. Emily's desk is 2 feet wide. How many inches is that?

Distance Around

A rabbit starts at point A. It goes all the way around. How many feet does it go?

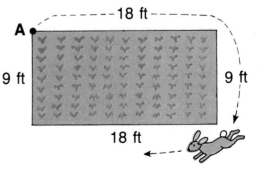

A

18 ft

9 ft

9 ft

18 ft

Yard

If you lay 3 one-foot rulers end to end, you will have a ruler **1 yard** long.

inches	inches	inches
1 2 3 4 5 6 7 8 9 10 11 12	1 2 3 4 5 6 7 8 9 10 11 12	1 2 3 4 5 6 7 8 9 10 11 12

Something that is 3 feet long is 1 yard long.

$$3 \text{ feet } = 1 \text{ yard}$$

You can write *1 yard* as **1 yd.**

These real objects are about 1 yard long.

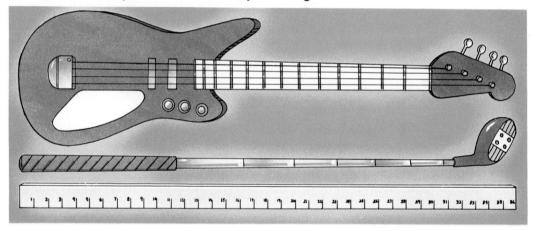

Exercises

Which is longer?

1. 1 yd or 2 ft

2. 1 yd or 12 ft

3. 1 yd or 1 ft

4. 1 yd or 5 ft

5. 1 yd or 6 ft

6. 1 yd or 4 ft

7. 2 yd or 12 ft

8. 2 yd or 5 ft

9. 2 yd or 7 ft

124

Would you use *inches* or *yards* to find these?

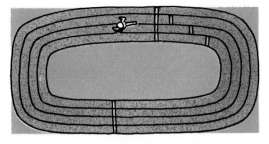

10. the distance you run around a track

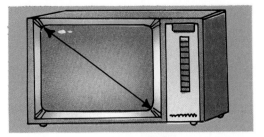

11. the distance across a TV screen, from corner to corner

12. the height of a telephone pole

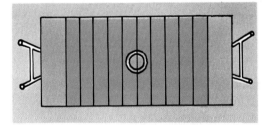

13. the length of a football field

14. A football team gained 16 yards on one play and 8 yards on the next play. How many yards were gained in both plays?

15. A store had 50 yards of material and sold 24 yards. How many yards were left?

Complete the table.

16.

Yards	1	2	3	4	5	6	7	8	9
Feet									

17. A piece of cloth is 1 yard long. How many inches is that?

18. A piece of cloth is 2 yards long. How many inches is that?

Area

You can find **area** by counting square units.

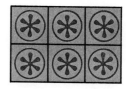

The tile is a square unit.

The area is 6 square units.

Exercises

Find the area. Use a tile as a square unit.

1.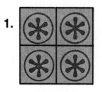

2.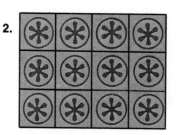

3.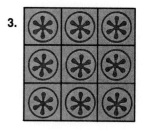

4.

5.

6.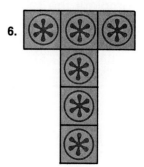

126

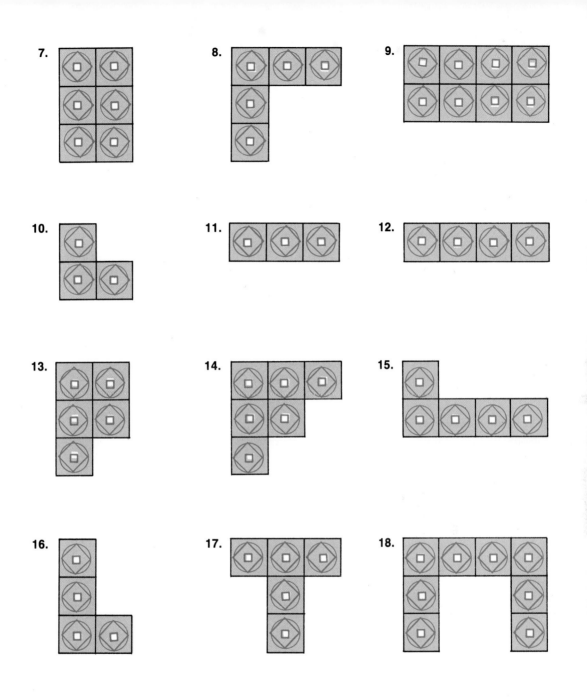

19. Draw a figure whose area is 6 square units.

20. Draw a figure whose area is 10 square units.

127

Square Centimeter

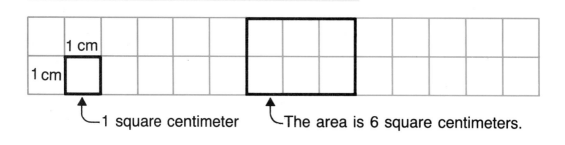

1 square centimeter   The area is 6 square centimeters.

Exercises

Find the area.

1.

2.

3.

4.

5.

6.

7.

8.

9.

Square Inch

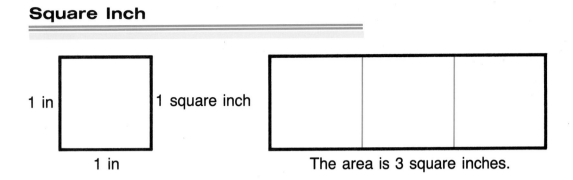

1 in | 1 square inch

1 in

The area is 3 square inches.

Exercises

Find the area.

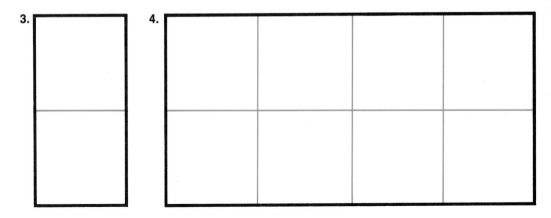

1.

2.

3.

4.

Area

Each of these is $\frac{1}{2}$ square centimeter.

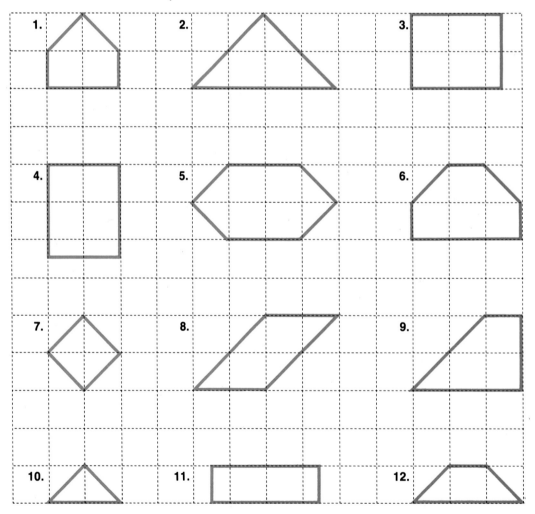

Exercises

Estimate the area in square centimeters.

Extra Practice—Set A, page 307

Add.

1. $\begin{array}{r} 20 \\ +30 \\ \hline \end{array}$
2. $\begin{array}{r} 50 \\ +40 \\ \hline \end{array}$
3. $\begin{array}{r} 42 \\ +23 \\ \hline \end{array}$
4. $\begin{array}{r} 85 \\ +14 \\ \hline \end{array}$
5. $\begin{array}{r} 79 \\ + 1 \\ \hline \end{array}$
6. $\begin{array}{r} 73 \\ + 8 \\ \hline \end{array}$

7. $\begin{array}{r} 34 \\ +29 \\ \hline \end{array}$
8. $\begin{array}{r} 43 \\ +48 \\ \hline \end{array}$
9. $\begin{array}{r} 28 \\ +37 \\ \hline \end{array}$
10. $\begin{array}{r} 69 \\ +16 \\ \hline \end{array}$
11. $\begin{array}{r} 57 \\ +27 \\ \hline \end{array}$
12. $\begin{array}{r} 29 \\ +59 \\ \hline \end{array}$

Subtract.

13. $\begin{array}{r} 80 \\ -20 \\ \hline \end{array}$
14. $\begin{array}{r} 90 \\ -90 \\ \hline \end{array}$
15. $\begin{array}{r} 68 \\ -32 \\ \hline \end{array}$
16. $\begin{array}{r} 55 \\ -42 \\ \hline \end{array}$
17. $\begin{array}{r} 42 \\ - 7 \\ \hline \end{array}$
18. $\begin{array}{r} 35 \\ - 8 \\ \hline \end{array}$

19. $\begin{array}{r} 55 \\ -17 \\ \hline \end{array}$
20. $\begin{array}{r} 67 \\ -28 \\ \hline \end{array}$
21. $\begin{array}{r} 70 \\ -46 \\ \hline \end{array}$
22. $\begin{array}{r} 64 \\ -37 \\ \hline \end{array}$
23. $\begin{array}{r} 53 \\ -36 \\ \hline \end{array}$
24. $\begin{array}{r} 80 \\ -49 \\ \hline \end{array}$

Multiply.

25. $\begin{array}{r} 2 \\ \times 8 \\ \hline \end{array}$
26. $\begin{array}{r} 1 \\ \times 5 \\ \hline \end{array}$
27. $\begin{array}{r} 7 \\ \times 9 \\ \hline \end{array}$
28. $\begin{array}{r} 5 \\ \times 7 \\ \hline \end{array}$
29. $\begin{array}{r} 9 \\ \times 4 \\ \hline \end{array}$
30. $\begin{array}{r} 7 \\ \times 7 \\ \hline \end{array}$

31. $\begin{array}{r} 9 \\ \times 6 \\ \hline \end{array}$
32. $\begin{array}{r} 6 \\ \times 4 \\ \hline \end{array}$
33. $\begin{array}{r} 6 \\ \times 0 \\ \hline \end{array}$
34. $\begin{array}{r} 8 \\ \times 3 \\ \hline \end{array}$
35. $\begin{array}{r} 7 \\ \times 8 \\ \hline \end{array}$
36. $\begin{array}{r} 8 \\ \times 9 \\ \hline \end{array}$

37. How many more votes did Jayne get than Ted?

38. Gerry got 5 times as many votes as Ted. How many votes did Gerry get?

Votes	
Jayne	34
Ted	7
Gerry	?

Cube

These real objects have the shape of a **cube.**

Each **face** of a cube is a square.

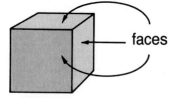

faces

How many faces does a cube have?

Exercises

Write *Yes* if the picture shows a cube.
Write *No* if it does not.

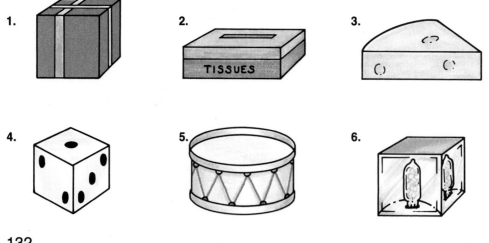

1.

2.

TISSUES

3.

4.

5.

6.

Write the number of cubes in each figure.

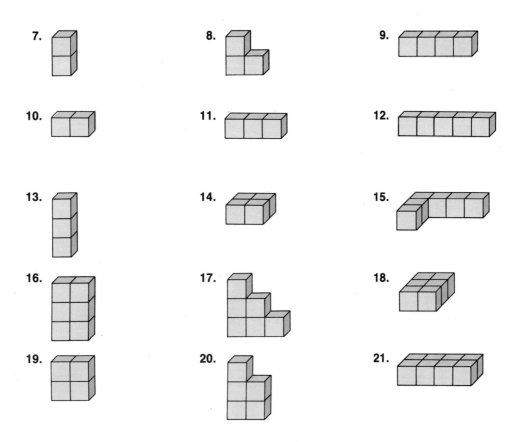

7.

8.

9.

10.

11.

12.

13.

14.

15.

16.

17.

18.

19.

20.

21.

Painted Faces

The outside is painted red. Then it is cut into 9 cubes.

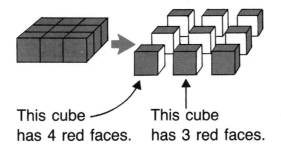

This cube — has 4 red faces.

This cube has 3 red faces.

How many cubes have only this many red faces?

1. 6 red faces

2. 5 red faces

3. 4 red faces

4. 3 red faces

5. 2 red faces

6. 1 red face

Volume

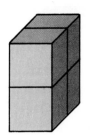

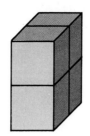

How many cubes
are in this figure?

How many cubes
are in this figure?

Think of sliding the two figures together.

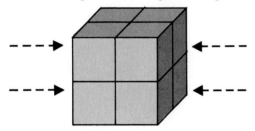

How many cubes are in the new figure?

Can you see all of them?

When you find how many cubes are in a
figure, you find its **volume.**

Exercises

Write the number of cubes in each figure.

1.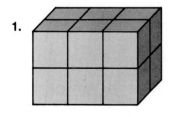

2.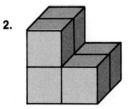

3.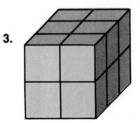

134

4.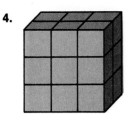

5.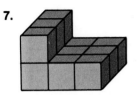

6.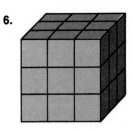

7.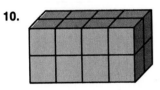

8.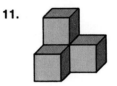

9.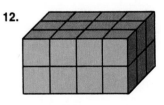

10.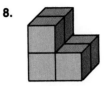

11.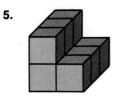

12.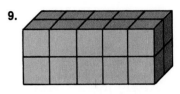

13.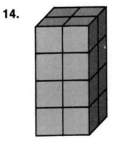

14.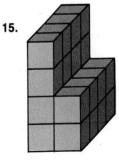

15.

16. Each block costs 9¢. Find how much it costs to buy the blocks needed to build the figure.

Extra Practice—Set B, page 307

CHAPTER REVIEW

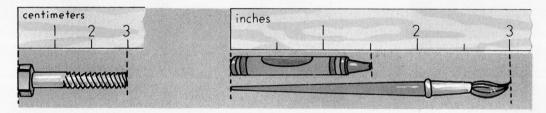

1. Give the length of the bolt in centimeters.

2. Give the length of the brush in inches.

3. Give the length of the crayon to the nearest $\frac{1}{2}$ inch.

Would you use *centimeters* or *meters* to find

4. the length of a pencil

5. the length of a bus

Which is longer?

6. 1 ft or 8 in

7. 1 yd or 4 ft

8. 2 yd or 5 ft

Find the area in square centimeters.

9.

10.

Write the number of cubes in each figure.

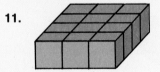

11.

12.

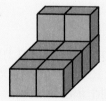

7 Addition

G. R. Roberts

Adding 10's and 100's

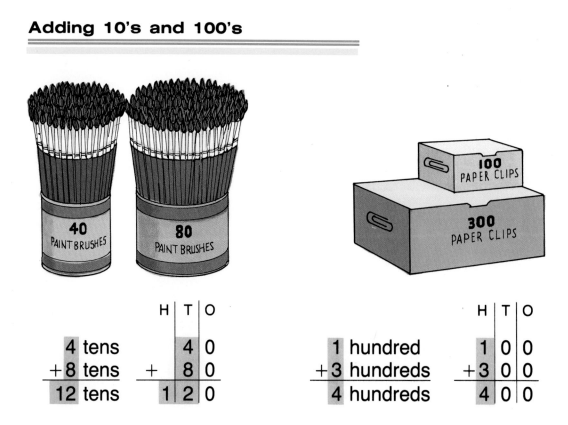

	H	T	O
4 tens		4	0
+8 tens	+	8	0
12 tens	1	2	0

There are 120 brushes in all.

	H	T	O
1 hundred	1	0	0
+3 hundreds	+3	0	0
4 hundreds	4	0	0

There are 400 clips in all.

Exercises

1. 5 tens   50
    +6 tens   +60

2. 7 tens   70
    +9 tens   +90

3. 8 tens   80
    +7 tens   +70

4. 5 hundreds   500
    +2 hundreds +200

5. 4 hundreds   400
    +1 hundred   +100

6. 3 hundreds   300
    +6 hundreds +600

138

7.	8.	9.	10.	11.
20 +90	50 +80	30 +90	50 +90	40 +90

12.	13.	14.	15.	16.
80 +60	30 +80	60 +60	90 +60	40 +70

17.	18.	19.	20.	21.
700 +200	100 +800	400 +300	200 +200	500 +400

22.	23.	24.	25.	26.
200 +300	400 +400	600 +200	300 +300	500 +300

27. There are 50 wide brushes.
There are 70 narrow ones.
How many brushes are there?

28. There are 200 jars of red paint.
There are 100 jars of blue paint.
How many jars are there?

29. First toss: 300 points
Second toss: 500 points
How many points were scored?

30. Gina's score: 80
Jack's score: 60
Find the combined score.

31. Abe has 200 pennies, Stephen
has 300 pennies, and Sarah has
400 pennies. How many pennies
do they have in all?

32. Franklin has 50 dimes, Eleanor
has 300 dimes, and Betty has
200 dimes. How many dimes
do they have in all?

Up and Down

1. 10, 40, 70, ___, ___

2. 80, ___, 60, 50, ___

3. 0, 200, 400, ___, ___

4. 900, 700, ___, ___, 100

Addition (no renaming)

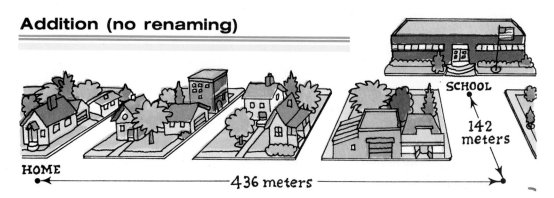

SCHOOL

142 meters

HOME

436 meters

How far is it from home to school?

Add the ones.	Add the tens.	Add the hundreds.
H T O	H T O	H T O
4 3 **6**	4 **3** 6	**4** 3 6
+1 4 **2**	+1 **4** 2	**+1** 4 2
8	**7** 8	**5** 7 8

It is 578 meters from home to school.

Exercises

1. 345
   +543

2. 538
   +241

3. 300
   +105

4. 660
   +239

5. 448
   +520

6. 222
   + 56

7. 372
   +415

8. 303
   +303

9. 654
   + 30

10. 747
   +111

11. 654
   +123

12. 417
   + 2

13. 211
   +600

14. 206
   +413

15. 100
   + 17

140

16.	125 +573	**17.**	453 +220	**18.**	503 + 96	**19.**	562 +326	**20.**	365 + 1
21.	810 + 41	**22.**	344 +213	**23.**	677 +321	**24.**	680 +117	**25.**	785 + 3
26.	352 +445	**27.**	141 +206	**28.**	904 + 4	**29.**	820 + 6	**30.**	236 +732

31. There are 131 math books.
There are 126 science books.
How many books are there?

32. 524 pupils buy their lunch.
114 pupils bring a lunch.
How many lunches are there?

33. If 320 more pounds of paper are collected, the school will reach its goal. How many pounds is the goal?

34. How many pupils attend Werner School?

Werner School
Pupils present: 615
Pupils absent: 23

Addition (renaming ones)

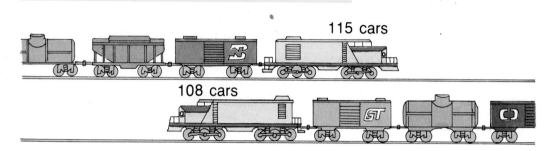

115 cars

108 cars

Add to find how many cars are on both trains.

Add the ones.	Add the tens.	Add the hundreds.

```
  H T O              H T O              H T O
    1                  1                  1
  1 1 5      5       1 1 5              1 1 5
+ 1 0 8    + 8     + 1 0 8            + 1 0 8
      3     13         2 3              2 2 3
```

223 cars are on both trains.

Exercises

1. 313 +628	**2.** 552 +229	**3.** 825 +136	**4.** 234 +747	**5.** 136 + 37
6. 405 +425	**7.** 349 +534	**8.** 646 +116	**9.** 123 + 59	**10.** 616 + 6
11. 273 +417	**12.** 572 + 18	**13.** 455 +337	**14.** 107 + 6	**15.** 249 +128

142

16.	613 +178	17.	362 +518	18.	724 + 69	19.	636 +258	20.	929 + 23

21.	463 + 19	22.	835 + 9	23.	544 +428	24.	946 + 44	25.	157 +737

26.	268 +524	27.	728 + 38	28.	356 + 19	29.	817 + 9	30.	379 + 11

31. 107 people got off a train. Then 8 more got off. How many people got off?

32. 236 seats are filled. 139 seats are empty. How many seats are there?

33. Mr. Perelman paid $126 for an adult ticket and $66 for a child's ticket. How much did he pay in all?

34. 105 adults were on the train. There were 75 more children than adults. How many children were on the train?

35. How far is it from the farm to the forest and then to the lake?

36. How far is it from the farm to the forest and then to the zoo?

37. How far is it from the lake to the zoo and then to the forest?

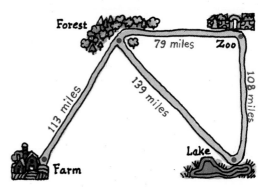

<, >, or =

1. 376 + 14 ● 358 + 33

2. 555 + 29 ● 568 + 14

3. 807 + 58 ● 829 + 36

4. 746 + 47 ● 779 + 13

Addition (renaming tens)

Mike counted 153 cars from their state.

Chris counted 72 cars from other states.

Add the ones.

```
  H T O
  1 5 3
+   7 2
      5
```

Add the tens.

```
    1
  H T O
  1 5 3
+   7 2        5 tens
  2 5          +7 tens
               12 tens
```

Add the hundreds.

```
    1
  H T O
  1 5 3
+   7 2
  2 2 5
```

They counted 225 cars in all.

Exercises

1. 778
   +141

2. 152
   +595

3. 376
   +261

4. 170
   + 32

5. 251
   + 82

6. 241
   +675

7. 390
   + 70

8. 765
   +144

9. 332
   +396

10. 653
   + 73

11. 485 +442	12. 544 +183	13. 546 + 92	14. 665 +253	15. 332 +387
16. 273 + 52	17. 423 +495	18. 831 + 73	19. 423 +184	20. 786 + 23
21. 147 +772	22. 194 + 95	23. 885 + 81	24. 398 +230	25. 252 +554
26. 760 + 92	27. 591 +144	28. 260 + 69	29. 487 +431	30. 640 + 67

David M. Campione/Taurus

31. Mike saw 137 road signs. Chris saw 182 road signs. How many signs were seen?

32. There were 225 cars and 91 trucks. How many cars and trucks were there?

33. They saw 64 station wagons. They saw 161 other cars. How many cars were seen?

34. Mom drove 185 miles. Dad drove 120 miles more than Mom. How many miles did Dad drive?

Addition (renaming twice)

I think there are 348 beans in the jar.

If you add 186 to your guess, you'll get the correct number.

Add the ones.	Add the tens.	Add the hundreds.

```
  H T O                    H T O                         H T O
    ⬚1⬚                     ⬚1⬚ 1                          1  1
  3 4 8          8        3 4 8          1 ten          3 4 8
+ 1 8 6        + 6      + 1 8 6          4 tens       + 1 8 6
  _____        ____       _____        + 8 tens         _____
      4        ⬚1⬚4         3 4        ⬚1⬚3 tens         5 3 4
```

There are 534 beans.

Exercises

1.	145	2.	234	3.	752	4.	373	5.	586
	+378		+568		+138		+175		+319

6.	307	7.	490	8.	237	9.	186	10.	361
	+325		+499		+508		+457		+580

11.	138 +247	**12.**	529 +383	**13.**	742 +168	**14.**	505 +275	**15.**	736 +217
16.	136 +492	**17.**	296 +307	**18.**	372 +428	**19.**	676 +239	**20.**	481 +246
21.	499 +281	**22.**	792 +125	**23.**	708 +193	**24.**	370 +270	**25.**	149 +248
26.	719 +162	**27.**	199 +111	**28.**	496 +218	**29.**	427 +317	**30.**	505 +395

31. How many beans are in jars *A* and *B*?

32. How many beans are in jars *B* and *C*?

33. How many beans are in jars *A* and *C*?

34. Jill guessed that there are 1000 beans in the three jars. Do you think her guess is too big or too small?

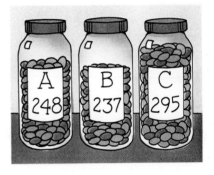

Be a Detective

Use these clues to find the number of beans in the jar.

- There are less than 400.

- There are more than 300.

- The tens digit is the same as the hundreds digit.

- The ones digit is twice the tens digit.

147

Addition (renaming twice)

Leona weighs 68 pounds. Her pony weighs 574 pounds. You can add to find their total weight.

Add the ones.

H	T	O
	1	
5	7	4
+	6	8
		2

4
+8
12

Add the tens.

H	T	O
1	1	
5	7	4
+	6	8
	4	2

1 ten
7 tens
+6 tens
14 tens

Add the hundreds.

H	T	O
1	1	
5	7	4
+	6	8
6	4	2

The total weight is 642 pounds.

Exercises

1.	137	2.	259	3.	598	4.	676	5.	745
	+ 74		+ 73		+ 83		+ 56		+ 66

6.	275	7.	166	8.	209	9.	868	10.	895
	+ 45		+ 39		+ 93		+ 59		+ 8

11. 149	12. 399	13. 348	14. 398	15. 236
+ 59	+ 16	+ 78	+ 6	+ 97

16. 457	17. 446	18. 158	19. 598	20. 267
+ 49	+ 88	+ 55	+ 54	+ 47

21. 278	22. 132	23. 572	24. 119	25. 663
+ 64	+ 89	+ 88	+ 84	+ 98

26. 126	27. 784	28. 697	29. 788	30. 208
+ 79	+ 89	+ 3	+ 22	+ 97

31. 285 tickets were sold today. 94 tickets were sold yesterday. How many were sold in all?

32. Julie saved $243. Marion saved $95 more than that. How much did Marion save?

33.

	Pounds
Mae	66
Her pony	+ 588
Total	

34.

	Pounds
Pony	568
Saddle	+ 32
Total	

35.

	Pounds
Bert	64
His pony	621
Saddle	+ 32
Total	

Puzzles

1. Copy the grid. Then put 1, 2, and 3 in each column so the sum for each column is 6 and the sum for each row is 6.

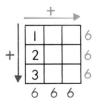

2. Copy the grid. Then put 1, 2, 3, and 4 in each column so the sum for each column is 10 and the sum for each row is 10.

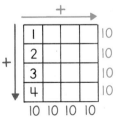

Addition Practice

1. 60
+70

2. 400
+300

3. 563
+122

4. 623
+149

5. 954
+ 24

6. 239
+ 24

7. 436
+286

8. 80
+90

9. 687
+212

10. 289
+207

11. 200
+600

12. 309
+397

13. 627
+ 42

14. 262
+523

15. 525
+184

16. 301
+189

17. 585
+ 13

18. 328
+ 17

19. 50
+80

20. 167
+ 6

21. 275
+343

22. 222
+678

23. 769
+ 57

24. 797
+ 3

25. 874
+114

26. 167
+471

27. 376
+ 39

28. 806
+ 98

29. 356
+482

30. 451
+336

31. 442
+ 56

32. 584
+207

33. 247
+ 86

34. 196
+308

35. 446
+ 81

36. 158
+ 75

37. 108
+ 3

38. 434
+274

39. 239
+186

40. 492
+ 48

41. 652
+298

42. 876
+ 24

43. 708
+108

44. 381
+289

45. 899
+ 1

World Record

The world's _?_ _?_ weighed 2859 pounds.
Find each sum. Use the code to find the letter
for that sum.

Code		First Word	Sum	Letter	Second Word	Sum	Letter
130	B	1. 235 + 3	238	L	8. 400 + 300	—	—
146	T	2. 146 + 28	—	—	9. 117 + 57	—	—
164	M	3. 118 + 209	—	—	10. 132 + 32	—	—
174	A	4. 159 + 89	—	—	11. 80 + 50	—	—
238	L	5. 335 + 92	—	—	12. 151 + 133	—	—
248	G	6. 240 + 132	—	—	13. 192 + 135	—	—
284	U	7. 124 + 22	—	—	14. 179 + 69	—	—
327	R				15. 361 + 66	—	—
372	S				16. 158 + 169	—	—
427	E						
700	H						

Addition (3-digit)

Add the ones.	Add the tens.	Add the hundreds.

Th	H	T	O
	7	2	6
+ 8	3	1
			7

Th	H	T	O
	7	2	6
+ 8	3	1
		5	7

Th	H	T	O
	7	2	6
+ 8	3	1
1	5	5	7

7 hundreds
+8 hundreds
15 hundreds

Exercises

1. 300
+900

2. 600
+700

3. 401
+874

4. 527
+932

5. 835
+841

6. 476
+912

7. 815
+923

8. 512
+643

9. 919
+340

10. 800
+300

11. 774
+721

12. 900
+200

13. 906
+901

14. 540
+757

15. 726
+672

16. 837
+521

17. 658
+621

18. 400
+700

19. 862
+313

20. 768
+811

21. 600
+800

22. 723
+924

23. 246
+922

24. 969
+610

25. 711
+425

26. How far is it to go from Chicago to Denver and back?

Denver ←——— 904 miles ———→ Chicago

Adding 1000's

	Th	H	T	O
2 thousands	2	0	0	0
+3 thousands	+3	0	0	0
5 thousands	5	0	0	0

Exercises

1.
```
  1 thousand        1000
+ 7 thousands     + 7000
```

2.
```
  4 thousands        4000
+ 2 thousands      + 2000
```

3.
```
  1000
+ 3000
```

4.
```
  3000
+ 2000
```

5.
```
  2000
+ 2000
```

6.
```
  2000
+ 4000
```

7.
```
  5000
+ 2000
```

8.
```
  7000
+ 1000
```

9.
```
  1000
+ 1000
```

10.
```
  3000
+ 4000
```

11.
```
  6000
+ 3000
```

12.
```
  4000
+ 1000
```

13.
```
  2000
+ 7000
```

14.
```
  2000
+ 1000
```

15.
```
  1000
+ 5000
```

16.
```
  3000
+ 3000
```

17.
```
  6000
+ 2000
```

18.
```
  4000
+ 5000
```

19.
```
  4000
+ 4000
```

20.
```
  8000
+ 1000
```

21.
```
  1000
+ 6000
```

22.
```
  3000
+ 5000
```

23. What number is 1000 more than 3000?

24. What number is 4000 more than 5000?

Addition (no renaming)

How far is it from New York to Honolulu if you stop over in San Francisco?

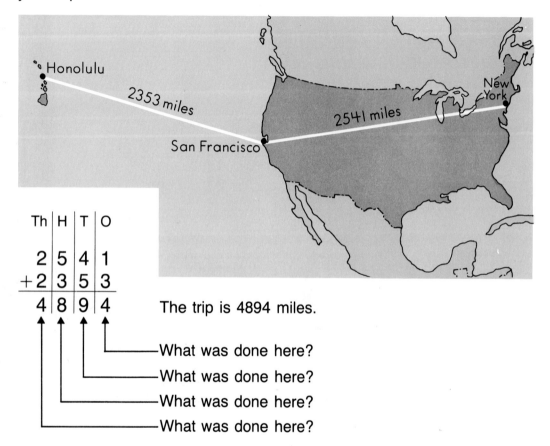

Th	H	T	O
2	5	4	1
+2	3	5	3
4	8	9	4

The trip is 4894 miles.

What was done here?
What was done here?
What was done here?
What was done here?

Exercises

1. 3472
    +4526

2. 2658
    +3321

3. 1746
    +6141

4. 4567
    +2300

5. 4004
    +4440

6. 1850
    +6011

7. 7381
    +1317

8. 8122
    +1610

9.   1683
  +1010

10.   7600
  +1115

11.   1761
  +2223

12.   2052
  +1202

13.   8536
  +1231

14.   2468
  +1201

15.   2115
  +5431

16.   3276
  +2423

17.   6457
  +2331

18.   3348
  +4541

19.   5120
  +4563

20.   7031
  +1466

21.   1364
  +1122

22.   4581
  +1312

23.   4473
  +5021

24.   5282
  +2711

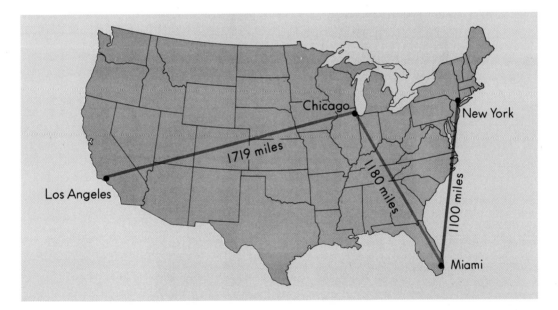

                    Miles   Miles

25. Los Angeles to Chicago   1719
    Chicago to Miami   +1180
    Total

26. New York to Miami   1100
    Miami to Chicago   +1180
    Total

27. How far is it from Los Angeles to Chicago
to Miami to New York?

155

Addition (4-digit)

How many people live in the two towns?

Add the ones and the tens.	Add the hundreds.		Add the thousands.

Th	H	T	O
4	8	3	2
+4	5	4	6
		7	8

Th	H	T	O
1			
4	8	3	2
+4	5	4	6
	3	7	8

8 hundreds
+5 hundreds
13 hundreds

Th	H	T	O
1			
4	8	3	2
+4	5	4	6
9	3	7	8

9378 people live in the two towns.

Exercises

1. 3721
    +1865

2. 1611
    +6974

3. 1813
    +7663

4. 2920
    +4291

5. 1501
    +1923

6. 2905
    +6393

7. 2844
    +6728

8. 3902
    +3719

9. 2729
    +2411

10. 2638
    +4702

11. 3787
    +5306

12. 4823
    +4928

13. 1584 +1509	14. 3803 +2328	15. 2715 +4516	16. 4626 +3407
17. 4534 +3671	18. 1725 +1580	19. 2616 +2492	20. 3890 +4387
21. 1968 +2435	22. 3784 +2356	23. 4586 +4444	24. 3376 +4645

Inventions

1783

The Bettmann Archive

120 years after the balloon

The Library of Congress

37 years after the airplane

Sikorsky Aircraft Information

25. When was this airplane invented?

26. When was this helicopter invented?

What Is Missing?

1. 5 8 6 9 + ■ 7 5 8 7 ■ 2 ■	2. 2 4 3 6 + 4 ■ 9 4 ■ 2 ■ 0	3. ■ 2 3 5 + 6 7 ■ 9 8 ■ 2 4	4. 3 2 1 ■ + 5 7 8 6 9 ■ ■ 5

Extra Practice—Set A, page 311

Solving Problems

Sydney Byrd/Photo Trends

1. The circus traveled 275 miles. It will travel 146 more miles. How many miles will it travel in all?

2. 476 children's tickets and 368 adult tickets were sold. How many tickets were sold in all?

3. The giant is 87 inches tall. The midget is 48 inches tall. How much taller is the giant?

4. One lion weighs 363 pounds. The other one weighs 385 pounds. How much do they weigh together?

5. The clown gave away 134 balloons. Then he gave away 29 more. How many did he give away in all?

6. One elephant weighs 4524 pounds. The other one weighs 4462 pounds. How much do they weigh together?

Subtract.

1. 46 − 9	**2.** 67 − 8	**3.** 58 −39	**4.** 85 −57	**5.** 60 −23	**6.** 74 −46

Multiply.

7. 3 ×4	**8.** 4 ×5	**9.** 0 ×8	**10.** 6 ×7	**11.** 8 ×3	**12.** 9 ×1
13. 4 ×9	**14.** 7 ×8	**15.** 8 ×6	**16.** 9 ×9	**17.** 9 ×7	**18.** 7 ×7

Write the letter of each figure that is

19. an angle   **20.** a rectangle   **21.** a square

22. a triangle   **23.** a circle

Write the letter of the figure for each of the following shapes:

24. cone   **25.** cube   **26.** cylinder   **27.** sphere

a   b   c   d

159

CHAPTER REVIEW

1. 60
    +90

2. 80
    +40

3. 300
    +200

4. 400
    +400

5. 890
    + 3

6. 703
    + 25

7. 327
    +102

8. 212
    +380

9. 415
    +426

10. 526
    + 37

11. 159
    +624

12. 362
    + 9

13. 672
    +174

14. 353
    + 86

15. 280
    + 35

16. 471
    +467

17. 565
    +247

18. 376
    +456

19. 478
    +494

20. 297
    + 37

21. 796
    + 7

22. 278
    + 58

23. 326
    +953

24. 665
    +823

25. 3000
    +6000

26. 1529
    +1360

27. 2335
    +2891

28. 4351
    +1789

29. Eric found 167 bottle caps. Jean found 43 bottle caps. How many were found in all?

30. There are 263 apple trees. There are 175 cherry trees. How many trees are there?

31. How far is it to go from Boston to Seattle and back?

Seattle

2496 miles

Boston

8 Subtraction

John Colwell/Grant Heilman

Subtracting 100's

Subtract to find how much more the big clown weighs.

3	hundreds	3	00
−1	hundred	−1	00
2	hundreds	2	00

The big clown weighs 200 pounds more.

300 pounds   100 pounds

Exercises

1. 5 hundreds   500
    − 2 hundreds   − 200

2. 7 hundreds   700
    − 3 hundreds   − 300

3. 600   4. 900   5. 400   6. 900   7. 800
    − 100   − 300   − 200   − 700   − 600

8. 900   9. 700   10. 900   11. 700   12. 800
    − 800   − 200   − 100   − 400   − 700

13. 600   14. 400   15. 800   16. 300   17. 900
     − 500   − 100   − 300   − 200   − 500

18. 800   19. 600   20. 900   21. 800   22. 800
     − 500   − 200   − 600   − 200   − 400

23. 700 −600	24. 900 −400	25. 700 −500	26. 600 −300	27. 900 −200
28. 700 −100	29. 800 −100	30. 600 −400	31. 500 −100	32. 500 −500

33. Chang collected 500 pennies. Su-Lee collected 300 pennies. How many more did Chang collect?

34. Mark had 700 stamps. He gave 200 to his sister. How many did he have left?

35. It takes 500 points to win. Flo has 100 points. How many more points does she need?

36. A lot can hold 800 cars. 600 cars are in the lot. How many more can it hold?

37. Bev threw yellow darts. Ron threw green darts. How many more points did Bev score?

38. The first person to make 800 points wins. How many more points does Bev need?

39. You have 2 books. Each book can hold 450 pictures. How many pictures can you put in the 2 books?

40. Suppose you put 600 pictures in the 2 books. How many more pictures could you put in?

Subtraction (no renaming)

So far we've made 138 pairs.

SHOES
SHOES
SHOES

Shoes to make: 258 pairs.

How many more pairs of shoes must the elves make?

Subtract the ones.	Subtract the tens.	Subtract the hundreds.

H	T	O		H	T	O		H	T	O
2	5	8		2	5	8		2	5	8
−1	3	8		−1	3	8		−1	3	8
		0			2	0		1	2	0

The elves must make 120 more pairs.

Exercises

1. 695
   −271

2. 764
   −354

3. 841
   −420

4. 439
   −   6

5. 352
   − 20

6. 952
   −721

7. 888
   − 88

8. 908
   −605

9. 526
   −510

10. 589
    −   1

164

11.	12.	13.	14.	15.
239	176	936	926	822
−128	− 25	−304	−723	− 2

16.	17.	18.	19.	20.
389	344	284	455	867
− 24	−232	−231	−345	−616

21.	22.	23.	24.	25.
578	659	572	495	433
− 5	−606	−340	− 42	−202

26.	27.	28.	29.	30.
537	683	798	742	628
− 27	−551	−464	−301	− 16

31. 268 pupils saw *The Elves and the Shoemaker* on Monday and 256 saw it on Tuesday. How many more saw it on Monday?

32. 137 pupils like funny stories and 25 like sports stories. How many more like funny stories?

33. There are 124 pages in a book. You read 102 pages. How many more pages are left to read?

34. 999 books are in a library. 109 books are checked out. How many books are left?

Find the End Number

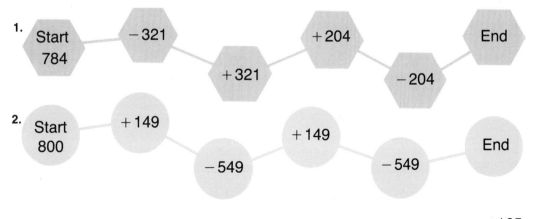

1. Start 784 − 321 + 321 + 204 − 204 End

2. Start 800 + 149 − 549 + 149 − 549 End

Extra Practice—Set A, page 312

Subtraction (renaming once)

82 pounds   375 pounds

How much less does the cub
weigh than the lion?

Subtract the ones.	Subtract the tens.	Subtract the hundreds.

H	T	O
3	7	5
−	8	2
		3

	2	17	
3	7̶	5
−	8	2
	9	3

	2	17	
3̶	7̶	5
−	8	2
2	9	3

Rename 3 hundreds,
7 tens as 2 hundreds,
17 tens.

The cub weighs 293 pounds less.

Exercises

1. 245
  − 63

2. 315
  − 132

3. 463
  − 226

4. 739
  − 654

5. 680
  − 62

6. 555
  − 60

7. 770
  − 227

8. 158
  − 9

9. 158
  − 90

10. 520
  − 140

166

11.	181 − 9	12.	200 − 10	13.	249 −153	14.	602 − 50	15.	891 −616
16.	677 −148	17.	353 − 70	18.	706 − 91	19.	975 − 91	20.	283 − 8
21.	418 − 82	22.	980 − 4	23.	208 − 90	24.	332 − 7	25.	485 −358
26.	730 − 60	27.	526 − 93	28.	527 − 35	29.	861 −452	30.	364 − 70

31. 275 pupils went to the zoo. 156 saw the dolphins. How many did not see the dolphins?

32. 794 people came yesterday. 9 fewer people came today. How many people came today?

33. Mom weighs 128 pounds. Ted weighs 72 pounds. How much less does Ted weigh?

34. Dad weighs 205 pounds. Tracy weighs 65 pounds. How much more does Dad weigh?

Looking Ahead

Write a numeral for each ▩.

Rename to get more ones.	Rename again to get more tens.

1.
H	T	O
	4	▩
6	5̸	3̸

H	T	O
	▩	
▩	4	13
6	5̸	3̸

2.
H	T	O
	0	▩
4	1̸	8̸

H	T	O
	▩	
▩	0	18
4̸	1̸	8̸

Subtraction (3-digit)

Baked: 360
Sold: 192

How many loaves are left?

Subtract the ones.	Subtract the tens.	Subtract the hundreds.

H	T	O
	5	10
3	6̶	0̶
−1	9	2
		8

Rename 6 tens,
0 ones as 5 tens,
10 ones.

H	T	O
	15	
2	5̶	10
3̶	6̶	0̶
−1	9	2
	6	8

Rename 3 hundreds,
5 tens as 2 hundreds,
15 tens.

H	T	O
	15	
2	5̶	10
3̶	6̶	0̶
−1	9	2
1	6	8

168 loaves are left.

Exercises

1.   581
    − 196

2.   478
    − 299

3.   567
    − 268

4.   616
    − 67

5.   360
    − 181

6.   555
    − 466

7.   911
    − 62

8.   774
    − 575

9.   820
    − 458

10.   921
    − 623

11.	511 −196	**12.**	723 −348	**13.**	314 −235	**14.**	853 − 75	**15.**	420 −131
16.	468 −279	**17.**	342 − 89	**18.**	355 −156	**19.**	325 −246	**20.**	884 −388
21.	715 −346	**22.**	912 −627	**23.**	680 −192	**24.**	830 −449	**25.**	651 −466
26.	420 −253	**27.**	650 − 58	**28.**	910 −813	**29.**	663 −374	**30.**	980 −791
31.	367 − 89	**32.**	975 −778	**33.**	788 −399	**34.**	691 −492	**35.**	812 −553
36.	356 −198	**37.**	448 −149	**38.**	530 −241	**39.**	423 − 65	**40.**	464 −377

41. A train has 432 seats. 246 seats are filled. How many are empty?

42. Ed's bowling score is 127. Joyce's score is 216. How much better is Joyce's score?

43. 543 people work in a factory. 398 of them are men. How many are women?

44. 470 points are needed to win. Your score is 87. How many more points do you need?

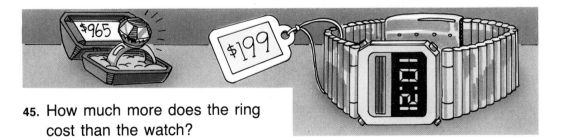

45. How much more does the ring cost than the watch?

Subtraction (3-digit)

This puzzle has 500 pieces.
128 of them are put together.
How many are not put together?

Rename to get some tens.	Rename again to get some ones.	Subtract.

```
      H | T | O                    H | T | O                  H | T | O
                                           9                          9
      4 |10 |                      4 |10 |10               4 |10 |10
      5 | 0 | 0                    5 | 0 | 0               5 | 0 | 0
    – 1 | 2 | 8                  – 1 | 2 | 8             – 1 | 2 | 8
                                                          3 | 7 | 2
```

Rename 5 hundreds,
0 tens as 4 hundreds,
10 tens.

Rename 10 tens,
0 ones as 9 tens,
10 ones.

372 pieces are not put together.

Exercises

Write a numeral for each ▧.

Rename to get some tens.	Rename again to get some ones.		

1.
```
  H | T | O              H | T | O
                                ▧
  ▧ |10 |                5 |10 |▧
  6 | 0 | 0              6 | 0 | 0
```

2.
```
  H | T | O              H | T | O
                                ▧
  ▧ |10 |                8 |10 |▧
  9 | 0 | 0              9 | 0 | 0
```

170

3. 600
    −468

4. 900
    −347

5. 800
    −259

6. 300
    −173

7. 400
    −184

8. 500
    −106

9. 700
    −645

10. 500
    − 51

11. 700
    −262

12. 900
    −591

13. 300
    − 49

14. 600
    −138

15. 900
    −606

16. 800
    −675

17. 300
    −188

18. 500
    −351

19. 400
    −317

20. 100
    − 17

21. 800
    −494

22. 900
    −791

23. 700
    −362

24. 300
    −124

25. 500
    −132

26. 400
    −243

27. 700
    −391

28. 100
    − 73

29. 600
    −285

30. 500
    −456

31. 100
    − 8

32. 800
    −504

33. How many more sheets of paper are in the Jumbo Pack than in the Regular Pack?

34. You buy the Jumbo Pack and use 198 sheets. How many sheets are left?

35. You buy 2 Regular Packs and use 482 sheets. How many sheets are left?

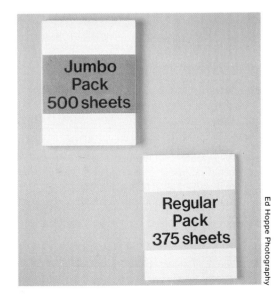

Jumbo
Pack
500 sheets

Regular
Pack
375 sheets

Ed Hoppe Photography

Subtraction Practice

1. 800 −500	2. 700 −600	3. 600 −500	4. 900 −200	5. 900 −600
6. 438 −226	7. 546 −442	8. 980 − 60	9. 875 − 3	10. 789 −567
11. 425 −134	12. 687 − 90	13. 501 −451	14. 463 − 7	15. 116 − 43
16. 526 −347	17. 870 −578	18. 444 − 55	19. 650 −281	20. 925 −777
21. 911 −747	22. 623 − 56	23. 786 −489	24. 384 −197	25. 612 −339
26. 500 −342	27. 600 −489	28. 700 −502	29. 800 − 33	30. 900 −899

31. 755 people rode a train today. 714 rode yesterday. How many more rode today?

32. 350 people were on a plane. 328 got off. How many stayed on the plane?

33. 500 points are needed to win. How many more points does Sara need to win?

34. How many fewer points does Jane have than Sara?

Scores

Sara	351 points
Jane	98 points

Basketball Baffler

What kind of a player are you?
Subtract the scores for each game.
Use the code to find the letter for each answer.

Flyers	110	Falcons	112	Hawks	108
Falcons	− 99	Owls	−106	Owls	− 98

First
word: 11
Y _____   _____   _____

Flyers	74	Falcons	103	Hawks	92
Hawks	−73	Hawks	− 95	Eagles	−89

Second
word: _____   _____   _____

Falcons	113	Flyers	101	Hawks	111
Eagles	−104	Owls	− 97	Jays	−108

Third
word: _____   _____   _____

Jerry Wachter/Focus on Sports

Flyers	81	Falcons	70	Eagles	88	Flyers	114	Falcons	100
Eagles	−79	Jays	−66	Jays	−87	Jays	−109	Flyers	− 93

Fourth
word: _____   _____   _____   _____   _____

Code:

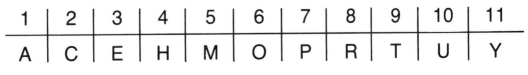

1	2	3	4	5	6	7	8	9	10	11
A	C	E	H	M	O	P	R	T	U	Y

Subtracting 1000's

How many more seats are on the main floor than in the balcony?

Balcony
1,000 seats

Main Floor
4,000 seats

4 thousands	4 000
− 1 thousand	− 1 000
3 thousands	3 000

3000 more seats are on the main floor.

Exercises

| 1. | 6 thousands | 6000 | 2. | 8 thousands | 8000 |
| | − 3 thousands | − 3000 | | − 2 thousands | − 2000 |

| 3. | 7000 | 4. | 6000 | 5. | 4000 | 6. | 9000 |
| | − 3000 | | − 1000 | | − 2000 | | − 7000 |

| 7. | 9000 | 8. | 5000 | 9. | 6000 | 10. | 8000 |
| | − 6000 | | − 1000 | | − 4000 | | − 7000 |

| 11. | 5000 | 12. | 3000 | 13. | 4000 | 14. | 3000 |
| | − 4000 | | − 2000 | | − 3000 | | − 1000 |

15. 7000
     − 6000

16. 8000
     − 3000

17. 9000
     − 8000

18. 8000
     − 8000

19. 3000 tickets went on sale. So far 1000 have been sold. How many have not been sold?

20. 9000 fans went to the game today. Yesterday 5000 went. How many more went today?

21. How much less does the blue box weigh than the yellow box?

22. How much less does the red box weigh than the blue box?

23. Stanley will carry the yellow box. Anne will carry the other two. How many more grams will Stanley carry than Anne?

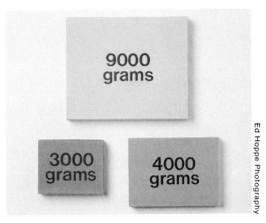

9000 grams

3000 grams

4000 grams

Ed Hoppe Photography

Looking Ahead

Write a numeral for each ▩.

	Rename to get some hundreds.	Rename again to get some tens.	Rename again to get some ones.

1.

Th	H	T	O
▩	10		
8̸	0̸	0	0

Th	H	T	O
	▩		
7	1̸0̸	10	
8̸	0̸	0̸	0

Th	H	T	O
		9	▩
7	1̸0̸	10	▩
8̸	0̸	0̸	0̸

2.

Th	H	T	O
▩	10		
5̸	0̸	0	0

Th	H	T	O
	▩		
4	1̸0̸	10	
5̸	0̸	0̸	0

Th	H	T	O
		9	▩
4	1̸0̸	10	▩
5̸	0̸	0̸	0̸

175

Subtraction (with renaming)

Start in New York. How much farther is it to travel to Los Angeles than to Chicago?

Subtract the ones and the tens.	Subtract the hundreds.	Subtract the thousands.

Th	H	T	O
2	4	5	4
−	7	1	3
		4	1

Th	H	T	O
	1	14	
2	4	5	4
−	7	1	3
	7	4	1

What is renamed?
Why is it renamed?

Th	H	T	O
	1	14	
2	4	5	4
−		7	1	3
1	7	4	1

It is 1741 miles farther.

Exercises

1. 3328
   −1513

2. 5846
   −2925

3. 7064
   − 941

4. 8489
   − 96

5. 7112
   −6212

6. 9368
   − 70

7. 6695
   −3833

8. 4007
   − 102

9. 2035
  − 904
	10. 5686
	  −3976
		11. 1692
		  − 861
			12. 7223
			  − 41

13. 2198
  − 244
	14. 9399
	  −8632
		15. 4845
		  − 933
			16. 3044
			  −1312

17. 3882
  − 951
	18. 8487
	  −2760
		19. 5096
		  − 572
			20. 2096
			  − 462

21. 3187
  − 874
	22. 4269
	  − 563
		23. 6475
		  − 93
			24. 7393
			  −3642

25. 2013
  −1101
	26. 4180
	  − 90
		27. 3057
		  − 320
			28. 1090
			  − 400

29. How much farther must the car go before it reaches Oma?

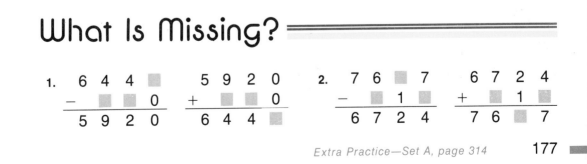

30. From Washington, D.C., it is 2329 miles to Seattle. It is 923 miles to Miami. How much farther is it to Seattle?

31. From Denver, it is 904 miles to Chicago. It is 1767 miles to Boston. How much farther is it to Boston?

What Is Missing?

1.
```
  6 4 4 ▦        5 9 2 0
-   ▦ ▦ 0     + ▦ ▦ ▦ 0
  5 9 2 0        6 4 4 ▦
```

2.
```
  7 6 ▦ 7        6 7 2 4
- ▦ 1 ▦        + ▦ 1 ▦
  6 7 2 4        7 6 ▦ 7
```

Subtraction (4-digit)

Ferris-Wheel Ride

Saturday	3204 people
Sunday	1386 people

How many more people rode on Saturday than on Sunday?

Rename to get some tens.

Th	H	T	O
	1	10	
3	2	0	4
−1	3	8	6

Rename 2 hundreds,
0 tens as 1 hundred,
10 tens.

Rename to get 10 more ones.

Th	H	T	O
		9	
	1	10	14
3	2	0	4
−1	3	8	6

Rename 10 tens,
4 ones as 9 tens,
14 ones.

Subtract.

Th	H	T	O
	11	9	
2	1	10	14
3	2	0	4
−1	3	8	6
1	8	1	8

What is renamed?
Why is it renamed?

1818 more people rode on Saturday.

Exercises

1. 5702
   −3274

2. 3506
   −1427

3. 8518
   −7009

4. 7703
   −3658

5. 3470
   −1659

6. 4812
   −3623

7. 6901
   −4466

8. 4204
   −2135

178

9.	3105 −1386	10.	9308 −7619	11.	3243 −1305	12.	6032 −4236
13.	8665 −8597	14.	6330 −3644	15.	9500 −5787	16.	7860 −4978
17.	4008 −2479	18.	7004 −2398	19.	5600 −4793	20.	8100 −5179
21.	4010 −1200	22.	6210 −2410	23.	8803 −3963	24.	8540 −8461
25.	8000 −4849	26.	5000 −1888	27.	4000 −3823	28.	6000 −2756

29. 5610 people came to the carnival on Saturday and 3723 came on Sunday. How many fewer came on Sunday?

30. 4723 people rode the roller coaster and 2878 rode the merry-go-round. How many more rode the roller coaster?

31. Walt Disney was born in 1901 and died in 1966. How many years did he live?

32. Disneyland opened in 1955. Disney World opened in 1971. How many years after Disneyland opened did Disney World open?

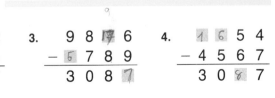

C. Ault/Photo Network

What Is Missing?

1.	4 3 2 1 − 1 2 3 4 3 0 8 7	2.	5 4 3 2 − 2 3 4 5 3 0 8 7	3.	9 8 7 6 − 5 7 8 9 3 0 8 7	4.	1 6 5 4 − 4 5 6 7 3 0 8 7

Solving Problems

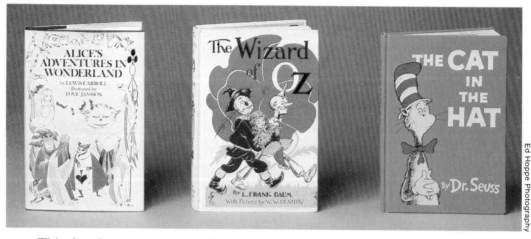

Ed Hoppe Photography

This book was written in 1865.

This book was written in 1900.

This book was written in 1957.

1. How many years after *The Wizard of Oz* was *The Cat in the Hat* written?

2. How many years after *Alice's Adventures in Wonderland* was *The Wizard of Oz* written?

3. L. Frank Baum was born in 1856. How old was he when he wrote *The Wizard of Oz?*

4. Lewis Carroll was born in 1832 and lived 66 years. In what year did he die?

5. 6 shows of *The Wizard of Oz* are put on each week. How many times is it put on in 7 weeks?

6. Dr. Seuss was 53 years old when he wrote *The Cat in the Hat.* In what year was he born?

Sir James Barrie wrote *Peter Pan.* He was born in 1860.

7. Sir James Barrie died in 1937. How many years did he live?

8. Sir James Barrie was 44 years old when he wrote *Peter Pan.* In what year did he write it?

Multiply.

1. 2 $\times 6$	**2.** 5 $\times 4$	**3.** 4 $\times 6$	**4.** 8 $\times 8$	**5.** 9 $\times 3$	**6.** 0 $\times 8$
7. 6 $\times 7$	**8.** 9 $\times 5$	**9.** 3 $\times 7$	**10.** 7 $\times 5$	**11.** 8 $\times 4$	**12.** 7 $\times 1$

Write the number of cubes in each figure.

13.   **14.**   **15.**

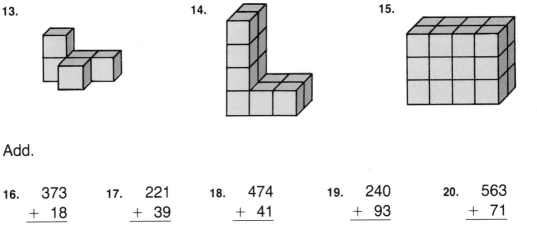

Add.

16. 373 + 18	**17.** 221 + 39	**18.** 474 + 41	**19.** 240 + 93	**20.** 563 + 71
21. 583 + 17	**22.** 672 + 69	**23.** 291 + 89	**24.** 348 +295	**25.** 373 +438
26. 591 +629	**27.** 485 +546	**28.** 3000 +4000	**29.** 1872 +1717	**30.** 7607 +1894

31. A phone book has 2675 white pages and 985 yellow pages. How many pages does it have?

32. There are 6 cages. 5 mice are in each cage. How many mice are there?

1. 700
   −300

2. 500
   −200

3. 624
   −121

4. 837
   −604

5. 368
   −174

6. 857
   − 9

7. 433
   −325

8. 908
   − 68

9. 515
   −186

10. 407
    −229

11. 640
    − 62

12. 300
    −135

13. 6000
    −4000

14. 8000
    −3000

15. 2074
    − 721

16. 5430
    −4620

17. 3051
    −1238

18. 7148
    −4671

19. 4200
    −2832

20. 8000
    −5694

21. Amy is 123 centimeters tall. Jimmy is 133 centimeters tall. How much taller is Jimmy?

22. Abraham Lincoln was born in 1809 and died in 1865. How many years did he live?

23. There are 365 days in a year. 186 of them are school days. How many are not school days?

24. You spend about 1100 hours in school each year. About 90 hours of that is for recess. How many hours are not for recess?

25. 607 pupils go to Lane School. 16 pupils are absent today. How many are in school today?

R. Terr/Taurus

9 Time, Weight, and Capacity

Artstreet

Calendar

This is what the month of March 1990 will look like.

This is what the month of April 1990 will look like.

March

S	M	T	W	T	F	S
				1	2	3
4	5	6	7	8	9	10
11	12	13	14	15	16	17
18	19	20	21	22	23	24
25	26	27	28	29	30	31

April

S	M	T	W	T	F	S
1	2	3	4	5	6	7
8	9	10	11	12	13	14
15	16	17	18	19	20	21
22	23	24	25	26	27	28
29	30					

Exercises

1. How many days are in March?

2. How many days are in April?

3. How many Fridays are in March?

4. How many Fridays are in April?

5. Do both months start on the same day of the week?

The *third* Wednesday in March is March 21.
Write the date for each of these days in March.

6. second Monday

7. third Saturday

8. fifth Thursday

Write the date for each of these days in April.

9. first Sunday

10. fourth Monday

11. third Wednesday

184

Write the day of the week for each of these dates.

12. March 12   **13.** March 22   **14.** March 31

15. April 7   **16.** April 15   **17.** April 30

18. How many days are in a week?

Write the date that will be one week after each of the following:

19. March 1   **20.** March 23   **21.** April 14

Write the date that will be one week before each of the following:

22. March 10   **23.** April 18   **24.** April 30

25. Write the date that will be one week after March 29.

26. Write the date that will be one week before April 3.

27. Write the day of the week for May 1, 1990.

Calendar Quiz

> 30 days has September,
> April, June, and November;
> All the rest have 31—
> But when February's done,
> It has just 28, I hear;
> Or 29 in a leap year.

1. How many months are in a year?

2. Which months have the most days?

3. Which month has the fewest days?

4. How many months have 30 days?

Telling Time

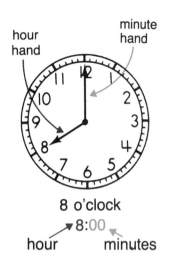

hour hand

minute hand

8 o'clock

8:00

hour · minutes

The minute hand moves this far in **1 minute.**

1 minute after 8
8:01

The minute hand moves this far in **7 minutes.**

7 minutes after 8
8:07

Exercises

The hands move this far in **1 hour.**

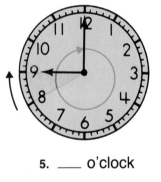

1. ___ minutes after 8

2. 8:___

3. ___ minutes after ___

4. ___:___

5. ___ o'clock

6. ___:___

How many minutes does it take for the minute hand to move from

7. 8 to 9

8. 4 to 7

9. 12 all the way around to 12

10. How many minutes are in 1 hour?

186

Write the time for each clock.
Do it as shown for the first clock.

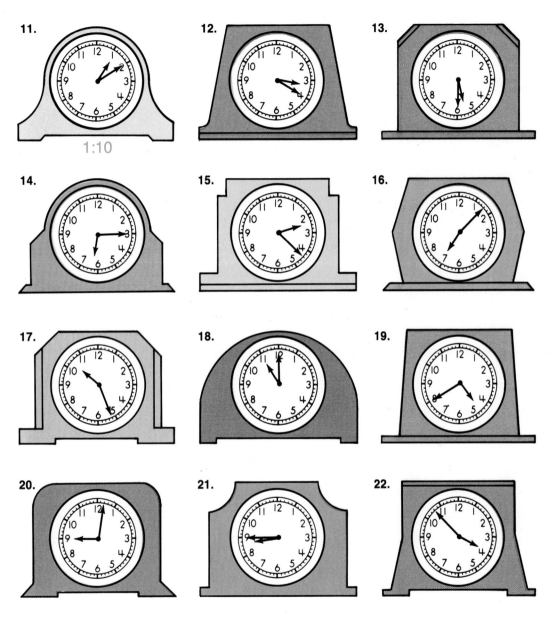

11.

1:10

12.

13.

14.

15.

16.

17.

18.

19.

20.

21.

22.

23. It is now 4:20. What time was it 20 minutes ago?

24. It is now 3:15. What time will it be 20 minutes from now?

Telling Time

The time on the clock is 4:40.

The minute hand has to move this far before it is 5:00.

You can also give the time as *20 minutes before 5.*

Exercises

Write each time two ways.

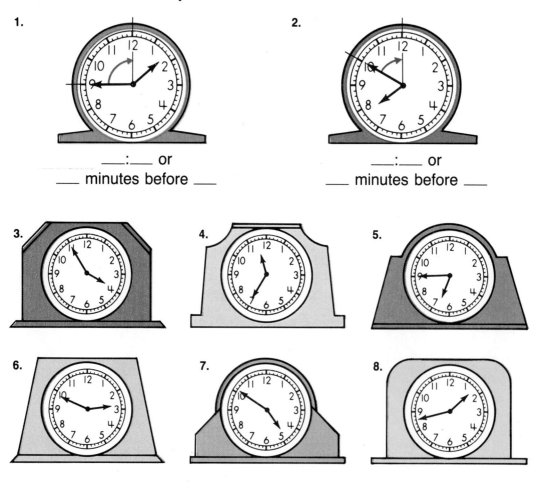

1.

___:___ or

___ minutes before ___

2.

___:___ or

___ minutes before ___

3.

4.

5.

6.

7.

8.

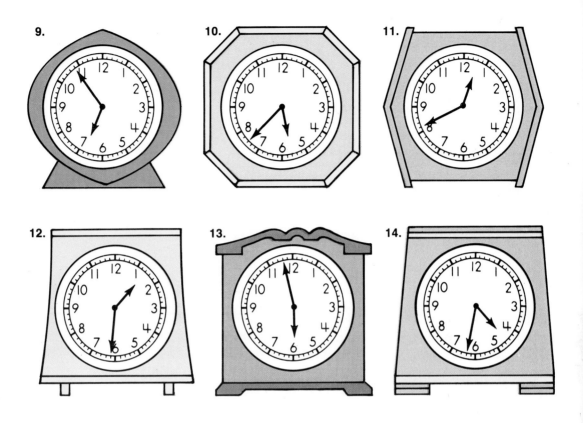

9. **10.** **11.**

12. **13.** **14.**

15. Mary got on a bus at 8:00. She got off at 8:22. How many minutes did she ride?

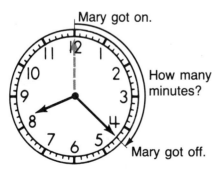

Mary got on.

How many minutes?

Mary got off.

16. A TV show started at 8:00. It lasted 30 minutes. When was it over?

17. School starts at 9:00. Jon came at 9:12. How many minutes late was he?

18. Recess started at 2:00. It lasted 15 minutes. When was it over?

19. Kate eats lunch at 12:35. She returns to class at 1:00. How long does she have for lunch?

20. Dan's math class ends at 24 minutes before 11. It begins at 10:00. How long does it last?

Other Clocks

Write the time for each clock.
Do it as shown for the first clock.

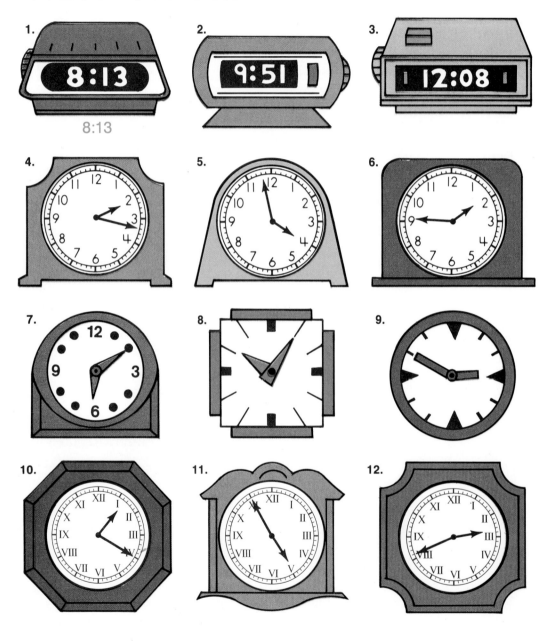

1. 8:13

8:13

2. 9:51

3. 12:08

Time

How many minutes is it from
6:50 to 7:06?

6:50 to 7:00 ⟶ 10 minutes
7:00 to 7:06 ⟶ + 6 minutes
                  16 minutes

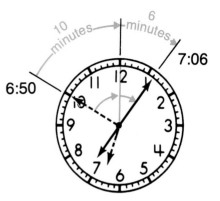

Exercises

How many minutes is it from

1. 8:45 to 9:05

    8:45 to 9:00 ⟶ ▮ minutes
    9:00 to 9:05 ⟶ + ▮ minutes
                  minutes

2. 1:30 to 2:25

    1:30 to 2:00 ⟶ ▮ minutes
    2:00 to 2:25 ⟶ + ▮ minutes
                  minutes

3. 6:50 to 7:10

4. 10:30 to 11:15

5. 2:40 to 3:10

6. 11:45 to 12:15

7. 8:59 to 9:01

8. 5:56 to 6:20

9. 10:55 to 11:12

10. 6:51 to 7:26

11. 3:32 to 4:03

12. 12:37 to 1:22

13. 7:48 to 8:08

14. 6:43 to 7:43

15. The movie started at 7:40.
It ended at 8:20.
How long did it last?

16. Rick put a pizza in at 8:35.
He took it out at 9:10.
How long did it bake?

17. Gwen went out at 6:50.
She came home at 7:25.
How long was she out?

18. The game started at 1:45.
It was over at 2:25.
How long did it last?

Time

You want to know how many minutes it is from 7:06 to 7:24.

24 is how much more than 6?
To find out, subtract 6 from 24.

$$\begin{array}{r} 24 \\ -6 \\ \hline 18 \end{array}$$

It is 18 minutes from 7:06 to 7:24.

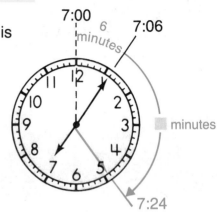

7:00
6 minutes
7:06

minutes

7:24

Exercises

1. $$\begin{array}{r} 50 \\ -20 \\ \hline \end{array}$$

2. How many minutes is it from 7:20 to 7:50?

3. $$\begin{array}{r} 31 \\ -26 \\ \hline \end{array}$$

4. How many minutes is it from 4:26 to 4:31?

5. $$\begin{array}{r} 40 \\ -8 \\ \hline \end{array}$$

6. How many minutes is it from 3:08 to 3:40?

How many minutes is it from

7. 2:01 to 2:44   8. 7:11 to 7:29   9. 10:30 to 10:55

10. 5:04 to 5:45   11. 2:06 to 2:19   12. 6:20 to 6:50

13. 7:17 to 7:47   14. 3:15 to 3:50   15. 6:27 to 6:42

16. 12:12 to 12:43   17. 5:37 to 5:46   18. 8:15 to 8:33

19. 1:23 to 1:51   20. 11:03 to 11:32   21. 1:18 to 1:40

22. 6:46 to 6:51   23. 9:29 to 9:48   24. 8:27 to 8:43

25. Renee got on a train at 4:20. She got off at 4:55. How many minutes did she ride?

26. The bell rang at 9:05. Wendell came at 9:14. How many minutes late was he?

27. The show started at 2:10. It was over at 2:35. How many minutes did it last?

28. A lesson started at 10:15. It was over at 10:50. How many minutes did it last?

29. It is now 9:35. What time was it 20 minutes ago?

30. It is now 11:23. What time was it 15 minutes ago?

A Dollar an Hour

You are to get a dollar every time a clock strikes the hour. You get the first dollar at 2:00. At what time will you get the fourth dollar?

Extra Practice—Set C, page 316

Hours and Minutes

What time will it be 2 hours after the time shown?

$$4:28 \longrightarrow \begin{array}{ll} 4 \text{ hours} & 28 \text{ minutes} \\ +2 \text{ hours} \\ \hline 6 \text{ hours} & 28 \text{ minutes} \end{array}$$

The time will be 6:28.

What time will it be 1 hour and 30 minutes after the time shown?

$$\begin{array}{ll} 4 \text{ hours} & 28 \text{ minutes} \\ +1 \text{ hour} & 30 \text{ minutes} \\ \hline 5 \text{ hours} & 58 \text{ minutes} \end{array}$$

The time will be 5:58.

Exercises

What time will it be 3 hours after each time given?

1. 6:10

2. 2:23

3. 5:35

4. 7:59

What time will it be 1 hour and 30 minutes after each time given?

5. 11:00

6. 6:15

7. 2:20

8. 8:07

9. It is now 1:45. It will take 2 hours to fix the car. What time will the car be ready?

10. Mrs. Spangler put a turkey in at 3:25. She took it out 2 hours and 30 minutes later. What time did she take it out?

194

SKILLS REVIEW

Multiply.

1.   1
   ×8
	2. 3
	  ×6
		3. 4
		  ×5
			4. 9
			  ×0
				5. 8
				  ×4
					6. 6
					  ×7

7.   0
  ×1
	8. 5
	  ×7
		9. 8
		  ×6
			10. 7
			  ×9
				11. 8
				  ×8
					12. 9
					  ×6

Add.

13.   746
  + 89
	14. 391
	  + 29
		15. 238
		  +464
			16. 544
			  +298

17.   509
  +692
	18. 5000
	  +3000
		19. 1691
		  +1385
			20. 2546
			  +1774

Subtract.

21.   958
  −236
	22. 504
	  − 90
		23. 731
		  −472
			24. 800
			  −359

25.   9000
  −7000
	26. 3063
	  − 582
		27. 6114
		  −1127
			28. 7000
			  −4183

29. The telephone was invented in 1876. The radio was invented 19 years later. In what year was the radio invented?

30. Elmer the elephant weighs 9540 pounds. Betty the bear weighs 1561 pounds. How much more does Elmer weigh?

Kilogram and Gram

Weight is measured in **kilograms** and **grams.**

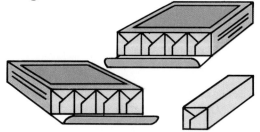

A one-dollar bill weighs about 1 gram.

This much margarine weighs about 1 kilogram.

1 kilogram = 1000 grams

You can write *1 gram* as **1 g.**

You can write *1 kilogram* as **1 kg.**

A raisin weighs about 1 gram.

7 baseballs weigh about 1 kilogram.

Exercises

Would you weigh these in *kilograms* or *grams?*

1.

2.

3.

4.

5.

6.

Guess the weight.

7.

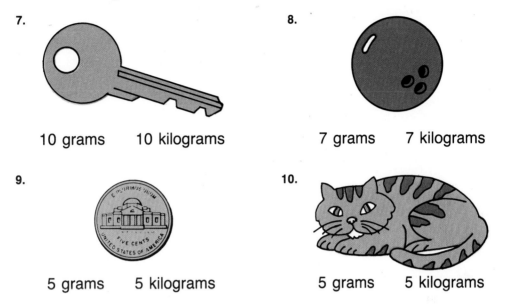

10 grams   10 kilograms

8.

7 grams   7 kilograms

9.

5 grams   5 kilograms

10.

5 grams   5 kilograms

On this scale, each mark shows 1 kilogram.
What weight is shown on each scale below?

11.

KILOGRAMS
0   10   20

12.

KILOGRAMS
60   70

13.

KILOGRAMS
30   40

14. Ray weighs 36 kilograms.
Sam weighs 27 kilograms.
They got on a scale together.
What should it read?

15. A golf ball weighs about 46
grams. A tennis ball weighs
about 57 grams. How much
lighter is a golf ball?

List things in the classroom that weigh

16. more than 1 kilogram

17. less than 50 grams

Pound and Ounce

Weight is also measured in **pounds** and **ounces.**

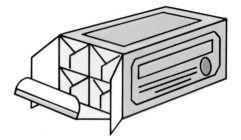

Five quarters weigh about
1 ounce.

This much butter weighs
1 pound.

1 pound = 16 ounces

You can write *1 pound* as **1 lb.**

You can write *1 ounce* as **1 oz.**

This book weighs about $1\frac{1}{2}$ pounds.

6 new pencils weigh about 1 ounce.

Exercises

Would you weigh these in *pounds* or *ounces*?

1.

2.

3.

4.

5.

6.

Guess the weight.

7.

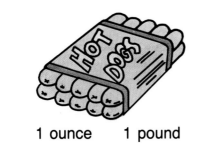

1 ounce   1 pound

8.

14 ounces   14 pounds

9.

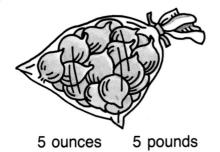

5 ounces   5 pounds

10.

5 ounces   5 pounds

On this scale, each mark shows 1 pound.
What weight is shown on each scale below?

11. POUNDS
50   60

12. POUNDS
80   90

13. POUNDS
70   80

14. Sheri weighs 51 pounds. Her little sister weighs 32 pounds. They got on a scale together. What should it read?

15. Tim weighs 72 pounds. Mark weighs 56 pounds. How much heavier is Tim?

List things in the classroom that weigh

16. more than 1 pound

17. less than 1 ounce

Liter

This carton holds **1 liter** of orange juice.

1 liter of orange juice is enough to fill 4 glasses.

Exercises

Tell whether each holds *more than 1 liter* or *less than 1 liter*.

1.

2.

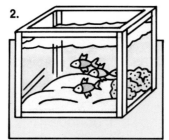

3.

4.

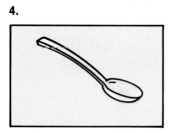

5.

6.

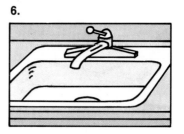

7. How much more water does Sue-Lee use taking a bath than taking a shower?

8. Sue-Lee washed her face 3 times today. How much water did she use?

Amount of Water Sue-Lee Uses	
taking a bath	105 liters
taking a shower	75 liters
washing her face	7 liters

Gallon, Quart, and Cup

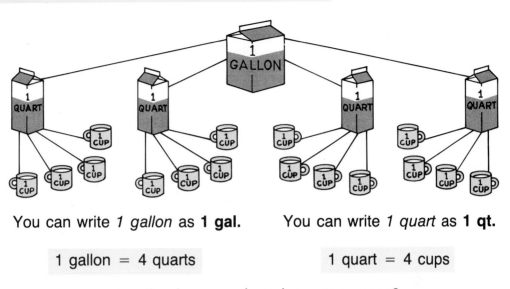

You can write *1 gallon* as **1 gal.**   You can write *1 quart* as **1 qt.**

1 gallon = 4 quarts   1 quart = 4 cups

1 gallon is as much as how many cups?

Exercises

Which is more?

1. 1 quart or 1 gallon

2. 3 quarts or 1 gallon

3. 6 cups or 1 quart

4. 8 cups or 1 gallon

5. 5 quarts or 1 gallon

6. 2 cups or 1 quart

Complete.

7. 1 quart = ___ cups

8. 4 quarts = ___ gallon

9. 1 gallon = ___ cups

10. 3 quarts = ___ cups

11. 8 cups = ___ quarts

12. 16 cups = ___ gallon

13. 8 quarts = ___ gallons

14. 2 gallons = ___ quarts

CHAPTER REVIEW

1. Write the date for the first Saturday in May.

2. Write the day of the week for May 7.

3. Write the date that is 1 week before May 8.

			May			
S	M	T	W	T	F	S
		1	2	3	4	5
6	7	8	9	10	11	12

Complete.

4. ___ minutes after ___

5. ___:___

6. ___ minutes before ___

7. ___:___

8. How many minutes is it from 7:35 to 8:10?

9. How many minutes is it from 5:09 to 5:52?

10. It is now 4:15. What time will it be in 1 hour and 30 minutes?

11. What weight is shown?

Complete.

12. 1 gallon = ___ quarts

13. 1 gallon = ___ cups

Choose the better answer.

14.

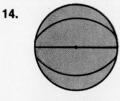

590 grams
590 kilograms

15.

1 ounce
1 pound

16.

less than 1 liter
more than 1 liter

10 Multiplication

Fredrik D. Bodin

Multiplying 10's

You want to buy these. How many cents are needed?

$$\begin{array}{r} 2 \text{ tens} \\ \times 4 \\ \hline 8 \text{ tens} \end{array} \qquad \begin{array}{r} 20 \\ \times 4 \\ \hline 80 \end{array}$$

You need 80 cents.

Discuss how 30 and 5 are multiplied below.

$$\begin{array}{r} 3 \text{ tens} \\ \times 5 \\ \hline 15 \text{ tens} \end{array} \qquad 10 \text{ tens} + 5 \text{ tens} \qquad \begin{array}{r} 30 \\ \times 5 \\ \hline 150 \end{array}$$

___ hundred + ___ tens

Exercises

1. $\begin{array}{r} 2 \text{ tens} \\ \times 3 \\ \hline 6 \text{ tens} \end{array} \rightarrow \begin{array}{r} 20 \\ \times 3 \\ \hline \end{array}$

2. $\begin{array}{r} 9 \text{ tens} \\ \times 4 \\ \hline \text{tens} \end{array} \rightarrow \begin{array}{r} 90 \\ \times 4 \\ \hline \end{array}$

3. $\begin{array}{r} 5 \text{ tens} \\ \times 2 \\ \hline \text{tens} \end{array} \rightarrow \begin{array}{r} 50 \\ \times 2 \\ \hline \end{array}$

4. $\begin{array}{r} 10 \\ \times 6 \\ \hline \end{array}$

5. $\begin{array}{r} 50 \\ \times 0 \\ \hline \end{array}$

6. $\begin{array}{r} 20 \\ \times 2 \\ \hline \end{array}$

7. $\begin{array}{r} 30 \\ \times 6 \\ \hline \end{array}$

8. $\begin{array}{r} 50 \\ \times 4 \\ \hline \end{array}$

9. $\begin{array}{r} 90 \\ \times 3 \\ \hline \end{array}$

10. $\begin{array}{r} 40 \\ \times 4 \\ \hline \end{array}$

11. $\begin{array}{r} 90 \\ \times 7 \\ \hline \end{array}$

12. $\begin{array}{r} 90 \\ \times 9 \\ \hline \end{array}$

13. $\begin{array}{r} 30 \\ \times 7 \\ \hline \end{array}$

14. $\begin{array}{r} 10 \\ \times 4 \\ \hline \end{array}$

15. $\begin{array}{r} 80 \\ \times 5 \\ \hline \end{array}$

16. $\begin{array}{r} 50 \\ \times 5 \\ \hline \end{array}$

17. $\begin{array}{r} 90 \\ \times 5 \\ \hline \end{array}$

18. $\begin{array}{r} 10 \\ \times 7 \\ \hline \end{array}$

19. $\begin{array}{r} 90 \\ \times 2 \\ \hline \end{array}$

20. $\begin{array}{r} 90 \\ \times 6 \\ \hline \end{array}$

21. $\begin{array}{r} 80 \\ \times 3 \\ \hline \end{array}$

22. $\begin{array}{r} 40 \\ \times 8 \\ \hline \end{array}$

23. $\begin{array}{r} 10 \\ \times 8 \\ \hline \end{array}$

24.	50 ×6	25.	90 ×8	26.	30 ×1	27.	20 ×8	28.	80 ×0

29.	20 ×1	30.	80 ×8	31.	50 ×1	32.	10 ×9	33.	90 ×0

34. You trade 8 dimes for pennies. How many pennies do you get?

35. You trade 9 dollars for dimes. How many dimes do you get?

36. There are 80 rows of chairs. Each row has 8 chairs. How many chairs are there in all?

37. A building has 60 floors. Each floor has 9 rooms. How many rooms are there in all?

38. 40 people can ride in each bus. How many people can ride in 5 buses?

39. Each toy car costs 90¢. How much does it cost to buy 8 toy cars?

Ways to Score 100

You threw 5 beanbags through the holes and scored 100 points. Show 5 different ways you could have scored 100 points.

	Nose 60 points	Eye 40 points	Hat 20 points	Mouth 0 points
1.	1	0	2	2
2.				
3.				
4.				
5.				

Multiplying 100's

Find how many sheets there are in all.

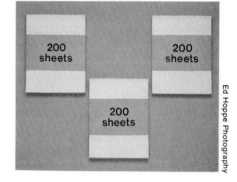

2 hundreds		200
×3		×3
6 hundreds		600

There are 600 sheets.

Look for a pattern in this example.

2		2 tens	20		2 hundreds	200
×4		×4	×4		×4	×4
8		8 tens	80		8 hundreds	800

The same pattern is shown in these examples.

4		4 tens	40		4 hundreds	400
×5		×5	×5		×5	×5
20		20 tens	200		20 hundreds	2000

7		7 tens	70		7 hundreds	700
×8		×8	×8		×8	×8
56		56 tens	560		56 hundreds	5600

Exercises

1. 3	2. 30	3. 300	4. 6	5. 60	6. 600
×3	×3	×3	×5	×5	×5

206

7. 50
×2

8. 500
×2

9. 20
×7

10. 200
×7

11. 400
×6

12. 800
×1

13. 800
×8

14. 600
×6

15. 700
×9

16. 200
×8

17. 500
×5

18. 300
×5

19. 100
×5

20. 200
×6

21. 700
×7

22. 200
×9

23. 80
×3

24. 100
×4

25. 800
×4

26. 300
×4

27. 600
×3

28. 900
×4

29. 90
×9

30. 60
×8

31. 500
×7

32. 500 sheets are in a box. How many sheets are in 8 boxes?

33. You trade 5 dollars for pennies. How many pennies do you get?

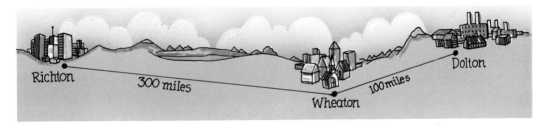

Richton — 300 miles — Wheaton — 100 miles — Dolton

34. Mr. Gorman went from Richton to Wheaton to Richton. He did that four times. How far did he go?

35. Mrs. Jandeska went from Dolton to Richton to Dolton. She did that six times. How far did she go?

Can You Do These?

1. 9000
×8

2. 5000
×9

3. 7000
×6

4. 5000
×8

Multiplication (2-digit by 1-digit)

	inches
Craig Cricket	21
Freddie Frog	
Katie Kangaroo	

Freddie Frog jumped 3 times as far as Craig Cricket. How far did he jump?

Multiply the ones by 3.	Multiply the tens by 3.

```
  T  O             T  O
  2  1             2  1        2 tens
×    3           ×    3       ×3
─────            ──────       ──────
     3             6  3        6 tens
```

He jumped 63 inches.

Katie Kangaroo jumped 8 times as far as Craig Cricket. How far did she jump?

Multiply the ones by 8.	Multiply the tens by 8.

```
  T  O          H  T  O
  2  1             2  1        2 tens
×    8           ×    8       ×8
─────           ────────      ──────
     8           1  6  8       16 tens
```

She jumped 168 inches.

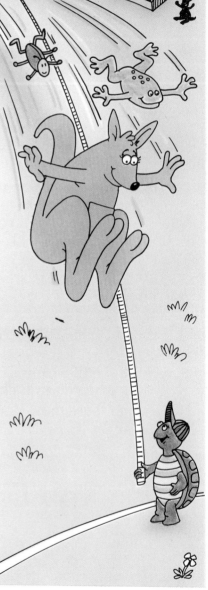

208

Exercises

1. 43
   ×2

2. 42
   ×2

3. 13
   ×2

4. 11
   ×5

5. 33
   ×3

6. 11
   ×9

7. 44
   ×2

8. 34
   ×2

9. 92
   ×2

10. 71
    ×8

11. 21
    ×8

12. 31
    ×7

13. 52
    ×2

14. 92
    ×3

15. 72
    ×3

16. 11
    ×8

17. 72
    ×2

18. 11
    ×6

19. 61
    ×6

20. 21
    ×9

21. 31
    ×6

22. 91
    ×2

23. 83
    ×3

24. 21
    ×7

25. 31
    ×9

26. 21
    ×6

27. 82
    ×4

28. 41
    ×9

29. 83
    ×2

30. 91
    ×3

31. 41
    ×8

32. 12
    ×3

33. 23
    ×3

34. 32
    ×4

35. 41
    ×5

There are 12 eggs in 1 dozen. How many eggs are in the following?

36. 2 dozen

37. 3 dozen

38. 4 dozen

39. 31 desks are in each of 9 rooms. How many desks are there?

What Is Missing?

1. ▦ 3
   × 2
   ───
   6 6

2. 7 4
   × ▦
   ───
   1 4 8

3. 6 ▦
   × 3
   ───
   1 8 9

4. ▦ 1
   × 6
   ───
   2 4 6

5. 5 2
   × ▦
   ───
   1 5 6

Extra Practice—Set A, page 318

Multiplication (2-digit by 1-digit)

How would you find how many tiles are on the floor?

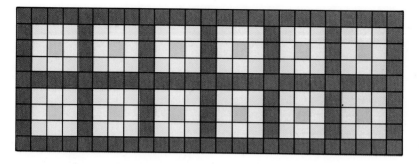

How many rows of tiles are there?   How many tiles are in each row?

You could multiply those numbers to find how many tiles there are.

Multiply the ones by 9.

T	O
4	
2	5
×	9
	5

9
× 5
4 5

Multiply the tens by 9.

H	T	O
	4	
	2	5
	×	9
2	2	5

2 tens
×9
18 tens
+ 4
22 tens

There are 225 tiles.

Exercises

Write a numeral for each ▦.

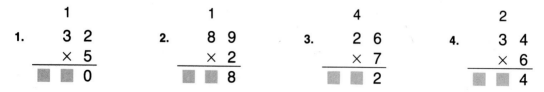

1.
```
  1
  3 2
× 5
▦ ▦ 0
```

2.
```
  1
  8 9
×   2
▦ ▦ 8
```

3.
```
  4
  2 6
×   7
▦ ▦ 2
```

4.
```
  2
  3 4
×   6
▦ ▦ 4
```

210

5. 55
   ×2
	6. 13
	   ×5
		7. 43
		   ×6
			8. 48
			   ×4
				9. 35
				   ×9

10. 82
   ×5
	11. 76
	   ×8
		12. 36
		   ×6
			13. 78
			   ×8
				14. 27
				   ×8

15. 25
   ×7
	16. 28
	   ×8
		17. 54
		   ×5
			18. 14
			   ×8
				19. 68
				   ×3

20. 19
   ×2
	21. 37
	   ×2
		22. 96
		   ×6
			23. 63
			   ×4
				24. 49
				   ×3

25. 65
   ×8
	26. 83
	   ×9
		27. 52
		   ×6
			28. 17
			   ×2
				29. 22
				   ×9

30. There are 24 hours in a day. There are 7 days in a week. How many hours are in a week?

31. There are 12 months in a year. How many months are there in 8 years?

32. There are 60 minutes in an hour. How many minutes are there in 8 hours?

33. There are 52 weeks in a year. How many weeks are there in 4 years?

Purple Tiles

Look at the tiles on page 210.

1. How many sections like this are there? How many tiles are in each section? How many tiles are in all the sections?

2. How many purple tiles are shown on page 210?

Solving Problems

1. How many yo-yos are in all the boxes shown?

2. How many marbles are in 6 bags?

3. 12 items are in a dozen. How many items are in 5 dozen?

4. How many toy cars are in all the boxes shown?

5. Yo-yos cost 49¢ each. Find the cost of 2 yo-yos.

6. Toy cars cost 87¢ each. Find the cost of 6 toy cars.

7. Find the cost of 8 hats.

8. Find the cost of 9 hats.

9. Find the cost of 6 bags of marbles.

10. How much more does a bag of marbles cost than a hat?

11. 600 toy cars are sold each month. How many toy cars are sold in 8 months?

12. Mother bought 2 boxes of toy cars and 1 box of yo-yos for prizes. How many prizes did she buy?

SKILLS REVIEW

Add.

1.   481
    +103

2.   309
    + 57

3.   427
    + 58

4.   263
    + 86

5.   161
    + 98

6.   172
    + 68

7.   749
    + 71

8.   545
    +179

9.   652
    +299

10. 916
    +882

Subtract.

11. 859
    −243

12. 793
    −572

13. 487
    − 90

14. 346
    − 81

15. 208
    − 16

16. 510
    −197

17. 624
    −287

18. 812
    −435

19. 300
    −159

20. 400
    −263

Write the time for each clock.

21.

22.

23.

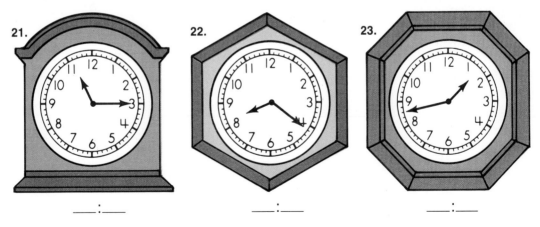

___:___

___:___

___:___

24. How many minutes is it from 6:48 to 7:02?

25. How many minutes is it from 1:19 to 1:31?

Multiplication (3-digit by 1-digit)

132 sticks were used to make this house.
How many sticks are needed to make 3
houses?

Multiply the ones by 3.	Multiply the tens by 3.	Multiply the hundreds by 3.

H	T	O
1	3	2
	×	3
		6

H	T	O
1	3	2
	×	3
	9	6

H	T	O
1	3	2
	×	3
3	9	6

1 hundred
×3
3 hundreds

396 sticks are needed.

Exercises

1. 114
   ×2

2. 142
   ×2

3. 240
   ×2

4. 224
   ×2

5. 321
   ×3

6. 140
   ×2

7. 203
   ×3

8. 312
   ×3

9. 401
   ×2

10. 313
    ×3

214

11. 431
    ×2

12. 423
    ×2

13. 313
    ×2

14. 110
    ×8

15. 334
    ×2

16. 222
    ×3

17. 302
    ×3

18. 444
    ×2

19. 211
    ×3

20. 111
    ×7

21. 323
    ×3

22. 331
    ×3

23. 433
    ×2

24. 404
    ×2

25. 213
    ×3

26. 411
    ×2

27. 333
    ×3

28. 220
    ×4

29. 212
    ×3

30. 311
    ×3

31. 410
    ×2

32. 201
    ×4

33. 122
    ×2

34. 143
    ×2

35. 102
    ×3

36. How many feet of string are in the rolls shown?

37. How many feet of string are in 4 rolls?

38. How many feet of string are in 6 rolls?

39. How many pencils are in the cartons shown?

40. Pencils cost 8¢ each. Find the cost of 111 pencils.

Multiplication (3-digit by 1-digit)

Multiply to find how many tickets there are in all.

Multiply the ones by 4.	Multiply the tens by 4.	Multiply the hundreds by 4.

H T O

2	1	5
×		4
		0

5
× 4
2 0

H T O

2

2	1	5
×		4
	6	0

1 ten
× 4
4 tens
+2 tens
6 tens

H T O

2

2	1	5
×		4
8	6	0

There are 860 tickets.

Exercises

1. 115
   ×6

2. 225
   ×3

3. 236
   ×2

4. 305
   ×3

5. 137
   ×2

6. 103
   ×9

7. 204
   ×4

8. 138
   ×2

9. 127
   ×3

10. 316
    ×3

11. 235 ×2	12. 226 ×3	13. 106 ×2	14. 139 ×2	15. 218 ×4
16. 118 ×5	17. 217 ×4	18. 228 ×3	19. 207 ×2	20. 318 ×3
21. 128 ×2	22. 107 ×4	23. 238 ×2	24. 136 ×2	25. 317 ×3
26. 206 ×4	27. 229 ×3	28. 135 ×2	29. 119 ×5	30. 319 ×3
31. 129 ×3	32. 227 ×3	33. 215 ×3	34. 239 ×2	35. 209 ×4

36. How many sheets of paper are in 2 notebooks?

37. How many sheets of paper are in 3 notebooks?

38. How many feet of tape are on 3 rolls?

39. How many feet of tape are on 6 rolls?

40. There is room for 120 rows of chairs in the gym. So far 104 rows have been put up. There are 9 chairs in each row. How many chairs have been put up?

41. How many more chairs can still be put up?

Multiplication (3-digit by 1-digit)

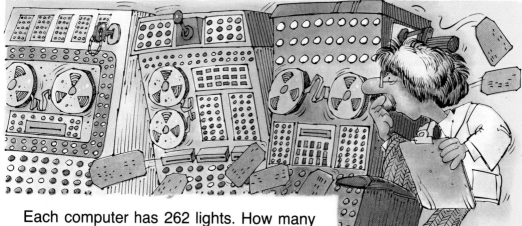

Each computer has 262 lights. How many lights are in the 3 computers?

Multiply the ones by 3.	Multiply the tens by 3.	Multiply the hundreds by 3.

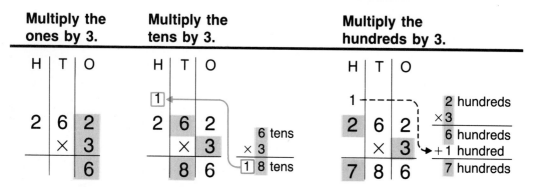

There are 786 lights in all.

Exercises

1. 151
   × 6

2. 262
   × 2

3. 351
   × 2

4. 191
   × 5

5. 362
   × 2

6. 130
   × 4

7. 490
   × 2

8. 260
   × 3

9. 163
   × 3

10. 272
    × 3

218

11. 162	12. 270	13. 152	14. 283	15. 252
×4	×3	×4	×3	×2

16. 251	17. 190	18. 282	19. 171	20. 352
×3	×5	×3	×5	×2

21. 170	22. 361	23. 182	24. 161	25. 192
×4	×2	×4	×6	×4

26. 253	27. 150	28. 263	29. 270	30. 363
×2	×6	×3	×2	×2

31. 281	32. 353	33. 180	34. 292	35. 291
×3	×2	×4	×2	×3

Photri

36. An airliner travels 472 miles in an hour. How many miles can it travel in 2 hours?

37. A small plane travels 160 miles in an hour. How many miles can it travel in 6 hours?

38. Find the cost of 2 adult tickets.

39. Find the cost of 3 child tickets.

40. Find the cost of 3 adult tickets and 4 child tickets.

DBS Airlines
Fly to Chicago.

Adult:	$283
Child:	$172

Multiplication (3-digit by 1-digit)

Jon is 2 years old today.
How many days has he lived?
(Use 365 days = 1 year.)

Multiply the ones by 2.	**Multiply the tens by 2.**	**Multiply the hundreds by 2.**

H	T	O
	[1]	
3	6	5
	×	2
		0

× 2 → 5 → [1]0

H	T	O	
	[1]	1- - -	6 tens
3	6	5	×2
	×	2	12 tens
	3	0	+ 1 ten
			[1]3 tens

H	T	O	
1	1		3 hundreds
3	6	5	×2
	×	2	6 hundreds
7	3	0	+1 hundred
			7 hundreds

Jon has lived 730 days.

Exercises

1. 155
   ×6

2. 255
   ×3

3. 256
   ×2

4. 165
   ×6

5. 265
   ×3

6. 122
   ×8

7. 132
   ×7

8. 197
   ×4

9. 198
   ×5

10. 175
    ×4

11. 258
    ×3

12. 156
    ×6

13. 167
    ×4

14. 186
    ×5

15. 196
    ×4

16. 157
    ×6

17. 188
    ×4

18. 179
    ×5

19. 169
    ×4

20. 195
    ×4

220

21. 177 ×2	22. 158 ×6	23. 187 ×2	24. 166 ×6	25. 259 ×3
26. 168 ×5	27. 159 ×6	28. 199 ×2	29. 178 ×5	30. 266 ×3

31. 168 hours are in a week. How many hours are in 5 weeks?

32. 128 plants are in each row. How many plants are in 7 rows?

33. Judy saved 135 pennies. Ralph saved 6 times that many. How many pennies did Ralph save?

34. There are 3 boys and 1 girl. Each person has 153 marbles. How many marbles are there?

Riddle Time

Little Jack Horner
Sat in a corner
Because he wa

Find each answer. Use the code to complete the riddle.

1.	234 ×4	2.	247 ×3	3.	8000 −7997	4.	4649 +3793	5.	270 ×2

936

W A ___   ___ ___ ___ ___   ___   ___ ___ ___ ___   ___ ___ ___

Code:	0	1	2	3	4	5	6	7	8	9
	Y	T	D	A	O	B	S	N	G	W

Multiplication Practice

1. 40
   ×6

2. 60
   ×4

3. 80
   ×7

4. 60
   ×9

5. 90
   ×8

6. 200
   ×4

7. 400
   ×5

8. 500
   ×9

9. 800
   ×8

10. 700
    ×8

11. 61
    ×7

12. 43
    ×3

13. 81
    ×6

14. 72
    ×3

15. 91
    ×6

16. 26
    ×5

17. 37
    ×7

18. 29
    ×9

19. 96
    ×3

20. 87
    ×9

21. 101
    ×8

22. 320
    ×3

23. 444
    ×2

24. 201
    ×4

25. 321
    ×2

26. 117
    ×5

27. 106
    ×8

28. 109
    ×7

29. 115
    ×6

30. 223
    ×4

31. 141
    ×7

32. 160
    ×6

33. 191
    ×5

34. 152
    ×4

35. 484
    ×2

36. 123
    ×8

37. 258
    ×3

38. 194
    ×4

39. 187
    ×4

40. 185
    ×5

41. 106
    ×6

42. 370
    ×2

43. 175
    ×5

44. 499
    ×2

45. 138
    ×7

46. 239
    ×4

47. 268
    ×3

48. 129
    ×7

49. 226
    ×4

50. 159
    ×6

Solving Problems

1. There are 6 teams. Each team has 25 players. How many players are there in all?

2. There are 6 refreshment stands. Each stand sold 160 hot dogs. How many hot dogs were sold?

3. 5740 fans came today and 3867 came yesterday. How many fans came during the 2 days?

4. Section A has 124 rows of seats. 8 seats are in each row. How many seats are there?

5. 300 seats are in Section B. Section C has 4 times that many seats. How many seats are in Section C?

6. 58 games will be on TV. 162 games will be on radio. How many more games will be on radio than on TV?

Mike Valeri/Picture Group

7. Find the cost of 125 adult tickets.

8. Find the cost of 275 child tickets.

9. Dad bought 2 adult and 4 child tickets. Find the total cost.

Tickets

Adult: $7

Child: $3

223

Multiplying Three Numbers

How would you find how many batteries there are in all?

Julio found the number of batteries like this.

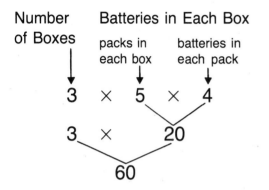

Karen found the number of batteries like this.

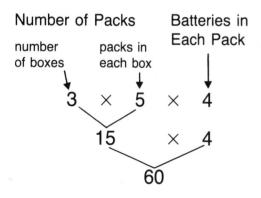

Are the answers the same?

Does it matter which two numbers you multiply first?

Exercises

1. $2 \times 5 \times 3$

2. $3 \times 5 \times 6$

3. $3 \times 5 \times 8$

4. $3 \times 8 \times 9$

5. $5 \times 8 \times 5$

6. $4 \times 5 \times 6$

7. $1 \times 16 \times 5$

8. $4 \times 9 \times 7$

9. $2 \times 7 \times 0$

10. $0 \times 4 \times 3$

11. $5 \times 6 \times 6$

12. $2 \times 4 \times 8$

13. $4 \times 5 \times 2$

14. $3 \times 5 \times 4$

15. $12 \times 5 \times 1$

16. $4 \times 2 \times 50$

17. $25 \times 2 \times 4$

18. $3 \times 0 \times 41$

19. $51 \times 2 \times 0$

20. $8 \times 1 \times 99$

21. $20 \times 5 \times 2$

22. $30 \times 5 \times 1$

23. $25 \times 4 \times 2$

24. $2 \times 3 \times 31$

25. $1 \times 14 \times 5$

26. $24 \times 2 \times 3$

27. $25 \times 4 \times 6$

28. $54 \times 0 \times 3$

29. $2 \times 4 \times 75$

30. $39 \times 2 \times 4$

31. $12 \times 5 \times 6$

32. $5 \times 25 \times 8$

33. $3 \times 3 \times 52$

34. There are 5 children. Each child has 3 dolls. There are 2 dresses for each doll. How many dresses are there in all?

35. There are 5 rows of desks and 5 desks in each row. There are 8 crayons on each desk. How many crayons are there in all?

What Is Missing?

1. $2 \times 3 \times \square = 24$

2. $\square \times 3 \times 3 = 9$

3. $\square \times 6 \times 8 = 0$

4. $1 \times 1 \times \square = 5$

5. $\square \times 3 \times 5 = 30$

6. $0 \times 8 \times \square = 0$

CHAPTER REVIEW

1. 10 ×7	2. 60 ×3	3. 70 ×7	4. 500 ×9	5. 600 ×7
6. 900 ×4	7. 31 ×3	8. 94 ×2	9. 61 ×8	10. 82 ×9
11. 47 ×6	12. 58 ×7	13. 321 ×2	14. 201 ×3	15. 120 ×4
16. 108 ×5	17. 109 ×6	18. 118 ×4	19. 329 ×3	20. 448 ×2
21. 140 ×7	22. 131 ×7	23. 160 ×6	24. 161 ×5	25. 172 ×4
26. 257 ×3	27. 128 ×6	28. 129 ×7	29. 124 ×8	30. 234 ×4

31. 36 apples are in a box. How many apples are in the boxes shown?

32. Last year 500 boxes of apples were sold. This year 6 times that many boxes were sold. How many boxes were sold this year?

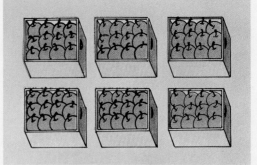

33. 105 tickets are in each roll. How many tickets are in 8 rolls?

34. 175 people paid $5 each. How much money was paid in all?

35. $9 \times 4 \times 2$

36. $9 \times 9 \times 8$

37. $57 \times 6 \times 0$

11 Division

Artstreet

Finding How Many Groups

There are 6 pencils. Put them into groups of 2 each.

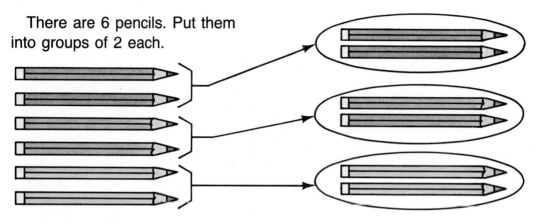

How many groups of 2 are there?

You can use **division** to find how many groups.

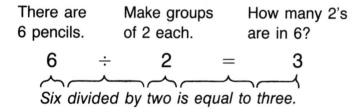

There are 6 pencils.	Make groups of 2 each.	How many 2's are in 6?

$$6 \div 2 = 3$$

Six divided by two is equal to three.

Exercises

1.

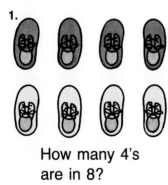

How many 4's are in 8?

$$8 \div 4 = \square$$

2.

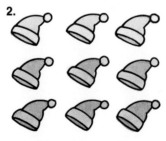

How many 3's are in 9?

$$9 \div 3 = \square$$

3.

How many 1's are in 2?

$$2 \div 1 = \square$$

228

4.

How many 5's are in 15?

15 ÷ 5 = ☐

5.

How many 6's are in 12?

12 ÷ 6 = ☐

6.

How many 5's are in 5?

5 ÷ 5 = ☐

7.

How many 8's are in 16?

16 ÷ 8 = ☐

8.

How many 7's are in 21?

21 ÷ 7 = ☐

9.

How many 9's are in 27?

27 ÷ 9 = ☐

10. How many 3's are in 12?

12 ÷ 3 = ☐

11. How many 3's are in 27?

27 ÷ 3 = ☐

12. How many 2's are in 14?

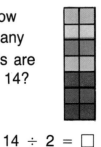

14 ÷ 2 = ☐

Multiplication and Division

Join 2 groups of 4 each.   Separate 8 into groups of 4.

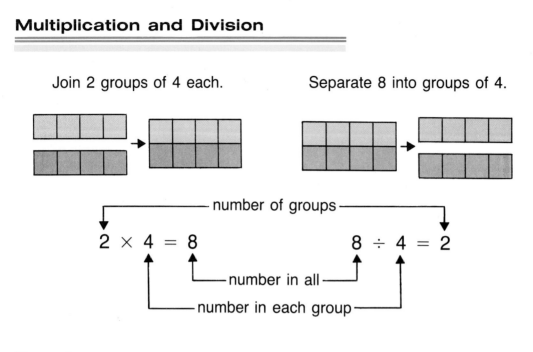

$$2 \times 4 = 8 \qquad 8 \div 4 = 2$$

number of groups

number in all

number in each group

Exercises

Write a numeral for each ☐.

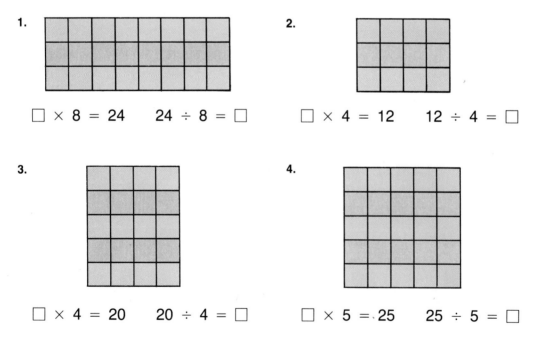

1.
☐ × 8 = 24   24 ÷ 8 = ☐

2.
☐ × 4 = 12   12 ÷ 4 = ☐

3.
☐ × 4 = 20   20 ÷ 4 = ☐

4.
☐ × 5 = 25   25 ÷ 5 = ☐

230

5.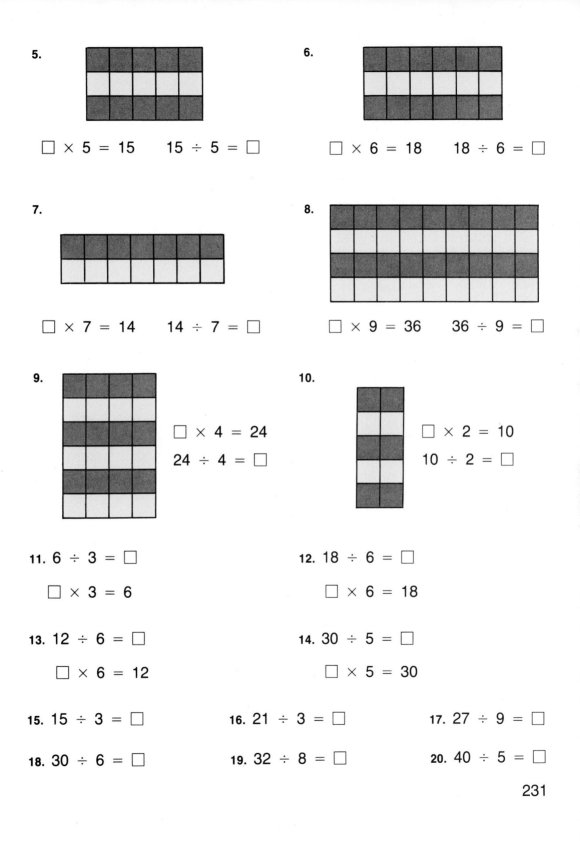

$\square \times 5 = 15$ $15 \div 5 = \square$

6.

$\square \times 6 = 18$ $18 \div 6 = \square$

7.

$\square \times 7 = 14$ $14 \div 7 = \square$

8.

$\square \times 9 = 36$ $36 \div 9 = \square$

9.

$\square \times 4 = 24$
$24 \div 4 = \square$

10.

$\square \times 2 = 10$
$10 \div 2 = \square$

11. $6 \div 3 = \square$

$\square \times 3 = 6$

12. $18 \div 6 = \square$

$\square \times 6 = 18$

13. $12 \div 6 = \square$

$\square \times 6 = 12$

14. $30 \div 5 = \square$

$\square \times 5 = 30$

15. $15 \div 3 = \square$

16. $21 \div 3 = \square$

17. $27 \div 9 = \square$

18. $30 \div 6 = \square$

19. $32 \div 8 = \square$

20. $40 \div 5 = \square$

Finding How Many in Each Group

There are 6 toy animals. Put the same number of animals in each of 2 boxes.

Can you put 1 animal in each box?

Can you put 2 animals in each box?

Can you put 3 animals in each box?

You can use division when the same number of objects is put into each group.

number in each group

$$6 \div 2 = 3$$

number in all ⎫   ⎫ number of groups

Exercises

Write a numeral for each □.

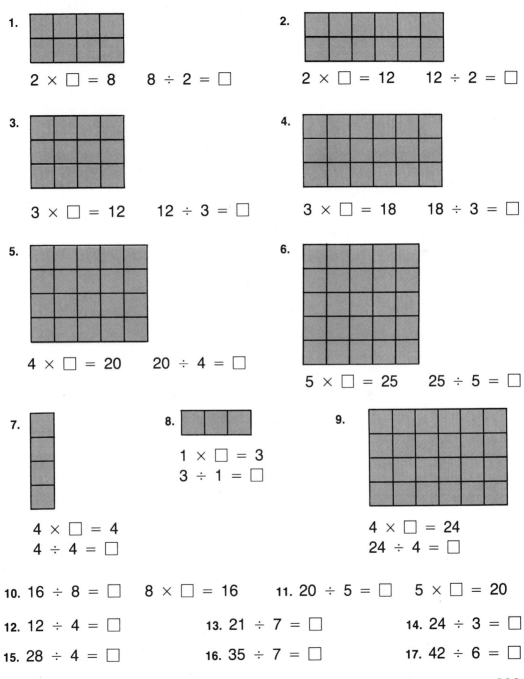

1. $2 \times \square = 8$ $8 \div 2 = \square$

2. $2 \times \square = 12$ $12 \div 2 = \square$

3. $3 \times \square = 12$ $12 \div 3 = \square$

4. $3 \times \square = 18$ $18 \div 3 = \square$

5. $4 \times \square = 20$ $20 \div 4 = \square$

6. $5 \times \square = 25$ $25 \div 5 = \square$

7. $4 \times \square = 4$
$4 \div 4 = \square$

8. $1 \times \square = 3$
$3 \div 1 = \square$

9. $4 \times \square = 24$
$24 \div 4 = \square$

10. $16 \div 8 = \square$ $8 \times \square = 16$

11. $20 \div 5 = \square$ $5 \times \square = 20$

12. $12 \div 4 = \square$

13. $21 \div 7 = \square$

14. $24 \div 3 = \square$

15. $28 \div 4 = \square$

16. $35 \div 7 = \square$

17. $42 \div 6 = \square$

233

Division Facts

There are 32 stamps.
8 stamps go on each page.
How many pages are needed?

$32 \div 8 = 4$ $4 \times 8 = 32$

4 pages will be needed.

36 plants will be planted in 4 rows. Each row will have the same number of plants. How many plants will be in each row?

$36 \div 4 = 9$ $4 \times 9 = 36$

9 plants will be in each row.

Exercises

1. $10 \div 2 = \square$

2. $12 \div 4 = \square$

3. $1 \div 1 = \square$

4. $2 \div 1 = \square$

5. $8 \div 1 = \square$

6. $6 \div 6 = \square$

7. $15 \div 3 = \square$

8. $8 \div 2 = \square$

9. $20 \div 4 = \square$

10. $24 \div 4 = \square$

11. $16 \div 8 = \square$

12. $12 \div 6 = \square$

13. $27 \div 9 = \square$

14. $21 \div 7 = \square$

15. $12 \div 3 = \square$

16. $30 \div 5 = \square$

17. $14 \div 7 = \square$

18. $16 \div 2 = \square$

19. $16 \div 4 = \square$

20. $18 \div 6 = \square$

21. $8 \div 8 = \square$

22. $27 \div 3 = \square$

23. $18 \div 9 = \square$

24. $25 \div 5 = \square$

25. $14 \div 2 = \square$ 26. $18 \div 3 = \square$ 27. $24 \div 6 = \square$

28. $20 \div 5 = \square$ 29. $28 \div 7 = \square$ 30. $32 \div 4 = \square$

31. $35 \div 5 = \square$ 32. $35 \div 7 = \square$ 33. $24 \div 3 = \square$

34. $40 \div 5 = \square$ 35. $42 \div 6 = \square$ 36. $28 \div 4 = \square$

37. $36 \div 9 = \square$ 38. $45 \div 5 = \square$ 39. $45 \div 9 = \square$

40. $24 \div 8 = \square$ 41. $30 \div 6 = \square$ 42. $48 \div 6 = \square$

43. $49 \div 7 = \square$ 44. $54 \div 6 = \square$ 45. $56 \div 7 = \square$

46. $72 \div 8 = \square$ 47. $63 \div 9 = \square$ 48. $81 \div 9 = \square$

Pencils 8¢ each

49. Marion has 56¢ to spend on pencils. How many can she buy?

50. These pupils will be put on 3 teams of the same size. How many will be put on each team?

Who Am I?

1. Divide me by 4. You get 8.

2. Divide me by 9. You get 4.

3. Divide me by 8. You get 4.

4. Divide me by 6. You get 6.

235

Division

12 ÷ 3 = 4   can be written as $3\overline{)12}$ with 4 above.

Both divisions shown above are read
"12 divided by 3 is equal to 4."

Exercises

1. ☐ × 5 = 10   2. 10 ÷ 5 = ☐   3. $5\overline{)10}$

4. ☐ × 4 = 16   5. 16 ÷ 4 = ☐   6. $4\overline{)16}$

7. ☐ × 8 = 24   8. 24 ÷ 8 = ☐   9. $8\overline{)24}$

10. ☐ × 7 = 49   11. 49 ÷ 7 = ☐   12. $7\overline{)49}$

13. ☐ × 9 = 9   14. 9 ÷ 9 = ☐   15. $9\overline{)9}$

16. ☐ × 1 = 8   17. 8 ÷ 1 = ☐   18. $1\overline{)8}$

19. ☐ × 7 = 42   20. 42 ÷ 7 = ☐   21. $7\overline{)42}$

22. $3\overline{)6}$ 23. $3\overline{)21}$ 24. $4\overline{)8}$ 25. $1\overline{)7}$

26. $4\overline{)20}$ 27. $3\overline{)27}$ 28. $5\overline{)25}$ 29. $9\overline{)18}$

30. $7\overline{)7}$ 31. $2\overline{)12}$ 32. $7\overline{)35}$ 33. $8\overline{)32}$

34. $3\overline{)24}$ 35. $6\overline{)30}$ 36. $8\overline{)40}$ 37. $6\overline{)48}$

38. $4\overline{)36}$ 39. $7\overline{)56}$ 40. $6\overline{)24}$ 41. $6\overline{)36}$

42. $9\overline{)81}$ 43. $5\overline{)45}$ 44. $6\overline{)42}$ 45. $9\overline{)54}$

46. $6\overline{)54}$ 47. $8\overline{)64}$ 48. $9\overline{)72}$ 49. $7\overline{)63}$

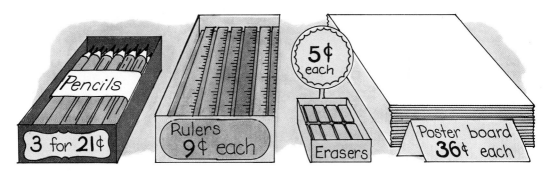

50. How much does 1 pencil cost?

51. How much do 9 pencils cost?

52. You have 36¢. How many rulers could you buy?

53. You have enough money to buy 9 erasers. How many rulers could you buy with your money?

54. You have 34¢. You buy 1 ruler and spend the rest on erasers. How many erasers do you get?

55. Al and 3 friends shared the cost of a poster board equally. How much did each pay?

Multiplication – Division Families

1. What do you notice about the three numbers used in each of the facts shown?

2. The two largest numbers in a family are 48 and 8. Find the other number.

3. The two smallest numbers in a family are 4 and 8. Find the other number.

$6 \times 9 = 54$

$9 \times 6 = 54$

$54 \div 6 = 9$

$54 \div 9 = 6$

Extra Practice—Set A, page 321   **237**

Remainders

There are 15 oranges. Put the same number of oranges in each of 6 trays.

How many oranges will be in each tray?
How many oranges will be left over?

Divide 15 by 6 to answer the questions.

Estimate how many 6's are in 15.		Multiply and subtract.	Write the remainder.

Can you put

1 on each tray? $1 \times 6 = 6$ Yes
2 on each tray? $2 \times 6 = 12$ Yes
3 on each tray? $3 \times 6 = 18$ No

The estimate is **2**.

$$6 \overline{\smash{)}15} \quad \begin{array}{r} 2 \\ \end{array}$$

$$\begin{array}{r} 2 \\ 6 \overline{\smash{)}15} \\ -12 \\ \hline 3 \end{array}$$
remainder┘
(number left)

$$\begin{array}{r} 2 \text{ R3} \\ 6 \overline{\smash{)}15} \\ -12 \\ \hline 3 \end{array}$$

There will be 2 oranges in each tray with 3 oranges left over.

Exercises

Write a digit for each ▧ and for each ☐.

$1 \times 5 = 5$
$2 \times 5 = 10$
$3 \times 5 = 15$
$4 \times 5 = 20$
$5 \times 5 = 25$
$6 \times 5 = 30$
$7 \times 5 = 35$
$8 \times 5 = 40$
$9 \times 5 = 45$

1.
$$\begin{array}{r} ▧ \text{ R}☐ \\ 5 \overline{\smash{)}32} \\ -30 \\ \hline 2 \end{array}$$

2.
$$\begin{array}{r} ▧ \text{ R}☐ \\ 5 \overline{\smash{)}39} \\ -35 \\ \hline 4 \end{array}$$

$1 \times 4 = 4$
$2 \times 4 = 8$
$3 \times 4 = 12$
$4 \times 4 = 16$
$5 \times 4 = 20$
$6 \times 4 = 24$
$7 \times 4 = 28$
$8 \times 4 = 32$
$9 \times 4 = 36$

3.
$$\begin{array}{r} ▧ \text{ R}☐ \\ 4 \overline{\smash{)}9} \\ -8 \\ \hline 1 \end{array}$$

4.
$$\begin{array}{r} ▧ \text{ R}☐ \\ 4 \overline{\smash{)}22} \\ -20 \\ \hline 2 \end{array}$$

5.
$$\begin{array}{r} ▧ \text{ R}☐ \\ 4 \overline{\smash{)}27} \\ -24 \\ \hline 3 \end{array}$$

6.
$$\begin{array}{r} ▧ \text{ R}☐ \\ 4 \overline{\smash{)}34} \\ -32 \\ \hline 2 \end{array}$$

Divide and find the remainder.

7. $6\overline{)7}$ 8. $3\overline{)8}$ 9. $2\overline{)9}$ 10. $2\overline{)7}$

11. $2\overline{)11}$ 12. $3\overline{)13}$ 13. $5\overline{)23}$ 14. $4\overline{)12}$

15. $6\overline{)13}$ 16. $7\overline{)32}$ 17. $4\overline{)26}$ 18. $3\overline{)23}$

19. $4\overline{)31}$ 20. $4\overline{)33}$ 21. $8\overline{)45}$ 22. $7\overline{)38}$

23. $6\overline{)35}$ 24. $7\overline{)50}$ 25. $8\overline{)54}$ 26. $7\overline{)47}$

27. $9\overline{)57}$ 28. $8\overline{)70}$ 29. $9\overline{)46}$ 30. $9\overline{)66}$

Each of 9 pupils will get the same number of pennies.

31. How many pennies will each pupil get if there are 37 pennies? How many will be left over?

32. How many pennies will each pupil get if there are 75 pennies? How many will be left over?

Remainder Clue

You put the checkers in stacks of 3 each. Could the number left over be

1. 0   2. 1

3. 2   4. 3

5. If you divide by 3, what do you know about the remainder?

You put the checkers in stacks of 4 each. Could the number left over be

6. 0   7. 1

8. 3   9. 4

10. If you divide by 4, what do you know about the remainder?

Extra Practice—Set B, page 321

Solving Problems

1. 4 pupils will share these cards equally. How many will each get?

2. Suppose 6 pupils share these cards equally. How many will each get?

3. Suppose 8 pupils share these cards equally. How many will each get? How many cards will be left over?

4. Thomas has 39 pennies to trade for nickels. How many nickels will he get? How many pennies will be left over?

5. You can put 8 bottles in a carton. You have 50 bottles. How many cartons can you fill? How many bottles will be left over?

6. How much does 1 surprise gift cost?

7. You buy 4 surprise gifts. You give the clerk 50¢. How much change should you get?

8. Mike bought 8 surprise gifts. Find the total cost.

9. You have 50 pears. You want to put the same number in each of 9 bags. How many pears will you put in each bag? How many pears will be left over?

10. 35 desks are in a room. You put them into rows of 6 desks each. How many rows can you make? How many desks are left over?

Using a Calculator

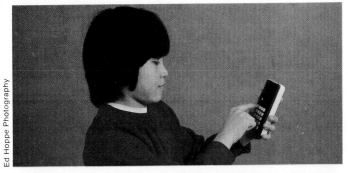

Ed Hoppe Photography

When you push a key, you tell the calculator what to do.

24	÷	4	=	6
Start with this.	Divide by	this number.	Show the answer.	Answer

What number key was pushed?

1. 15 ÷ ? = 3
2. 48 ÷ ? = 6
3. 21 ÷ ? = 7
4. 40 ÷ ? = 5
5. 56 ÷ ? = 8
6. 72 ÷ ? = 9

Was +, −, ×, or ÷ pushed?

7. 6 ? 3 = 2
8. 6 ? 3 = 9
9. 6 ? 3 = 3
10. 6 ? 3 = 18
11. 28 ? 7 = 4
12. 28 ? 7 = 196
13. 18 ? 9 = 27
14. 81 ? 9 = 9
15. 28 ? 0 = 28
16. 9 ? 1 = 9

241

SKILLS REVIEW

Add.

| 1. | 287 +102 | 2. | 358 +321 | 3. | 474 + 16 | 4. | 639 + 90 | 5. | 231 + 87 |

| 6. | 592 + 59 | 7. | 868 + 77 | 8. | 234 +579 | 9. | 146 +486 | 10. | 725 +842 |

Subtract.

| 11. | 336 −120 | 12. | 548 −226 | 13. | 719 − 75 | 14. | 976 − 84 | 15. | 452 − 91 |

| 16. | 654 −399 | 17. | 865 −588 | 18. | 901 −437 | 19. | 500 −312 | 20. | 400 −198 |

Multiply.

| 21. | 21 ×4 | 22. | 84 ×2 | 23. | 24 ×4 | 24. | 59 ×3 | 25. | 98 ×6 |

| 26. | 120 ×3 | 27. | 133 ×2 | 28. | 112 ×6 | 29. | 121 ×7 | 30. | 167 ×5 |

31. It costs $45 a night to stay at a hotel. How much does it cost to stay there 7 nights?

32. 456 pupils attend a school. There are 228 boys. How many girls are there?

33. 925 people came yesterday. 75 people more than that came today. How many people came today?

34. A small TV costs $150. A large TV costs 6 times that much. How much does a large TV cost?

242

Dividing 10's

$$6 \div 2 = 3 \qquad 2\overline{)6}^{\,3}$$

$$6 \text{ tens} \div 2 = 3 \text{ tens} \qquad 2\overline{)60}^{\,30}$$
$$60 \div 2 = 30$$

$$5 \div 5 = 1 \qquad 5\overline{)5}^{\,1}$$

$$5 \text{ tens} \div 5 = 1 \text{ ten} \qquad 5\overline{)50}^{\,10}$$
$$50 \div 5 = 10$$

Exercises

1. $9\overline{)9}$ 2. $9\overline{)90}$ 3. $2\overline{)8}$ 4. $2\overline{)80}$

5. $2\overline{)6}$ 6. $2\overline{)60}$ 7. $7\overline{)7}$ 8. $7\overline{)70}$

9. $3\overline{)3}$ 10. $3\overline{)30}$ 11. $2\overline{)4}$ 12. $2\overline{)40}$

13. $5\overline{)5}$ 14. $5\overline{)50}$ 15. $6\overline{)6}$ 16. $6\overline{)60}$

17. $4\overline{)4}$ 18. $4\overline{)40}$ 19. $8\overline{)8}$ 20. $8\overline{)80}$

21. $3\overline{)6}$ 22. $3\overline{)60}$ 23. $1\overline{)7}$ 24. $1\overline{)70}$

25. $1\overline{)8}$ 26. $1\overline{)80}$ 27. $3\overline{)9}$ 28. $3\overline{)90}$

29. $2\overline{)20}$ 30. $1\overline{)90}$ 31. $4\overline{)80}$ 32. $1\overline{)60}$

33. 5 roses will go in each vase. There are 50 roses in all. How many vases will be used?

34. 60 pupils are marching in the band. The same number of pupils are in each of 3 rows. How many are in each row?

Division (2-digit by 1-digit)

There are 8 dimes and 4 pennies. Six pupils will share the money equally.

How much money will each pupil get?

You can use these steps to divide 84 by 6.

Estimate the tens digit.	Multiply and subtract.	Bring down the 4 ones.	Estimate the ones digit.	Multiply and subtract.
Can each pupil get	T | O	T | O		T | O
1 dime?	1	1		1 | 4
1 ten × 6 = 6 tens	6)8 | 4	6)8 | 4		6)8 | 4
Yes	−6	−6 ↓		−6
2 dimes?	2	2 | 4	4 × 6 = 24 →	2 | 4
2 tens × 6 = 12 tens				−2 | 4
No				0
The tens digit is 1.				

Each pupil will get 14¢.

Exercises

Estimate the tens digit.

1. 3)4 2

2. 4)5 6

3. 3)8 7

4. 2)7 6

Estimate the ones digit.

5.
$$\begin{array}{r} 1\ \blacksquare \\ 2\overline{)3\ 8} \\ -2\ \downarrow \\ \hline 1\ 8 \end{array}$$

6.
$$\begin{array}{r} 1\ \blacksquare \\ 3\overline{)4\ 5} \\ -3\ \downarrow \\ \hline 1\ 5 \end{array}$$

7.
$$\begin{array}{r} 2\ \blacksquare \\ 3\overline{)8\ 1} \\ -6\ \downarrow \\ \hline 2\ 1 \end{array}$$

8.
$$\begin{array}{r} 1\ \blacksquare \\ 5\overline{)6\ 0} \\ -5\ \downarrow \\ \hline 1\ 0 \end{array}$$

Divide.

9. $2\overline{)32}$

10. $2\overline{)78}$

11. $5\overline{)65}$

12. $4\overline{)56}$

13. $2\overline{)50}$

14. $2\overline{)36}$

15. $3\overline{)72}$

16. $2\overline{)54}$

17. $2\overline{)30}$

18. $3\overline{)57}$

19. $3\overline{)78}$

20. $5\overline{)75}$

21. $3\overline{)42}$

22. $2\overline{)90}$

23. $2\overline{)74}$

24. $4\overline{)68}$

25. $5\overline{)90}$

26. $7\overline{)91}$

27. $5\overline{)70}$

28. $7\overline{)84}$

29. 72 birds are in cages. There are 6 birds in each cage. How many cages are there?

30. Kevin has 95 cents. It is all in nickels. How many nickels does he have?

31. Rosa put 48 beads on 3 strings. The same number of beads were put on each string. How many beads were put on each string?

32. 94 pupils will ride in 2 buses. Each bus will carry the same number of pupils. How many pupils will ride in each bus?

33. There are 47 boys and 49 girls. 8 children are put on each team to play games. How many teams are there?

34. The games began at 10:00 and ended at 10:52. There were 4 games in all. Each lasted the same amount of time. How long did each game last?

Division (2-digit by 1-digit)

69 prizes will be bought for a party. Three prizes come in a package. How many packages are needed?

You can use these steps to divide 69 by 3.

Estimate the tens digit.	Multiply and subtract.	Bring down the 9 ones.	Estimate the ones digit.	Multiply and subtract.

1 ten × 3 = 3 tens
The tens digit could be 1.
 	
2 tens × 3 = 6 tens
2 is just right.
 	
The tens digit is 2.
	T O
	   2
	3) 6 9
	  −6
	   0
		T O
		   2
		3) 6 9
		  −6 ↓
		   0 9
			3 × 3 = 9 ⟶	T O
				   2 3
				3) 6 9
				  −6
				   0 9
				   − 9
				     0

23 packages are needed.

Exercises

Estimate the tens digit.

1. 2) 6 4

2. 5) 5 5

3. 3) 9 6

4. 4) 8 0

Estimate the ones digit.

5.
```
    2 ▨
3) 6  3
  −6 ↓
   0  3
```

6.
```
    2 ▨
4) 8  8
  −8 ↓
   0  8
```

7.
```
    2 ▨
2) 4  6
  −4 ↓
   0  6
```

8.
```
    3 ▨
3) 9  0
  −9 ↓
   0  0
```

246

Divide.

9. $2\overline{)86}$ 10. $2\overline{)66}$ 11. $3\overline{)33}$ 12. $4\overline{)80}$

13. $2\overline{)26}$ 14. $2\overline{)62}$ 15. $2\overline{)60}$ 16. $3\overline{)93}$

17. $9\overline{)99}$ 18. $4\overline{)68}$ 19. $3\overline{)51}$ 20. $9\overline{)90}$

21. $5\overline{)65}$ 22. $4\overline{)84}$ 23. $6\overline{)78}$ 24. $7\overline{)98}$

25. $5\overline{)80}$ 26. $2\overline{)86}$ 27. $4\overline{)96}$ 28. $6\overline{)84}$

29. 6 pupils will share 66 crayons equally. How many crayons will each pupil get?

30. Tim is paid $4 for mowing each lawn. Last week he earned $48. How many did he mow?

31. 90 magazines are put into stacks of 6 each. How many stacks are there?

32. 52 cards are dealt to 4 players. How many cards does each player get?

∩umber Fun

1. Pick a number less than 30.

2. Add 6.

3. Multiply by 3.

4. Subtract 15.

5. Divide by 3.

6. Subtract the number you started with.

Try this with several different numbers. Do you always end with the same number? If so, what is that number?

Jacqueline Durand

Remainders

You have 31 slices of bread. You use 2 slices for each sandwich.

How many sandwiches can you make?

How many slices will be left?

You can use these steps to divide 31 by 2.

Estimate the tens digit.	Multiply and subtract.	Bring down the ones.	Estimate the ones digit.	Multiply and subtract. Write the remainder.

1 ten × 2 = 2 tens
  The tens digit could be 1.
2 tens × 2 = 4 tens
  TOO BIG!
  The tens digit is 1.
	T | O
	  1
	2)3 1
	  −2
	  1
		T | O
		  1
		2)3 1
		  −2 ↓
		  1 1
			5 × 2 = 10
			  Could be 5.
			6 × 2 = 12
			  TOO BIG!
			  The ones digit is 5.
				T | O
				  1 5 R1
				2)3 1
				  −2
				  1 1
				  −1 0
				  1

You can make 15 sandwiches. There will be 1 slice left.

Exercises

Complete each division and write the remainder.

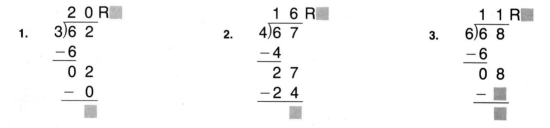

1.
```
   2 0 R▓
3)6 2
 −6
  0 2
 −  0
    ▓
```

2.
```
   1 6 R▓
4)6 7
 −4
  2 7
 −2 4
    ▓
```

3.
```
   1 1 R▓
6)6 8
 −6
  0 8
 − ▓
    ▓
```

248

```
     2 ▧  R▧              2 ▧  R▧            ▧ ▧  R▧
4. 4)8 3             5. 3)8 2            6. 5)5 4
   −8                  −6                  −▧
     ▧ ▧                 ▧ ▧                ▧ ▧
   − ▧                  − ▧                − ▧
   ─────               ─────              ─────
     ▧                   ▧                  ▧
```

Divide and find the remainder.

7. 4)42   8. 3)31   9. 2)41   10. 3)62

11. 5)53   12. 4)51   13. 2)61   14. 3)74

15. 6)65   16. 5)80   17. 4)81   18. 6)68

19. 5)84   20. 2)81   21. 2)29   22. 3)92

23. 5)60   24. 3)51   25. 9)69   26. 5)51

27. 9)58   28. 4)63   29. 5)72   30. 4)80

31. 3)61   32. 7)99   33. 2)95   34. 3)94

35. 3)50   36. 7)75   37. 8)90   38. 4)46

39. 2)93   40. 7)91   41. 8)87   42. 7)88

43. You have 96 beads. You make
    bracelets having 6 beads each.
    How many bracelets can you
    make? How many beads will
    be left?

44. Suppose you make bracelets
    having 7 beads each. How
    many bracelets can you make?
    How many beads will be left?

45. Suppose you make bracelets
    having 9 beads each. How
    many bracelets can you make?
    How many beads will be left?

Division Practice

Complete each division fact.

1. $1\overline{)9}$
2. $3\overline{)24}$
3. $5\overline{)40}$
4. $4\overline{)36}$

5. $6\overline{)48}$
6. $9\overline{)45}$
7. $8\overline{)72}$
8. $7\overline{)49}$

9. $6\overline{)42}$
10. $9\overline{)81}$
11. $7\overline{)56}$
12. $8\overline{)56}$

13. $9\overline{)63}$
14. $6\overline{)54}$
15. $8\overline{)64}$
16. $7\overline{)63}$

Divide.

17. $4\overline{)13}$
18. $5\overline{)19}$
19. $2\overline{)17}$
20. $3\overline{)25}$

21. $6\overline{)38}$
22. $7\overline{)30}$
23. $8\overline{)45}$
24. $9\overline{)83}$

25. $3\overline{)60}$
26. $4\overline{)80}$
27. $2\overline{)80}$
28. $3\overline{)90}$

29. $2\overline{)32}$
30. $2\overline{)54}$
31. $3\overline{)48}$
32. $4\overline{)56}$

33. $5\overline{)70}$
34. $6\overline{)72}$
35. $4\overline{)60}$
36. $3\overline{)57}$

37. $3\overline{)96}$
38. $4\overline{)48}$
39. $5\overline{)55}$
40. $2\overline{)86}$

41. $4\overline{)94}$
42. $3\overline{)62}$
43. $5\overline{)64}$
44. $2\overline{)97}$

45. $7\overline{)80}$
46. $4\overline{)83}$
47. $8\overline{)99}$
48. $9\overline{)95}$

49. A building has 96 windows. Each floor has 8 windows. How many floors are there?

50. 9 pupils share 75 marbles equally. How many does each get? How many are left over?

250

Solving Problems

1. There are 98 plants. 7 plants are in each row. How many rows are there?

2. A train went 52 miles each hour. How many miles did it go in 4 hours?

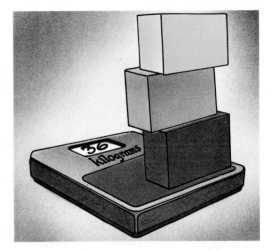

3. Each bag weighs 6 pounds. How many bags are there?

4. Each box weighs the same. How much does 1 box weigh?

5. Andy saved $27 in 9 weeks. He saved the same amount each week. How much did he save each week?

6. 6 bottles fill a carton. You have 68 bottles. How many cartons can you fill? How many bottles will be left over?

7. You have 90¢. How many comic books can you buy? How much money will you have left?

8. You buy 8 comic books. Find the total cost.

9. You buy 5 comic books. You give the clerk 50¢. How much change should you get?

CHAPTER REVIEW

1. $16 \div 2 = \square$ **2.** $28 \div 4 = \square$ **3.** $42 \div 6 = \square$

4. $5\overline{)40}$ **5.** $7\overline{)56}$ **6.** $3\overline{)21}$ **7.** $8\overline{)32}$

8. 12 shells are shared equally among 4 boys. How many does each get?

9. Beth had 30 stamps. She put 6 in each row. How many rows were there?

10. $3\overline{)7}$ **11.** $5\overline{)13}$ **12.** $2\overline{)19}$ **13.** $3\overline{)26}$

14. $9\overline{)41}$ **15.** $5\overline{)49}$ **16.** $3\overline{)60}$ **17.** $2\overline{)80}$

18. $6\overline{)90}$ **19.** $3\overline{)54}$ **20.** $3\overline{)48}$ **21.** $4\overline{)68}$

22. $2\overline{)22}$ **23.** $8\overline{)88}$ **24.** $4\overline{)80}$ **25.** $3\overline{)99}$

26. Dino has 36 rabbits. He keeps 3 in each pen. How many pens are there?

27. 57¢ is shared equally among 3 girls. How much money does each girl get?

28. $5\overline{)53}$ **29.** $6\overline{)75}$ **30.** $7\overline{)93}$ **31.** $3\overline{)92}$

32. Michelle has 85¢. How many clickers can she buy? How much money will she have left?

33. 83 clickers are put into bags of 4 each. How many bags are filled? How many clickers are left over?

Clickers 7¢ each

12 Fractions and Decimals

Fredrik D. Bodin

Fractions

Every figure in this lesson is separated into parts of the same size.

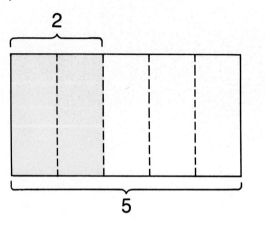

2 ← There are 2 parts colored.

5 ← There are 5 parts in all.

2 out of 5 parts are colored.

$\frac{2}{5}$ of the figure is colored.

$\frac{2}{5}$ is a **fraction.**

Exercises

Choose the fraction that tells how much is colored.

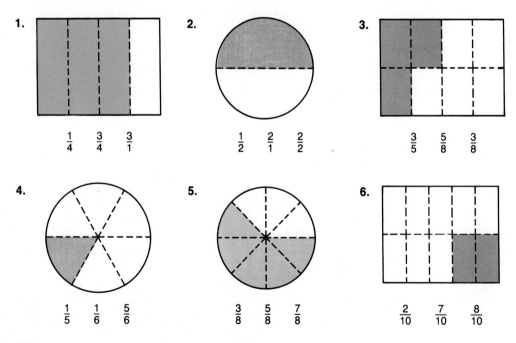

1.

$\frac{1}{4}$ $\frac{3}{4}$ $\frac{3}{1}$

2.

$\frac{1}{2}$ $\frac{2}{1}$ $\frac{2}{2}$

3.

$\frac{3}{5}$ $\frac{5}{8}$ $\frac{3}{8}$

4.

$\frac{1}{5}$ $\frac{1}{6}$ $\frac{5}{6}$

5.

$\frac{3}{8}$ $\frac{5}{8}$ $\frac{7}{8}$

6.

$\frac{2}{10}$ $\frac{7}{10}$ $\frac{8}{10}$

254

7. $\frac{4}{1}$ $\frac{4}{5}$ $\frac{1}{5}$

8. $\frac{3}{8}$ $\frac{3}{6}$ $\frac{5}{8}$

9. $\frac{1}{3}$ $\frac{2}{3}$ $\frac{3}{1}$

10. $\frac{3}{10}$ $\frac{7}{10}$ $\frac{8}{10}$

11. $\frac{1}{4}$ $\frac{3}{4}$ $\frac{4}{3}$

12. $\frac{2}{2}$ $\frac{2}{1}$ $\frac{1}{2}$

13. $\frac{1}{10}$ $\frac{1}{8}$ $\frac{9}{10}$

14. $\frac{1}{3}$ $\frac{2}{3}$ $\frac{2}{1}$

15. $\frac{6}{1}$ $\frac{1}{6}$ $\frac{6}{6}$

16. $\frac{1}{4}$ $\frac{3}{4}$ $\frac{4}{1}$

17. $\frac{1}{4}$ $\frac{4}{4}$ $\frac{4}{1}$

18. $\frac{4}{8}$ $\frac{8}{4}$ $\frac{5}{8}$

19. $\frac{4}{6}$ $\frac{4}{10}$ $\frac{6}{10}$

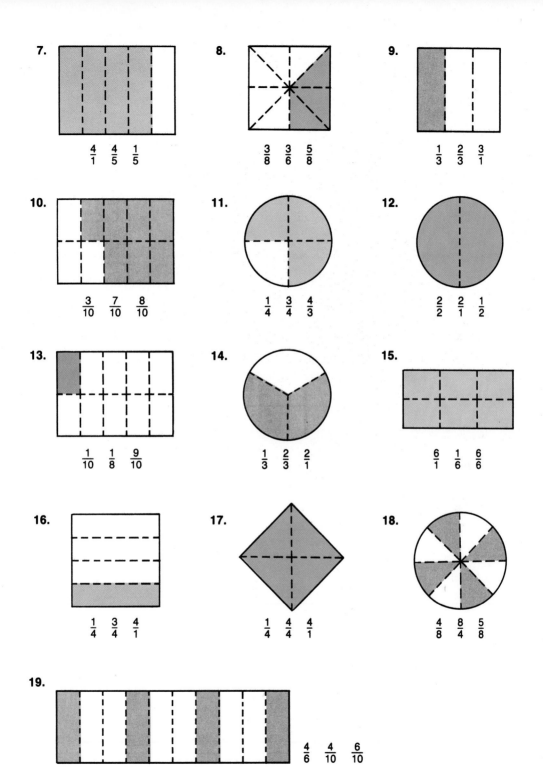

255

Reading Fractions

$\dfrac{2}{3}$ → two thirds $\dfrac{3}{5}$ → three fifths

Exercises

Read these fractions.

1. $\dfrac{1}{4}$ 2. $\dfrac{3}{3}$ 3. $\dfrac{2}{5}$ 4. $\dfrac{7}{10}$ 5. $\dfrac{1}{2}$ 6. $\dfrac{5}{8}$

Write as a fraction.

7. one third   8. three fourths   9. two eighths

10. nine tenths   11. four fifths   12. one half

13. four fourths   14. three eighths   15. three tenths

16. one tenth   17. six tenths   18. six eighths

Half Past the Hour

Write the time for each clock.
Do it as shown for the first clock.

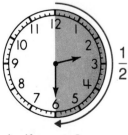      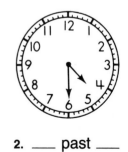

half past 2   1. ___ past ___   2. ___ past ___

Why or Why Not?

1. Does this show $\frac{1}{3}$?

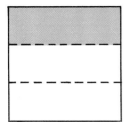

2. Does this show $\frac{1}{3}$?

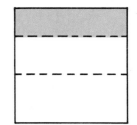

3. Does this show $\frac{1}{3}$?

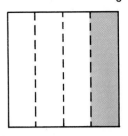

4. Does this show $\frac{1}{4}$?

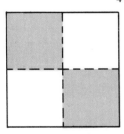

5. Does this show $\frac{1}{4}$?

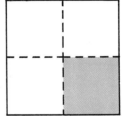

6. Does this show $\frac{1}{4}$?

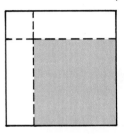

7. Does this show $\frac{1}{2}$?

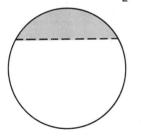

8. Does this show $\frac{1}{2}$?

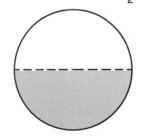

9. Does this show $\frac{1}{2}$?

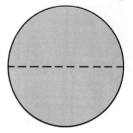

10. Does this show $\frac{2}{5}$?

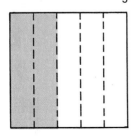

11. Does this show $\frac{2}{5}$?

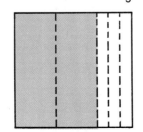

12. Does this show $\frac{2}{5}$?

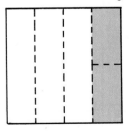

257

Writing Fractions

Every figure in this lesson is separated into parts of the same size.

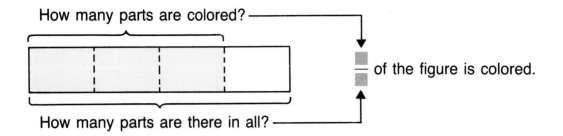

How many parts are colored?

$\frac{\blacksquare}{\blacksquare}$ of the figure is colored.

How many parts are there in all?

Exercises

Write a fraction to tell how much is colored.

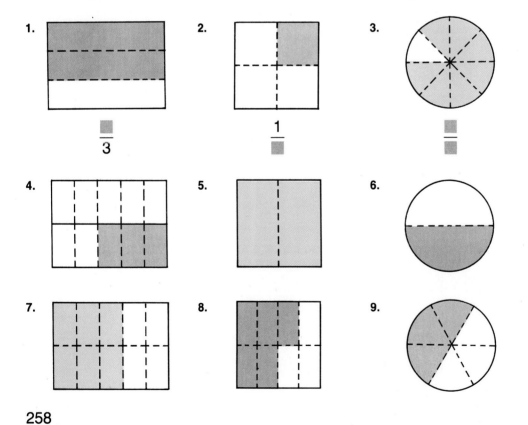

1.

$\dfrac{\blacksquare}{3}$

2.

$\dfrac{1}{\blacksquare}$

3.

$\dfrac{\blacksquare}{\blacksquare}$

4.

5.

6.

7.

8.

9.

258

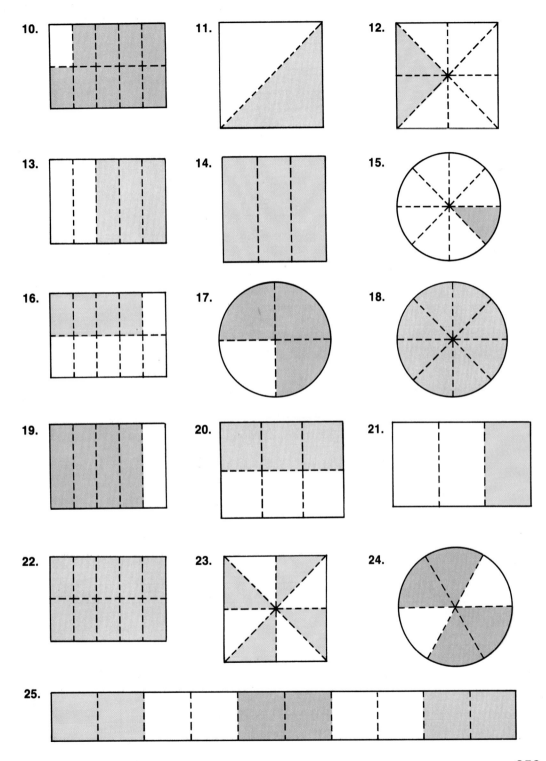

10.

11.

12.

13.

14.

15.

16.

17.

18.

19.

20.

21.

22.

23.

24.

25.

Writing Fractions

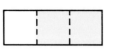

2 out of 3 parts are colored.
Each part has the same size.
$\frac{2}{3}$ of the figure is colored.

1 out of 3 parts is not colored.
Each part has the same size.
$\frac{1}{3}$ of the figure is not colored.

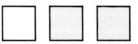

2 out of 3 squares are colored.
$\frac{2}{3}$ of the squares are colored.

1 out of 3 squares is not colored.
$\frac{1}{3}$ of the squares are not colored.

Exercises

Write a fraction to tell how many are colored.

1.

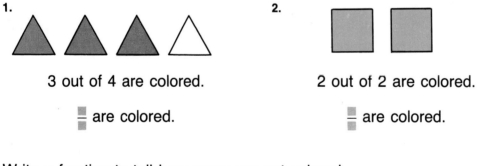

3 out of 4 are colored.

$\frac{}{}$ are colored.

2.

2 out of 2 are colored.

$\frac{}{}$ are colored.

Write a fraction to tell how many are not colored.

3.

2 out of 5 are not colored.

$\frac{}{}$ are not colored.

4.

4 out of 4 are not colored.

$\frac{}{}$ are not colored.

Write a fraction to tell how many are colored.
Then write a fraction to tell how many are not colored.

5.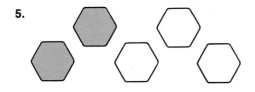

6.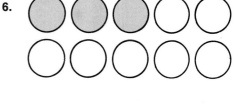

7.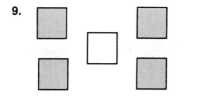

8.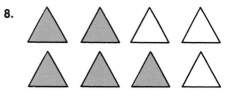

9.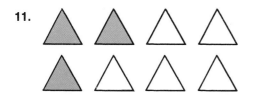

10.

11.

12.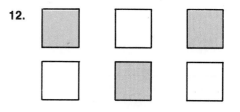

13.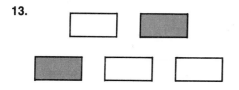

14.

261

Writing Fractions

How many books are open? ⟶ 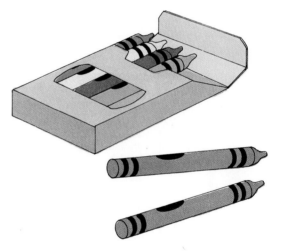

How many books are there in all? ⟶ $\dfrac{\blacksquare}{\blacksquare}$ of the books are open.

Exercises

Complete.

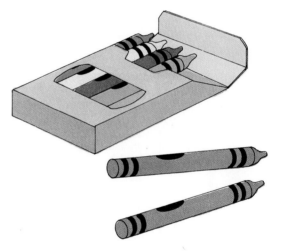

1. ___ crayons in the box

2. ___ crayons not in the box

3. ___ crayons in all

4. $\dfrac{\blacksquare}{\blacksquare}$ are in the box.

5. $\dfrac{\blacksquare}{\blacksquare}$ are not in the box.

Write a fraction for each $\dfrac{\blacksquare}{\blacksquare}$.

6.

$\dfrac{\blacksquare}{\blacksquare}$ have flowers.

$\dfrac{\blacksquare}{\blacksquare}$ do not have flowers.

7.

$\dfrac{\blacksquare}{\blacksquare}$ have flags.

$\dfrac{\blacksquare}{\blacksquare}$ do not have flags.

262

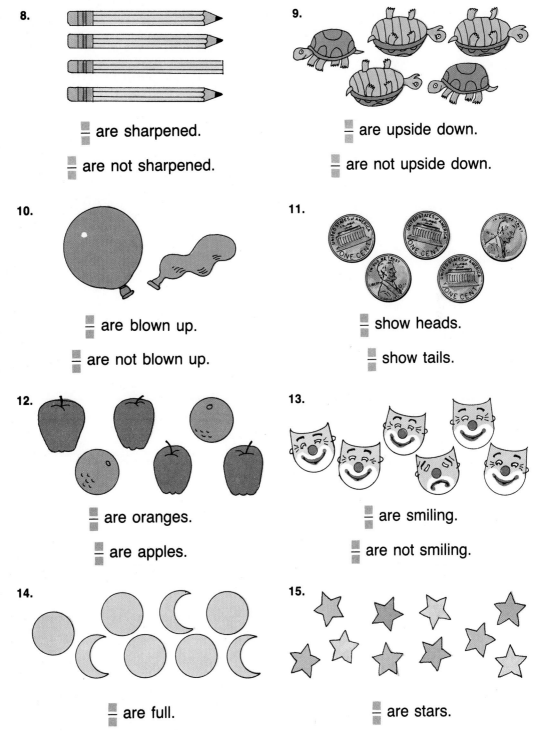

8.

$\frac{}{}$ are sharpened.

$\frac{}{}$ are not sharpened.

9.

$\frac{}{}$ are upside down.

$\frac{}{}$ are not upside down.

10.

$\frac{}{}$ are blown up.

$\frac{}{}$ are not blown up.

11.

$\frac{}{}$ show heads.

$\frac{}{}$ show tails.

12.

$\frac{}{}$ are oranges.

$\frac{}{}$ are apples.

13.

$\frac{}{}$ are smiling.

$\frac{}{}$ are not smiling.

14.

$\frac{}{}$ are full.

15.

$\frac{}{}$ are stars.

263

Writing Fractions

Count the children.

Then write a fraction for each $\frac{\blacksquare}{\blacksquare}$.

1. $\frac{\blacksquare}{\blacksquare}$ are skating.

2. $\frac{\blacksquare}{\blacksquare}$ are not skating.

3. $\frac{\blacksquare}{\blacksquare}$ are sitting down.

4. $\frac{\blacksquare}{\blacksquare}$ are not sitting down.

5. $\frac{\blacksquare}{\blacksquare}$ are wearing red coats.

6. $\frac{\blacksquare}{\blacksquare}$ are not wearing red coats.

7. $\frac{\blacksquare}{\blacksquare}$ are wearing green coats.

8. $\frac{\blacksquare}{\blacksquare}$ are wearing coats.

9. $\frac{\blacksquare}{\blacksquare}$ are wearing blue hats.

10. $\frac{\blacksquare}{\blacksquare}$ are not wearing blue hats.

11. $\frac{\blacksquare}{\blacksquare}$ are wearing red hats.

12. $\frac{\blacksquare}{\blacksquare}$ are not wearing red hats.

13. $\frac{\blacksquare}{\blacksquare}$ are wearing yellow hats.

14. $\frac{\blacksquare}{\blacksquare}$ are wearing hats.

Extra Practice—Set B, page 323

Use a $ and . to write the value.

1. 1 dollar, 4 dimes, 7 pennies   2. 2 dollars, 6 dimes

3. 5 dollars, 4 pennies   4. 2 dimes, 9 pennies

Subtract.

5. 781	6. 516	7. 668	8. 553	9. 800
-290	-444	-499	-264	-132

Multiply.

10. 23	11. 24	12. 18	13. 324	14. 132
$\times 2$	$\times 4$	$\times 5$	$\times 2$	$\times 3$
46	96 96	90		

15. 216	16. 281	17. 192	18. 167	19. 159
$\times 4$	$\times 3$	$\times 4$	$\times 4$	$\times 5$

Divide.

20. $2\overline{)18}$ 21. $3\overline{)24}$ 22. $5\overline{)30}$ 23. $7\overline{)49}$ 24. $8\overline{)56}$

25. $6\overline{)50}$ 26. $6\overline{)98}$ 27. $6\overline{)78}$ 28. $4\overline{)88}$ 29. $3\overline{)93}$

30. $2\overline{)80}$ 31. $8\overline{)96}$ 32. $7\overline{)96}$ 33. $6\overline{)75}$ 34. $3\overline{)83}$

35. 48 pupils can ride in each bus. How many pupils can ride in 6 buses?

36. 96 pennies are shared equally among 6 pupils. How many pennies does each pupil get?

265

Equal Amounts

Fold a square piece of paper in half and open it. Color 1 part.

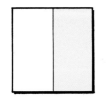

1 out of 2 parts is colored.
$\frac{1}{2}$ of the paper is colored.

Fold the piece of paper as before and then fold it in half again. Open it.

2 out of 4 parts are colored.
$\frac{2}{4}$ of the paper is colored.

Do both pictures show the same amount colored?

$\frac{1}{2}$ and $\frac{2}{4}$ name the same amount.

$$\frac{1}{2} = \frac{2}{4}$$

Exercises

Complete.

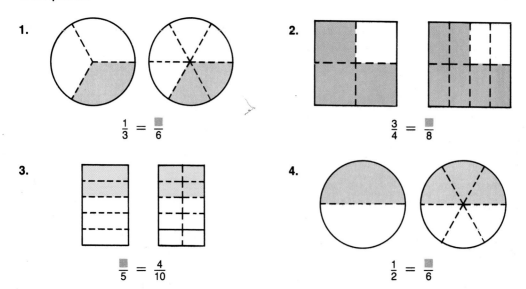

1. $\frac{1}{3} = \frac{\blacksquare}{6}$

2. $\frac{3}{4} = \frac{\blacksquare}{8}$

3. $\frac{\blacksquare}{5} = \frac{4}{10}$

4. $\frac{1}{2} = \frac{\blacksquare}{6}$

266

5.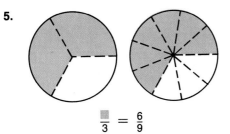

$$\frac{\blacksquare}{3} = \frac{6}{9}$$

6.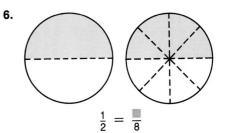

$$\frac{1}{2} = \frac{\blacksquare}{8}$$

7.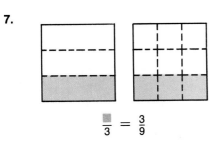

$$\frac{\blacksquare}{3} = \frac{3}{9}$$

8.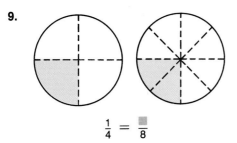

$$\frac{\blacksquare}{4} = \frac{4}{8}$$

9.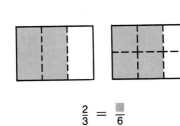

$$\frac{1}{4} = \frac{\blacksquare}{8}$$

10.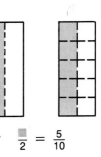

$$\frac{\blacksquare}{2} = \frac{5}{10}$$

11.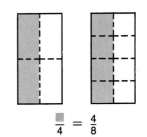

$$\frac{2}{3} = \frac{\blacksquare}{6}$$

12.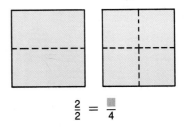

$$\frac{2}{2} = \frac{\blacksquare}{4}$$

Complete the Pattern

$$\frac{1}{2}, \quad \frac{2}{4}, \quad \frac{3}{6}, \quad \frac{\blacksquare}{\blacksquare}, \quad \frac{\blacksquare}{\blacksquare}, \quad \frac{\blacksquare}{\blacksquare}$$

Extra Practice—Set A, page 324   **267**

Mixed Numerals

2 waffles $\frac{3}{4}$ waffle

2 + $\frac{3}{4}$ waffles

$2\frac{3}{4}$ or *two and three-fourths* waffles are shown.

$2\frac{3}{4}$ is a **mixed numeral.**

Exercises

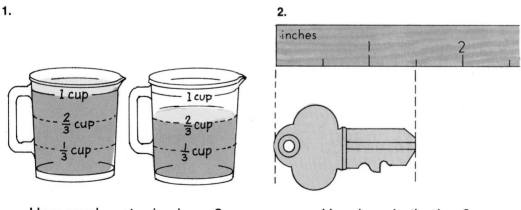

1.

How much water is shown?

2.

How long is the key?

Write a mixed numeral for each ___.

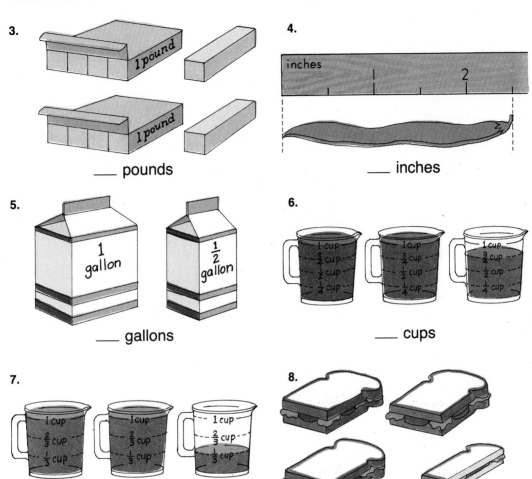

3.

___ pounds

4.

inches

2

___ inches

5.

1 gallon

½ gallon

___ gallons

6.

1 cup
¾ cup
½ cup
¼ cup

___ cups

7.

1 cup
⅔ cup
⅓ cup

___ cups

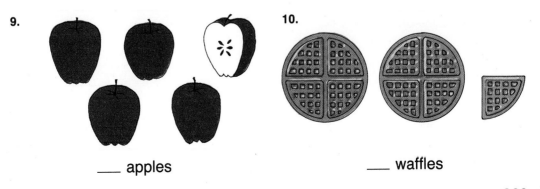

8.

___ sandwiches

9.

___ apples

10.

___ waffles

Comparing Fractions

The two boxes are the same size.

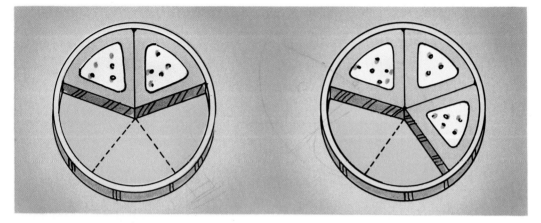

This box is $\frac{2}{5}$ full.

Which box has less cheese?

$\frac{2}{5}$ is less than $\frac{3}{5}$.

$$\frac{2}{5} < \frac{3}{5}$$

This box is $\frac{3}{5}$ full.

Which box has more cheese?

$\frac{3}{5}$ is more than $\frac{2}{5}$.

$$\frac{3}{5} > \frac{2}{5}$$

Exercises

Write < or > for each ⬤.

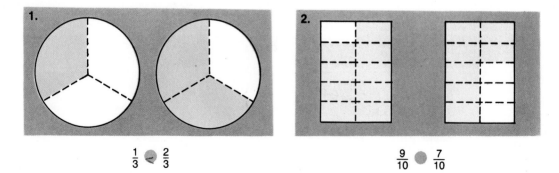

1.

$\frac{1}{3}$ ⬤ $\frac{2}{3}$

2.

$\frac{9}{10}$ ⬤ $\frac{7}{10}$

3.

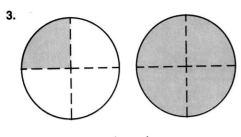

$\dfrac{1}{4}$ ⊚< $\dfrac{4}{4}$

4.

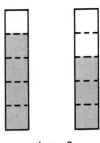

$\dfrac{4}{5}$ ⊚ $\dfrac{3}{5}$

5.

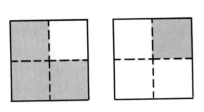

$\dfrac{3}{4}$ ⊚ $\dfrac{1}{4}$

6.

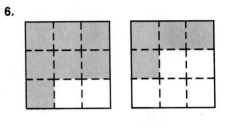

$\dfrac{7}{9}$ ⊚ $\dfrac{4}{9}$

7.

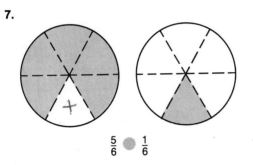

$\dfrac{5}{6}$ ⊚ $\dfrac{1}{6}$

8.

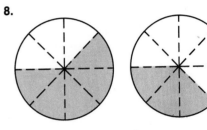

$\dfrac{5}{8}$ ⊚ $\dfrac{3}{8}$

9.

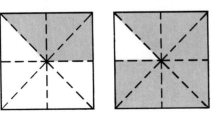

$\dfrac{3}{8}$ ⊚ $\dfrac{7}{8}$

10.

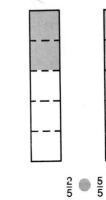

$\dfrac{2}{5}$ ⊚ $\dfrac{5}{5}$

Fraction Practice

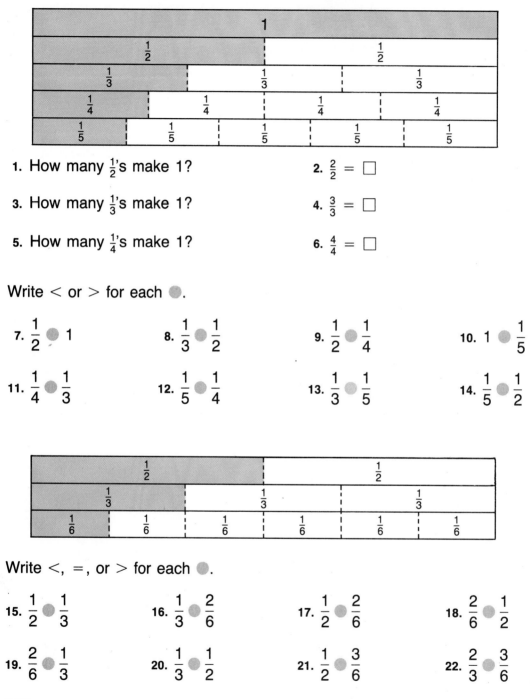

1. How many $\frac{1}{2}$'s make 1?

2. $\frac{2}{2} = \square$

3. How many $\frac{1}{3}$'s make 1?

4. $\frac{3}{3} = \square$

5. How many $\frac{1}{4}$'s make 1?

6. $\frac{4}{4} = \square$

Write $<$ or $>$ for each ●.

7. $\frac{1}{2}$ ● 1

8. $\frac{1}{3}$ ● $\frac{1}{2}$

9. $\frac{1}{2}$ ● $\frac{1}{4}$

10. 1 ● $\frac{1}{5}$

11. $\frac{1}{4}$ ● $\frac{1}{3}$

12. $\frac{1}{5}$ ● $\frac{1}{4}$

13. $\frac{1}{3}$ ● $\frac{1}{5}$

14. $\frac{1}{5}$ ● $\frac{1}{2}$

Write $<$, $=$, or $>$ for each ●.

15. $\frac{1}{2}$ ● $\frac{1}{3}$

16. $\frac{1}{3}$ ● $\frac{2}{6}$

17. $\frac{1}{2}$ ● $\frac{2}{6}$

18. $\frac{2}{6}$ ● $\frac{1}{2}$

19. $\frac{2}{6}$ ● $\frac{1}{3}$

20. $\frac{1}{3}$ ● $\frac{1}{2}$

21. $\frac{1}{2}$ ● $\frac{3}{6}$

22. $\frac{2}{3}$ ● $\frac{3}{6}$

272

Stop and Think

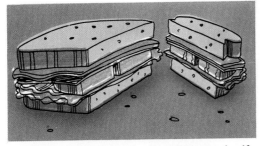

1. Dom said he got the bigger half of the sandwich. Can he be right?

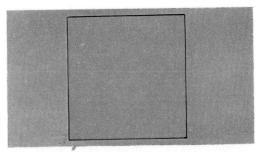

2. Draw some squares. How many ways can you cut a square in half?

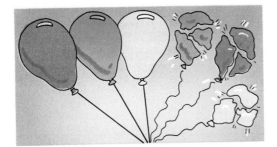

3. Leon said $\frac{1}{2}$ of the balloons broke. Dessa said $\frac{3}{6}$ of them broke. Can they both be right?

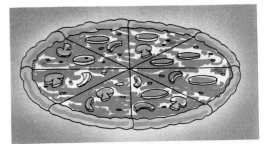

4. Gina is going to share a pizza with seven friends. Why did she cut it into pieces of the same size?

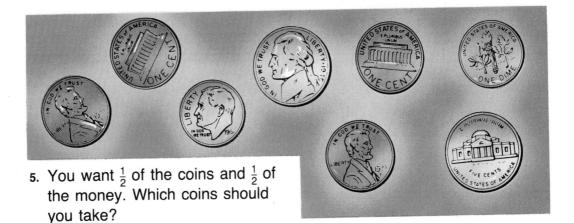

5. You want $\frac{1}{2}$ of the coins and $\frac{1}{2}$ of the money. Which coins should you take?

Tenths

The box is $\frac{7}{10}$ filled.

$\frac{7}{10}$ can be written 0.7.

$$\frac{7}{10} = 0.7$$

0.7 is called a **decimal.**

0 is used to show that there are no ones.

decimal point

$\frac{7}{10}$ and 0.7 are read "seven tenths."

Give a decimal to tell how much of the box is not filled.

Exercises

Write a decimal to tell how much is colored.

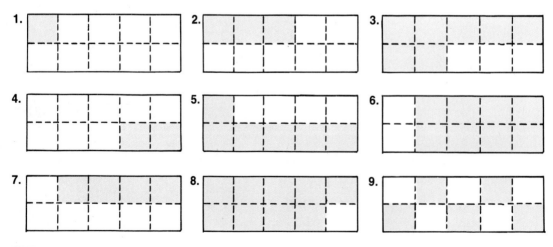

1.

2.

3.

4.

5.

6.

7.

8.

9.

Write a decimal for each fraction.

10. $\dfrac{5}{10}$ 11. $\dfrac{2}{10}$ 12. $\dfrac{1}{10}$ 13. $\dfrac{4}{10}$

14. $\dfrac{8}{10}$ 15. $\dfrac{7}{10}$ 16. $\dfrac{9}{10}$ 17. $\dfrac{6}{10}$

Write a fraction for each decimal.

18. 0.9 19. 0.3 20. 0.1 21. 0.7

22. 0.2 23. 0.4 24. 0.5 25. 0.6

Write a decimal for each word name.

26. one tenth 27. five tenths 28. four tenths

29. seven tenths 30. two tenths 31. three tenths

32. eight tenths 33. six tenths 34. nine tenths

Tenths of a Centimeter

1 millimeter or 0.1 centimeter

1 mm = 0.1 cm

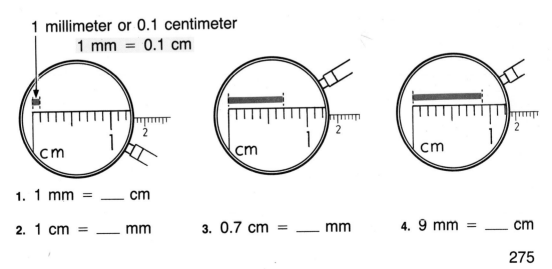

1. 1 mm = ___ cm

2. 1 cm = ___ mm 3. 0.7 cm = ___ mm 4. 9 mm = ___ cm

Decimals

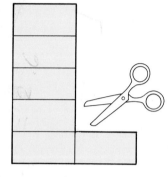

2 sheets $\frac{6}{10}$ sheet

$2\frac{6}{10}$ sheets

$2\frac{6}{10}$ can be written 2.6.

$$2\frac{6}{10} = 2.6$$

$2\frac{6}{10}$ and 2.6 are read "two and six tenths."

Exercises

Write a decimal to tell how much is colored.

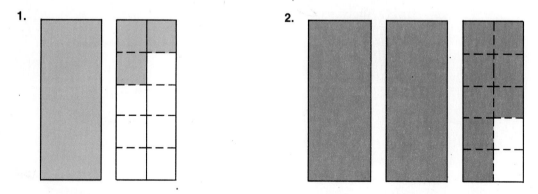

1.   2.

276

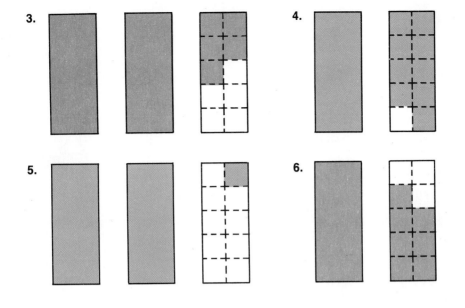

3.

4.

5.

6.

Write as a decimal.

7. $3\frac{2}{10}$

8. $2\frac{9}{10}$

9. $4\frac{4}{10}$

10. $10\frac{1}{10}$

11. $2\frac{7}{10}$

12. $5\frac{6}{10}$

13. $23\frac{3}{10}$

14. $1\frac{5}{10}$

15. Jose ran the 50-yard dash in $7\frac{3}{10}$ seconds.

16. Becky put $15\frac{9}{10}$ gallons of gasoline in the car.

17. Your body temperature is $98\frac{6}{10}$ degrees.

Write as a mixed numeral.

18. 3.8

19. 4.5

20. 1.3

21. 7.7

22. 2.4

23. 22.2

24. 10.9

25. 55.1

26. The world's largest tomato weighed 6.5 pounds.

27. The car odometer read 1687.8 miles.

CHAPTER REVIEW

Write a fraction to tell how much is colored.

1. ___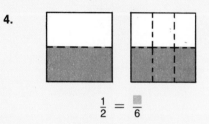

2. ___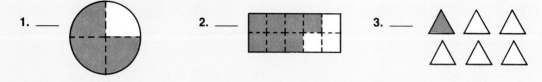

3. ___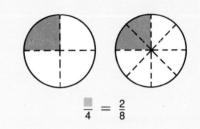

Complete.

4.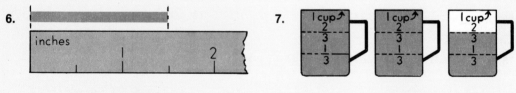

$$\frac{1}{2} = \frac{\blacksquare}{6}$$

5.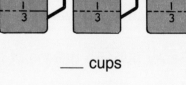

$$\frac{\blacksquare}{4} = \frac{2}{8}$$

Write a mixed numeral for each ___.

6.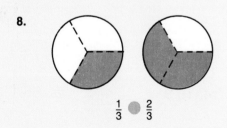

___ inches

7.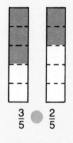

___ cups

Write < or > for each ●.

8.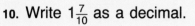

$$\frac{1}{3} \; ● \; \frac{2}{3}$$

9.

$$\frac{3}{5} \; ● \; \frac{2}{5}$$

10. Write $1\frac{7}{10}$ as a decimal.

11. Write 0.9 as a fraction.

13 Graphs

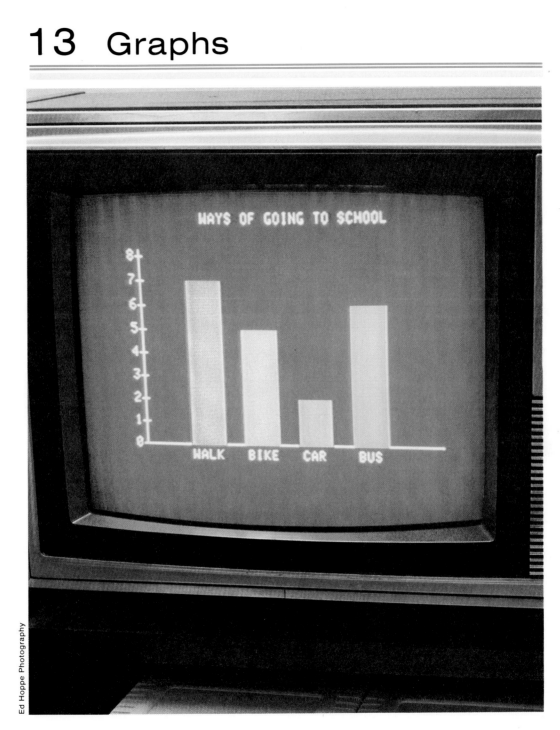

Ed Hoppe Photography

279

Picture Graph

This graph is called a **picture graph.** It shows the number of books read by each pupil.

Each 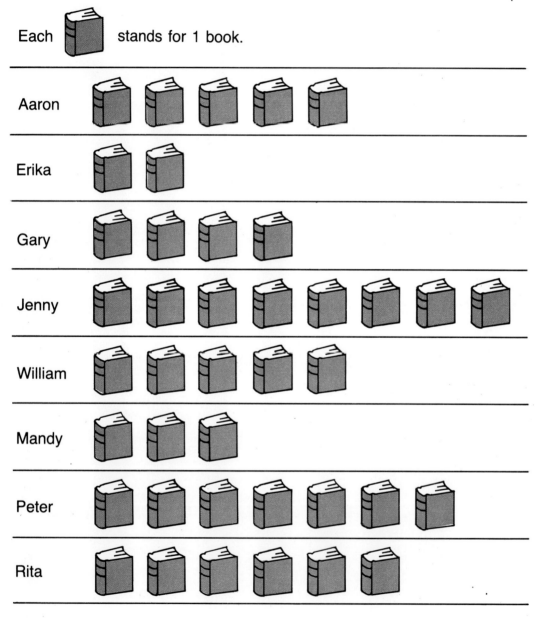 stands for 1 book.

Aaron	📕📕📕📕📕
Erika	📕📕
Gary	📕📕📕📕
Jenny	📕📕📕📕📕📕📕📕
William	📕📕📕📕📕
Mandy	📕📕📕
Peter	📕📕📕📕📕📕📕
Rita	📕📕📕📕📕📕

280

Exercises

How many books were read by each pupil?

1. Aaron

2. Rita

3. Mandy

4. Gary

5. Peter

6. Jenny

7. William

8. Erika

Tell who read each number of books.

9. 8 books

10. 2 books

11. 4 books

12. 7 books

13. Who read the most books?

14. Who read the fewest books?

15. Which two pupils read the same number of books?

Each ✏ stands for 1 lesson finished.

Alba	✏ ✏ ✏ ✏ ✏ ✏
Olga	✏ ✏
Vince	✏ ✏ ✏ ✏
Ron	✏ ✏ ✏

How many lessons were finished by

16. Alba

17. Ron

18. Olga

19. Vince

Tell who finished each number of lessons.

20. 3 lessons

21. 6 lessons

22. 2 lessons

23. 4 lessons

24. Who finished twice as many lessons as Olga?

25. How many more lessons must Ron finish if he wants 8 ✏ 's?

Making a Picture Graph

Favorite Colors	
Color	Number of pupils
Red	4
Orange	3
Yellow	2
Green	5
Blue	6
Purple	4

Pupils raised their hand when the teacher named their favorite color.

This table shows how many pupils chose each color.

Exercises

1. Make the following on grid paper:

Favorite Colors

Red	●	●	●	●	
Orange					
Yellow					
Green					
Blue					
Purple					

2. The table shows that 4 pupils chose red. Draw 4 ● 's after *Red* as shown.

3. How many ● 's should be drawn after *Orange?*

4. Complete the picture graph for favorite colors. You can use colored ● 's.

5. Make a picture graph to show the number of perfect papers each pupil has. Draw a ★ to stand for 1 perfect paper.

Perfect Papers

Pupil	Number
Bonnie	4
Hans	2
Manuel	3
Naomi	1
Tess	5

6. Make a picture graph to show the number of games each team won. Draw a 🏈 to stand for 1 game.

Games Won

Team	Number
Flyers	2
Martians	6
Rockets	3
Stars	5

Picture This

Copy and complete this picture graph to show how many houses each pupil passes.

Each 🏠 stands for 3 houses.

Tom	🏠 🏠 🏠 🏠
Laurie	
Alison	
Cara	
Robert	
Gene	

Pupil	Number of houses passed on the way to school
Tom	12
Laurie	3
Alison	15
Cara	9
Robert	6
Gene	18

Row-Seat

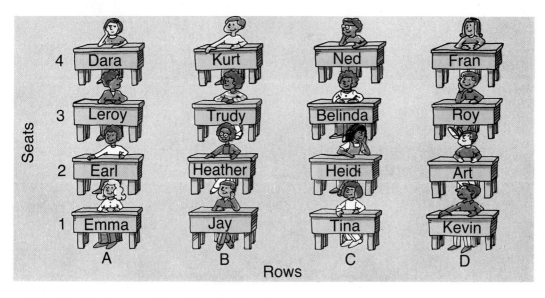

Trudy sits in row B and seat 3.
A short way to write this is B3.

row ⤒⤒ seat

Exercises

Tell who sits at each seat.

1. A2
2. B4
3. D2
4. A1
5. C3

6. A3
7. C1
8. B1
9. C4
10. D3

11. C2
12. D4
13. B2
14. A4
15. D1

Give the row and seat for each pupil.

16. Earl
17. Emma
18. Trudy
19. Art

20. Tina
21. Leroy
22. Belinda
23. Fran

24. Kürt	**25.** Heather	**26.** Kevin	**27.** Dara
28. Jay	**29.** Ned	**30.** Heidi	**31.** Roy

Copy the seating chart.
Then write these names in the proper spaces.

32. Arlene sits at A2.   **33.** Herb sits at C1.

34. Steven sits at C2.   **35.** Barb sits at B2.

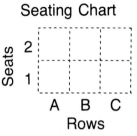

Seating Chart

"Tickets, Please"

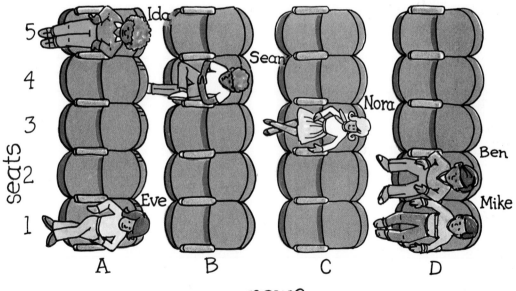

rows

Six pupils went to the movie. Who had each ticket below?

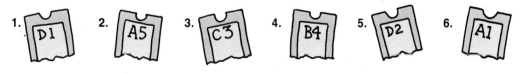

1. D1   2. A5   3. C3   4. B4   5. D2   6. A1

285

Games on a Grid

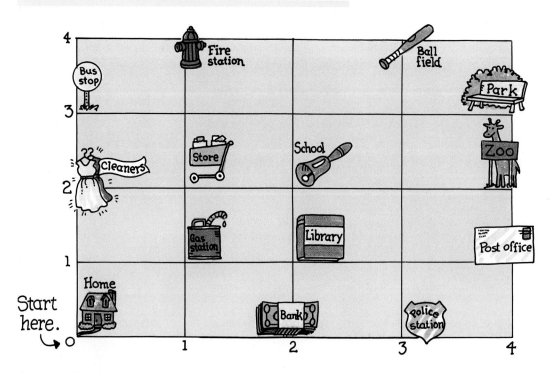

Start at home.

The library is 2 blocks → and 1 block ↑.
A short way to write this is 2 → 1 ↑.

Exercises

Start at home. Tell where each pair of moves takes you.

1. 3 → 4 ↑

2. 4 → 3 ↑

3. 3 → 0 ↑

4. 1 → 4 ↑

5. 4 → 1 ↑

6. 2 → 2 ↑

7. 0 → 3 ↑

8. 1 → 2 ↑

9. 1 → 1 ↑

10. 4 → 2 ↑

11. 0 → 2 ↑

12. 2 → 0 ↑

From home, tell how to get to each place.

13. ball field

14. park

15. bus stop

16. gas station

17. police station

18. store

19. cleaners

20. post office

21. school

22. fire station

23. zoo

24. bank

Dear Mom,

Each pair of moves takes you to a letter.
Make the moves to find what this note says.

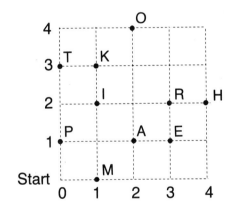

First word $1 \rightarrow 2\uparrow$

Second word $2 \rightarrow 1\uparrow$ $1 \rightarrow 0\uparrow$

Third word $2 \rightarrow 1\uparrow$ $0 \rightarrow 3\uparrow$

Fourth word $0 \rightarrow 3\uparrow$ $4 \rightarrow 2\uparrow$ $3 \rightarrow 1\uparrow$

Fifth word $0 \rightarrow 1\uparrow$ $2 \rightarrow 1\uparrow$ $3 \rightarrow 2\uparrow$ $1 \rightarrow 3\uparrow$

Bar Graph

This graph is called a **bar graph.** The heights of the bars show how many pupils come to school by walking, by riding a bike, by car, or by bus.

Each ▨ stands for 1 pupil.

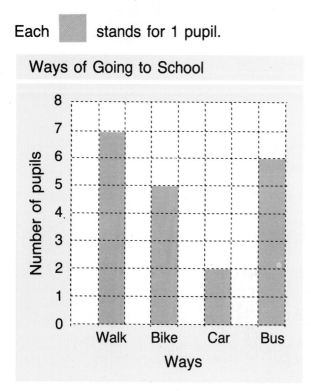

Exercises

How many pupils

1. walk   2. ride a bike   3. come by car   4. come by bus

Which way is used

5. by 5 pupils   6. by 6 pupils   7. by 2 pupils

8. by 7 pupils   9. the most   10. the least

This graph shows how many pupils chose apples, bananas, cherries, grapes, oranges, or pears as their favorite fruit.

Each 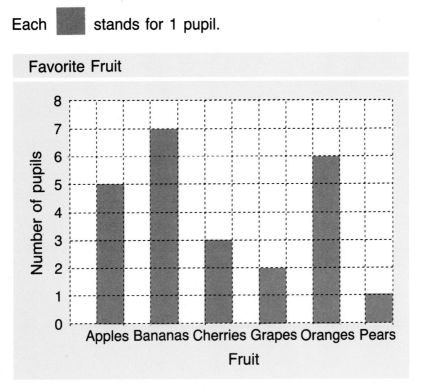 stands for 1 pupil.

Favorite Fruit

How many pupils chose each fruit?

11. apples

12. grapes

13. pears

14. cherries

15. bananas

16. oranges

Which fruit was chosen

17. by 3 pupils

18. by 2 pupils

19. by 6 pupils

20. by 5 pupils

21. by 1 pupil

22. by 7 pupils

23. the most

24. the least

Making a Bar Graph

Birthday Months			
Month	Pupils	Month	Pupils
Jan.	1	July	2
Feb.	0	Aug.	2
March	5	Sept.	1
April	4	Oct.	3
May	2	Nov.	1
June	4	Dec.	3

Pupils raised their hand when the teacher named their birthday month.

This table shows how many pupils have birthdays each month.

Exercises

1. Make the following on grid paper:

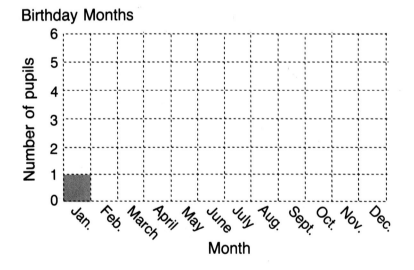

2. The table shows that 1 pupil has a birthday in January. Color 1 ⬜ above *Jan.* as shown.

3. How many ⬜ 's should be colored above *Feb.?*

4. Complete the bar graph for birthday months.

290

5. Make this on grid paper. Then make a bar graph to show favorite seasons.

Color 1 ▢ for each pupil.

Favorite Seasons

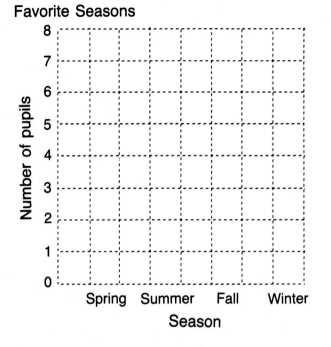

Favorite Seasons	
Season	Pupils
Spring	5
Summer	8
Fall	4
Winter	3

6. Make a bar graph to show favorite foods. Color 1 ▢ for each pupil.

Favorite Foods	
Food	Pupils
Hamburger	8
Hot dog	5
Pizza	7
Tacos	2

7. Make a bar graph to show favorite pets. Color 1 ▢ for each pupil.

Favorite Pets	
Pet	Pupils
Cat	8
Dog	7
Fish	2
Bird	4
Duck	1

Chance

You put in a quarter and turn the handle.
Guess the color of the *Crazy Ball* you will get.

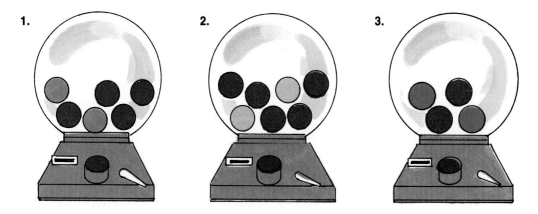

1.   2.   3.

You win if you guess the color on which the
pointer stops. Which color would you guess?

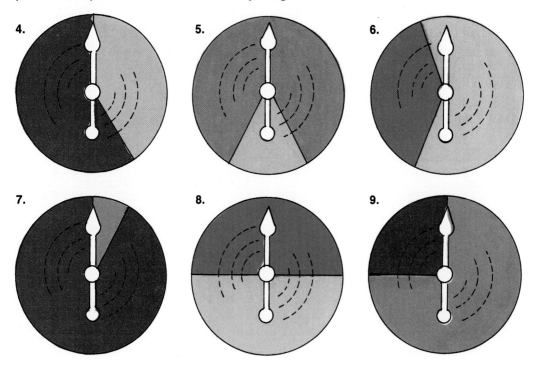

4.   5.   6.

7.   8.   9.

You are to close your eyes and pick up a pencil.
Which color do you think you will get?

10.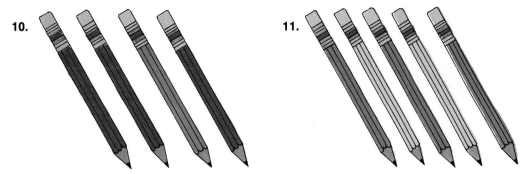

11.

You are to pull one string to get a prize.

12. What are you most likely to get?

13. What are you least likely to get?

SKILLS REVIEW

Add.

1.	601 +283	**2.**	822 +104	**3.**	234 + 45	**4.**	365 +528	**5.**	716 + 7
6.	183 +762	**7.**	179 +351	**8.**	458 +494	**9.**	632 +667	**10.**	754 +935

Subtract.

11.	576 −266	**12.**	487 −201	**13.**	795 −317	**14.**	384 −193	**15.**	349 − 30
16.	932 −693	**17.**	608 −439	**18.**	555 − 57	**19.**	700 −674	**20.**	400 −128

Multiply.

21.	322 ×3	**22.**	102 ×4	**23.**	214 ×4	**24.**	108 ×3	**25.**	317 ×2
26.	290 ×3	**27.**	172 ×2	**28.**	257 ×3	**29.**	168 ×5	**30.**	143 ×6

Divide.

31. $6\overline{)31}$ **32.** $7\overline{)60}$ **33.** $2\overline{)92}$ **34.** $3\overline{)39}$ **35.** $3\overline{)51}$

36. $5\overline{)69}$ **37.** $4\overline{)54}$ **38.** $4\overline{)87}$ **39.** $3\overline{)75}$ **40.** $2\overline{)35}$

CHAPTER REVIEW

How many pupils have a

1. dog   **2.** cat

Which pet is owned by

3. 2 pupils   **4.** 3 pupils

5. the most pupils

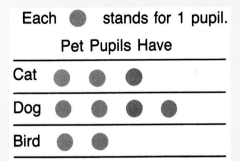

Each ● stands for 1 pupil.

Pet Pupils Have

Cat	● ● ●
Dog	● ● ● ●
Bird	● ●

Each pair of moves takes you to a letter. Tell the letter for each pair of moves.

6. 1 → 2 ↑   **7.** 1 → 3 ↑

8. 2 → 0 ↑   **9.** 2 → 1 ↑

10. 3 → 1 ↑   **11.** 3 → 3 ↑

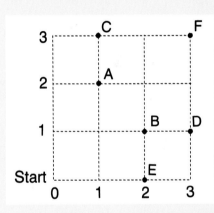

This graph shows how many pupils chose cherry, lemon, or lime as their favorite flavor.

How many pupils chose

12. cherry   **13.** lemon

Which flavor was chosen

14. the most   **15.** the least

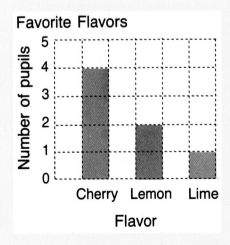

Favorite Flavors

REVIEW AND PRACTICE

Set A (Use after page 13.)

8 +6 14	**1.** 5 +5	**2.** 6 +4	**3.** 8 +0	**4.** 1 +7	**5.** 7 +3
6. 5 +8	**7.** 6 +6	**8.** 3 +9	**9.** 9 +2	**10.** 7 +9	**11.** 0 +9
12. 8 +8	**13.** 9 +4	**14.** 6 +8	**15.** 4 +8	**16.** 5 +9	**17.** 6 +7
18. 7 +6	**19.** 8 +3	**20.** 9 +9	**21.** 1 +9	**22.** 4 +7	**23.** 5 +7
24. 9 +6	**25.** 7 +8	**26.** 8 +9	**27.** 9 +7	**28.** 7 +7	**29.** 9 +8

Set B (Use after page 15.)

5 4 +6 15	**1.** 4 4 +4	**2.** 2 0 +9	**3.** 1 6 +3	**4.** 6 4 +6	**5.** 6 3 +7
6. 5 5 +4	**7.** 7 1 +9	**8.** 6 2 +7	**9.** 8 8 +0	**10.** 5 5 +5	**11.** 9 1 +9
12. 3 6 +3	**13.** 0 7 +7	**14.** 5 4 +5	**15.** 6 2 +6	**16.** 4 1 +7	**17.** 9 0 +9

	17	1.	9	2.	8	3.	7	4.	10	5.	12
	− 8		−1		−8		−0		− 2		− 6
	9										

6.	13	7.	11	8.	12	9.	10	10.	11	11.	13
	− 4		− 1		− 3		− 9		− 7		− 5

12.	14	13.	15	14.	13	15.	15	16.	9	17.	16
	− 7		− 5		− 8		− 9		−9		− 7

18.	11	19.	13	20.	12	21.	17	22.	16	23.	14
	− 5		− 7		− 9		− 7		− 9		− 6

24.	8	25.	12	26.	14	27.	16	28.	15	29.	11
	−0		− 5		− 9		− 8		− 7		− 6

30.	14	31.	19	32.	11	33.	15	34.	13	35.	13
	− 8		− 9		− 8		− 6		− 3		− 6

36.	15	37.	12	38.	18	39.	13	40.	17	41.	18
	− 8		− 7		− 9		− 9		− 9		− 8

Set B (Use after page 27.)

Write < or > for each ●.

9 > 6

1. 8 ● 5
2. 4 ● 1
3. 5 ● 7
4. 2 ● 3
5. 7 ● 2
6. 6 ● 8
7. 0 ● 4
8. 3 ● 10
9. 12 ● 7
10. 8 ● 0
11. 18 ● 9

Name the following in this word: **Wednesday**

first letter   W   1. fourth letter   2. eighth letter

3. sixth letter   4. second letter   5. ninth letter

6. third letter   7. seventh letter   8. fifth letter

40 + 9 = 49   1. 60 + 7 = ___   2. 80 + 6 = ___

3. 50 + 8 = ___   4. 70 + 4 = ___   5. 70 + 5 = ___

6. 60 + 2 = ___   7. 80 + 1 = ___   8. 90 + 3 = ___

Give the place value of the colored digit.

3571   tens   1. 3091   2. 5692   3. 9184

4. 7009   5. 2351   6. 8319   7. 6040

Write the numeral.

2000 + 200 + 80 + 3 = 2283   8. 9000 + 800 + 20 + 5

9. 6000 + 900 + 90 + 1   10. 3000 + 400 + 1

11. 800 + 80 + 4   12. 7000 + 700

13. 2000 + 70 + 3   14. 9000 + 800 + 90

15. 400 + 3   16. 4000 + 3

Use a $ and . to write the value.

1 dollar, 3 dimes, 7 pennies $1.37

1. 1 dollar, 4 dimes

2. 1 dollar, 9 dimes, 1 penny

3. 2 dollars, 2 pennies

4. 5 dollars, 7 dimes

5. 9 dimes, 9 pennies

6. 9 dimes

7. 9 pennies

8. 1 dollar and 25 cents

9. 7 dollars and 46 cents

10. 8 dollars and 30 cents

11. 3 dollars and 6 cents

12. 78 cents

13. 1 dollar, 10 dimes

Find the most *hundreds.* From what is left, find the most *tens.* The rest will be *ones.*

	Number	Hundreds	Tens	Ones
	153	1	5	3
1.	426			
2.	307			
3.	240			
4.	39			
5.	581			

Find the most *tens.* The rest will be *ones.*

	Number	Tens	Ones
	235	23	5
6.	193		
7.	400		
8.	730		
9.	93		
10.	1		

299

Set A (Use after page 57.)

34 +45 79	1. 20 +30	2. 30 +30	3. 10 +80	4. 40 +60	5. 13 + 3
6. 13 +26	7. 84 + 4	8. 73 +15	9. 25 +30	10. 26 +50	11. 17 +41
12. 60 + 7	13. 14 +22	14. 38 +11	15. 50 +19	16. 43 + 6	17. 12 +72
18. 26 +11	19. 52 +20	20. 60 +19	21. 78 +20	22. 87 +12	23. 36 + 3

Set B (Use after page 59.)

55 +28 83	1. 19 + 9	2. 16 +46	3. 47 +37	4. 89 + 7	5. 23 +49
6. 18 + 6	7. 27 +36	8. 35 +15	9. 64 +27	10. 78 + 8	11. 33 +38
12. 25 +59	13. 39 +41	14. 48 + 7	15. 56 +35	16. 64 +16	17. 36 +57
18. 33 +19	19. 22 +68	20. 48 +34	21. 53 +18	22. 79 + 6	23. 17 +37
24. 22 +69	25. 13 +57	26. 34 +49	27. 55 + 7	28. 48 +29	29. 49 +49

Set A (Use after page 63.)

	78 −46 32	1.	50 −20	2.	80 −10	3.	60 −60	4.	27 −10	5.	76 − 6
6.	38 −35	7.	27 − 1	8.	75 −52	9.	79 −62	10.	68 − 7	11.	97 −71
12.	85 −11	13.	94 −52	14.	63 −31	15.	19 − 2	16.	70 − 0	17.	81 −40
18.	99 − 7	19.	96 − 4	20.	88 −32	21.	47 − 7	22.	79 −24	23.	37 −20

Set B (Use after page 67.)

	90 −16 74	1.	45 −27	2.	27 −18	3.	36 − 9	4.	48 −29	5.	50 − 4
6.	81 −54	7.	31 − 7	8.	42 −26	9.	50 −32	10.	33 −17	11.	45 −26
12.	72 − 4	13.	44 −25	14.	63 − 9	15.	84 −48	16.	95 −59	17.	71 −22
18.	66 −18	19.	54 − 7	20.	73 −35	21.	92 −48	22.	31 −16	23.	63 −46
24.	70 −19	25.	97 −39	26.	85 − 8	27.	66 −27	28.	50 −13	29.	88 −79

Set A (Use after page 79.)

$3 \times 2 = 6$

1. $5 \times 2 = \square$

2. $8 \times 2 = \square$

3. $6 \times 2 = \square$

4. $2 \times 2 = \square$

5. $7 \times 2 = \square$

6. $9 \times 2 = \square$

7. $4 \times 2 = \square$

8. $3 \times 3 = \square$

9. $8 \times 3 = \square$

10. $7 \times 3 = \square$

11. $9 \times 3 = \square$

12. $5 \times 3 = \square$

13. $4 \times 3 = \square$

14. $6 \times 3 = \square$

Set B (Use after page 83.)

$$\begin{array}{r} 4 \\ \times 6 \\ \hline 24 \end{array}$$

1. $\begin{array}{r} 4 \\ \times 4 \\ \hline \end{array}$
2. $\begin{array}{r} 4 \\ \times 1 \\ \hline \end{array}$
3. $\begin{array}{r} 4 \\ \times 5 \\ \hline \end{array}$
4. $\begin{array}{r} 4 \\ \times 8 \\ \hline \end{array}$
5. $\begin{array}{r} 4 \\ \times 2 \\ \hline \end{array}$

6. $\begin{array}{r} 4 \\ \times 3 \\ \hline \end{array}$
7. $\begin{array}{r} 4 \\ \times 9 \\ \hline \end{array}$
8. $\begin{array}{r} 4 \\ \times 7 \\ \hline \end{array}$
9. $\begin{array}{r} 5 \\ \times 1 \\ \hline \end{array}$
10. $\begin{array}{r} 5 \\ \times 5 \\ \hline \end{array}$
11. $\begin{array}{r} 5 \\ \times 2 \\ \hline \end{array}$

12. $\begin{array}{r} 5 \\ \times 4 \\ \hline \end{array}$
13. $\begin{array}{r} 5 \\ \times 8 \\ \hline \end{array}$
14. $\begin{array}{r} 5 \\ \times 3 \\ \hline \end{array}$
15. $\begin{array}{r} 5 \\ \times 7 \\ \hline \end{array}$
16. $\begin{array}{r} 5 \\ \times 6 \\ \hline \end{array}$
17. $\begin{array}{r} 5 \\ \times 9 \\ \hline \end{array}$

Set C (Use after page 87.)

$$\begin{array}{r} 6 \\ \times 9 \\ \hline 54 \end{array}$$

1. $\begin{array}{r} 6 \\ \times 1 \\ \hline \end{array}$
2. $\begin{array}{r} 6 \\ \times 6 \\ \hline \end{array}$
3. $\begin{array}{r} 6 \\ \times 4 \\ \hline \end{array}$
4. $\begin{array}{r} 6 \\ \times 2 \\ \hline \end{array}$
5. $\begin{array}{r} 6 \\ \times 5 \\ \hline \end{array}$

6. $\begin{array}{r} 6 \\ \times 8 \\ \hline \end{array}$
7. $\begin{array}{r} 6 \\ \times 7 \\ \hline \end{array}$
8. $\begin{array}{r} 6 \\ \times 3 \\ \hline \end{array}$
9. $\begin{array}{r} 7 \\ \times 1 \\ \hline \end{array}$
10. $\begin{array}{r} 7 \\ \times 5 \\ \hline \end{array}$
11. $\begin{array}{r} 7 \\ \times 2 \\ \hline \end{array}$

12. $\begin{array}{r} 7 \\ \times 7 \\ \hline \end{array}$
13. $\begin{array}{r} 7 \\ \times 4 \\ \hline \end{array}$
14. $\begin{array}{r} 7 \\ \times 3 \\ \hline \end{array}$
15. $\begin{array}{r} 7 \\ \times 9 \\ \hline \end{array}$
16. $\begin{array}{r} 7 \\ \times 6 \\ \hline \end{array}$
17. $\begin{array}{r} 7 \\ \times 8 \\ \hline \end{array}$

Set A (Use after page 91.)

8 ×5 40	1. 8 ×3	2. 8 ×1	3. 8 ×6	4. 8 ×2	5. 8 ×7
6. 8 ×8	7. 8 ×4	8. 8 ×9	9. 9 ×1	10. 9 ×8	11. 9 ×2
12. 9 ×6	13. 9 ×3	14. 9 ×5	15. 9 ×4	16. 9 ×9	17. 9 ×7

Set B (Use after page 93.)

0 ×1 0	1. 1 ×7	2. 5 ×1	3. 8 ×0	4. 2 ×6	5. 4 ×3
6. 5 ×7	7. 3 ×6	8. 6 ×2	9. 8 ×3	10. 2 ×9	11. 4 ×7
12. 7 ×3	13. 0 ×8	14. 9 ×3	15. 7 ×5	16. 1 ×8	17. 3 ×5
18. 6 ×6	19. 9 ×4	20. 2 ×8	21. 4 ×8	22. 6 ×7	23. 5 ×9
24. 7 ×7	25. 8 ×9	26. 4 ×0	27. 9 ×6	28. 8 ×8	29. 6 ×4
30. 5 ×8	31. 8 ×6	32. 9 ×0	33. 9 ×7	34. 8 ×7	35. 9 ×9

Write the letter of each angle that is

1. a right angle   2. smaller than a right angle

3. larger than a right angle

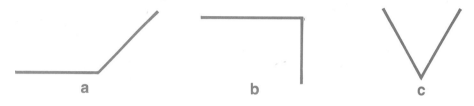

4. Write the letter of each figure that is a rectangle.

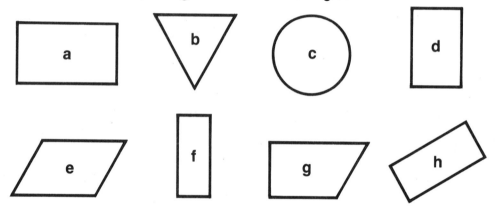

5. Write the letter of each figure that is a square.

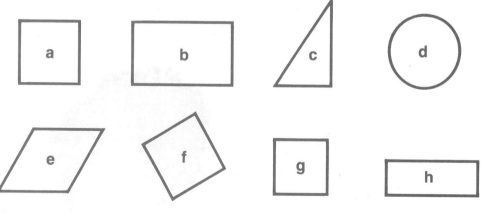

304

1. Write the letter of each figure that is a circle.

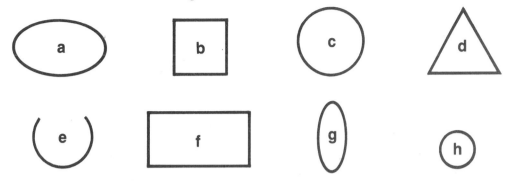

2. Write the letter of each figure that is a triangle.

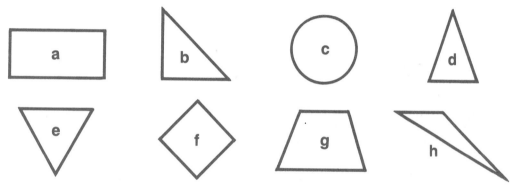

Write the letter of the figure for each of the following shapes:

1. cube   2. cone   3. sphere   4. cylinder

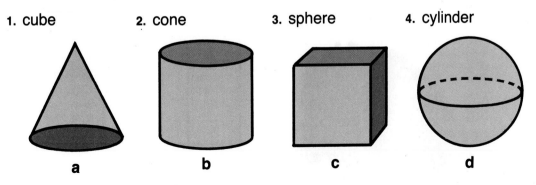

Use a centimeter ruler to find the length of
each picture.

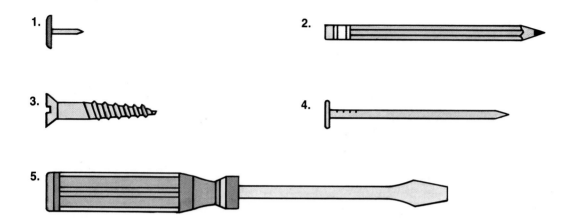

1.

2.

3.

4.

5.

Find each length to the nearest $\frac{1}{2}$ inch.

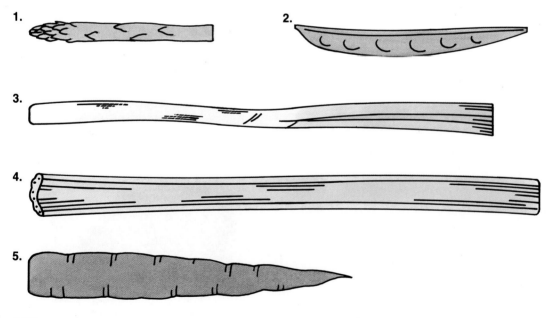

1.

2.

3.

4.

5.

Set A (Use after page 130.)

Find the area.

Each ⬚ is 1 square centimeter.

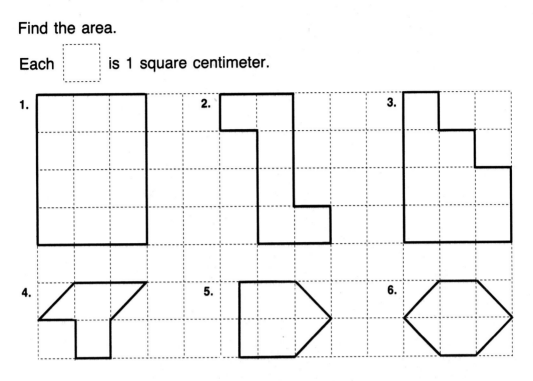

1.

2.

3.

4.

5.

6.

Set B (Use after page 135.)

Write the number of cubes in each figure.

1.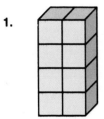

2.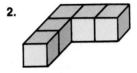

3.

4.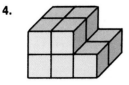

5.

6.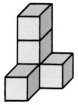

	253	1.	107	2.	344	3.	328	4.	216
	+146		+ 2		+254		+521		+ 62
	399								

5.	142	6.	239	7.	388	8.	497	9.	805
	+420		+310		+301		+302		+ 73

10.	861	11.	790	12.	676	13.	569	14.	700
	+107		+ 4		+213		+210		+100

15.	173	16.	484	17.	415	18.	550	19.	622
	+125		+402		+350		+201		+ 32

	326	1.	257	2.	544	3.	833	4.	915
	+ 16		+138		+346		+139		+ 77
	342								

5.	125	6.	123	7.	638	8.	767	9.	868
	+829		+ 37		+148		+ 7		+ 19

10.	614	11.	235	12.	346	13.	459	14.	409
	+ 59		+715		+528		+ 9		+477

15.	904	16.	702	17.	501	18.	702	19.	106
	+ 47		+ 88		+129		+ 39		+859

20.	265	21.	523	22.	177	23.	318	24.	408
	+ 26		+ 8		+616		+ 34		+ 45

Set A (Use after page 145.)

	353 + 64 417	1.	264 +284	2.	471 +477	3.	582 +182	4.	363 + 76
5.	242 + 65	6.	189 + 20	7.	178 +730	8.	697 + 42	9.	754 + 85
10.	831 + 85	11.	290 +533	12.	318 + 91	13.	465 +363	14.	846 + 72
15.	726 + 91	16.	645 + 80	17.	554 + 72	18.	160 +696	19.	453 + 53

Set B (Use after page 149.)

	552 + 68 620	1.	774 +187	2.	489 +389	3.	366 + 97	4.	327 +597
5.	643 + 67	6.	455 +385	7.	164 +788	8.	215 + 97	9.	838 + 99
10.	767 +169	11.	539 + 85	12.	479 +244	13.	391 + 9	14.	178 + 53
15.	562 + 69	16.	848 + 88	17.	186 +467	18.	277 + 78	19.	299 + 9
20.	739 +173	21.	845 + 95	22.	669 + 68	23.	184 +356	24.	269 + 97

	343 +368 711	1.	794 +107	2.	675 +227	3.	546 +187	4.	569 +297
5.	744 +193	6.	180 +126	7.	309 +279	8.	337 +178	9.	468 +258
10.	652 +153	11.	461 +164	12.	298 +159	13.	307 +587	14.	120 +193
15.	531 +299	16.	272 +370	17.	185 +650	18.	366 +386	19.	251 +480
20.	104 +649	21.	561 +158	22.	272 +437	23.	385 +220	24.	493 +316
25.	109 +970	26.	223 +934	27.	334 +824	28.	407 +981	29.	516 +513
30.	502 +732	31.	211 +845	32.	624 +865	33.	621 +652	34.	730 +732
35.	410 +630	36.	710 +861	37.	330 +954	38.	421 +778	39.	805 +860
40.	808 +540	41.	320 +743	42.	931 +647	43.	510 +982	44.	625 +764
45.	416 +851	46.	623 +543	47.	954 +934	48.	930 +769	49.	817 +910

```
     1357        1.  5000       2.  7000       3.  3119
   + 2938          + 3000         + 2000         + 2420
     4295
```

```
 4.  6408        5.  7326       6.  8135       7.  1020
   + 1340          + 2622         + 1011         + 1003
```

```
 8.  8217        9.  4427      10.  7336      11.  5655
   + 1340          + 2462         + 1530         + 2340
```

```
12.  3157       13.  2342      14.  1032      15.  5005
   + 4610          + 1102         + 1800         + 2190
```

```
16.  1906       17.  5885      18.  6897      19.  1858
   + 1136          + 3286         + 1498         + 4344
```

```
20.  4718       21.  2723      22.  7934      23.  2949
   + 3843          + 3981         + 1974         + 2828
```

```
24.  3918       25.  4629      26.  3939      27.  2847
   + 3690          + 4653         + 1554         + 4534
```

```
28.  2886       29.  1595      30.  2654      31.  5766
   + 5862          + 2660         + 6786         + 1737
```

```
32.  5677       33.  6754      34.  6673      35.  5725
   + 2857          + 1550         + 2493         + 1399
```

```
36.  1934       37.  3406      38.  4470      39.  4578
   + 1295          + 2733         + 3929         + 4500
```

Set A (Use after page 165.)

	1.	2.	3.	4.
646 −134 512	798 − 4	388 −286	699 − 42	542 −540

5.	6.	7.	8.	9.
857 −201	979 −325	897 −170	784 − 30	473 −131

10.	11.	12.	13.	14.
238 −100	685 −251	766 −530	858 −728	967 − 7

15.	16.	17.	18.	19.
929 −619	597 −304	439 − 21	355 −154	236 −136

Set B (Use after page 167.)

	1.	2.	3.	4.
924 − 53 871	615 − 8	556 −127	847 −308	770 − 59

5.	6.	7.	8.	9.
733 − 71	876 −793	969 − 83	983 − 68	688 − 93

10.	11.	12.	13.	14.
804 − 61	750 − 2	439 − 58	369 −195	507 −244

15.	16.	17.	18.	19.
417 − 52	682 − 8	548 −497	355 − 46	461 −158

20.	21.	22.	23.	24.
211 − 30	331 −127	522 − 3	447 − 75	692 − 77

	654	1.	915	2.	613	3.	631	4.	432
	− 475		− 729		− 294		− 142		− 267
	179								

5.	945	6.	726	7.	925	8.	812	9.	822
	− 667		− 178		− 438		− 578		− 246

10.	725	11.	954	12.	823	13.	743	14.	532
	− 396		− 296		− 468		− 585		− 399

15.	944	16.	646	17.	524	18.	582	19.	571
	− 157		− 179		− 149		− 393		− 283

20.	613	21.	514	22.	413	23.	473	24.	362
	− 236		− 148		− 267		− 199		− 175

25.	900	26.	800	27.	900	28.	700	29.	900
	− 795		− 696		− 213		− 492		− 181

30.	800	31.	900	32.	800	33.	900	34.	700
	− 514		− 687		− 274		− 525		− 179

35.	900	36.	800	37.	700	38.	700	39.	600
	− 428		− 482		− 563		− 336		− 461

40.	900	41.	800	42.	800	43.	600	44.	700
	− 339		− 341		− 157		− 348		− 257

45.	500	46.	500	47.	400	48.	600	49.	600
	− 121		− 337		− 259		− 108		− 262

	5018 − 312 4706	1.	4982 −1291	2.	8854 −7573	3.	9736 − 182
4.	6139 − 623	5.	2929 − 54	6.	4377 −1614	7.	5465 − 704
8.	3659 − 802	9.	2477 − 92	10.	3096 −2853	11.	6283 −5430
12.	7628 − 68	13.	9178 −7837	14.	8397 − 486	15.	7686 − 764

	7715 −4807 2908	1.	6405 −4282	2.	5406 −3309	3.	7212 −5049
4.	8331 −6737	5.	4311 −2509	6.	8600 −5928	7.	6217 −3850
8.	3423 −1509	9.	9504 −7624	10.	4225 −1328	11.	5515 −2935
12.	9400 −6667	13.	9300 −5924	14.	3000 −1415	15.	8000 −4679
16.	7000 −3258	17.	9000 −2135	18.	4000 −1976	19.	5000 −2482

Give the date.

	S	M	T	W	T	F	S
JULY							
		1	2	3	4	5	6
	7	8	9	10	11	12	13

1. first Thursday

2. second Saturday

3. first Sunday

4. second Tuesday

Give the day of the week.

5. July 8

6. July 3

7. July 2

8. July 6

9. July 12

10. July 11

Write the time as shown for the first clock.

8:15

1.

2.

3.

4.

5.

Set A (Use after page 189.)

Write the time as shown for the first clock.

20 minutes before 12

1.

2.

3.

4.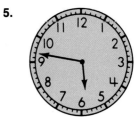

5.

Set B (Use after page 191.)

How many minutes is it from

    1:55 to 2:18   23

1. 2:50 to 3:10

2. 2:45 to 3:15

3. 6:55 to 7:21

4. 8:49 to 9:05

5. 10:32 to 11:12

6. 5:37 to 6:07

7. 3:48 to 4:29

8. 4:41 to 5:32

Set C (Use after page 193.)

How many minutes is it from

    1:03 to 1:17   14

1. 3:10 to 3:37

2. 6:49 to 6:59

3. 8:14 to 8:25

4. 9:27 to 9:54

5. 12:08 to 12:23

6. 2:22 to 2:31

7. 4:38 to 4:46

8. 5:09 to 5:36

Set A (Use after page 197.)

Guess the weight.

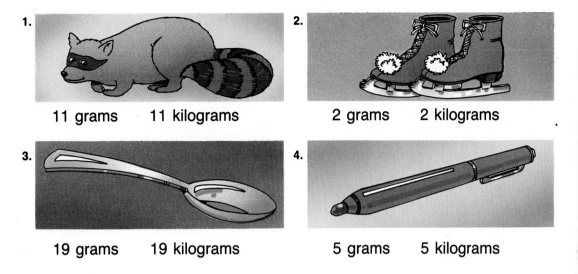

1. 11 grams   11 kilograms

2. 2 grams   2 kilograms

3. 19 grams   19 kilograms

4. 5 grams   5 kilograms

Set B (Use after page 199.)

Guess the weight.

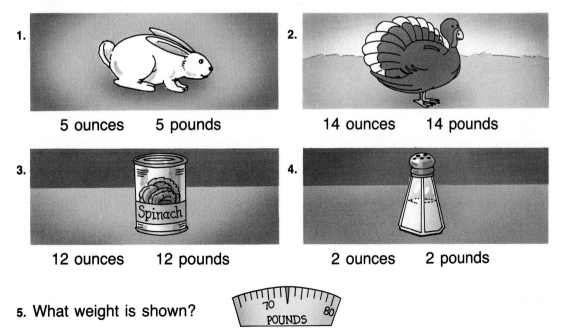

1. 5 ounces   5 pounds

2. 14 ounces   14 pounds

3. 12 ounces   12 pounds

4. 2 ounces   2 pounds

5. What weight is shown?

317

Set A (Use after page 209.)

	51 ×9 459	**1.** 12 ×2	**2.** 21 ×4	**3.** 31 ×3	**4.** 13 ×3
5.	51 ×6	**6.** 62 ×3	**7.** 81 ×9	**8.** 73 ×3	**9.** 53 ×3
10.	91 ×5	**11.** 41 ×7	**12.** 61 ×7	**13.** 71 ×7	**14.** 81 ×4
15.	51 ×5	**16.** 91 ×6	**17.** 81 ×8	**18.** 71 ×9	**19.** 81 ×3

Set B (Use after page 211.)

	83 ×6 498	**1.** 62 ×5	**2.** 74 ×4	**3.** 57 ×9	**4.** 25 ×8
5.	49 ×2	**6.** 95 ×4	**7.** 67 ×2	**8.** 58 ×3	**9.** 68 ×4
10.	59 ×5	**11.** 67 ×6	**12.** 19 ×9	**13.** 17 ×3	**14.** 24 ×9
15.	19 ×6	**16.** 87 ×7	**17.** 98 ×8	**18.** 19 ×3	**19.** 35 ×7
20.	75 ×5	**21.** 76 ×6	**22.** 98 ×6	**23.** 78 ×7	**24.** 47 ×4

Set A (Use after page 215.)

112 ×4 448	1. 221 ×3	2. 133 ×3	3. 214 ×2	4. 332 ×3
5. 103 ×3	6. 141 ×2	7. 202 ×4	8. 113 ×2	9. 101 ×6
10. 232 ×2	11. 124 ×2	12. 104 ×2	13. 344 ×2	14. 130 ×3
15. 121 ×3	16. 131 ×2	17. 123 ×3	18. 413 ×2	19. 340 ×2

Set B (Use after page 217.)

123 ×4 492	1. 112 ×8	2. 326 ×3	3. 114 ×6	4. 248 ×2
5. 223 ×4	6. 116 ×5	7. 146 ×2	8. 117 ×5	9. 104 ×4
10. 118 ×4	11. 102 ×8	12. 338 ×2	13. 113 ×7	14. 112 ×7
15. 237 ×2	16. 349 ×2	17. 115 ×5	18. 109 ×9	19. 104 ×5
20. 206 ×2	21. 106 ×5	22. 106 ×4	23. 112 ×8	24. 103 ×5

Set A (Use after page 219.)

	1.	2.	3.	4.
153 ×3 459	293 ×3	160 ×5	274 ×2	482 ×2
5. 354 ×2	6. 150 ×5	7. 382 ×2	8. 261 ×3	9. 451 ×2
10. 161 ×4	11. 461 ×2	12. 172 ×4	13. 374 ×2	14. 151 ×5
15. 190 ×4	16. 181 ×5	17. 273 ×3	18. 391 ×2	19. 492 ×2

Set B (Use after page 221.)

	1.	2.	3.	4.
276 ×3 828	287 ×3	176 ×5	355 ×2	149 ×6
5. 148 ×6	6. 126 ×7	7. 368 ×2	8. 147 ×4	9. 487 ×2
10. 185 ×5	11. 136 ×4	12. 189 ×5	13. 138 ×7	14. 499 ×2
15. 296 ×3	16. 125 ×7	17. 475 ×2	18. 146 ×4	19. 128 ×6
20. 134 ×5	21. 147 ×6	22. 238 ×4	23. 139 ×7	24. 119 ×8

Set A (Use after page 237.)

$$\overset{5}{3)\overline{15}}$$

1. $2)\overline{4}$ 2. $1)\overline{5}$ 3. $6)\overline{6}$

4. $5)\overline{35}$ 5. $1)\overline{7}$ 6. $3)\overline{27}$ 7. $7)\overline{63}$

8. $3)\overline{9}$ 9. $4)\overline{4}$ 10. $9)\overline{72}$ 11. $9)\overline{45}$

12. $8)\overline{8}$ 13. $2)\overline{12}$ 14. $5)\overline{30}$ 15. $8)\overline{64}$

16. $4)\overline{20}$ 17. $2)\overline{16}$ 18. $2)\overline{8}$ 19. $6)\overline{42}$

20. $9)\overline{36}$ 21. $5)\overline{45}$ 22. $7)\overline{42}$ 23. $8)\overline{56}$

24. $7)\overline{56}$ 25. $9)\overline{63}$ 26. $6)\overline{54}$ 27. $9)\overline{81}$

Set B (Use after page 239.)

$$\overset{2\ R2}{5)\overline{12}}$$

1. $3)\overline{20}$ 2. $4)\overline{5}$ 3. $2)\overline{5}$

4. $5)\overline{6}$ 5. $3)\overline{25}$ 6. $7)\overline{62}$ 7. $6)\overline{10}$

8. $4)\overline{27}$ 9. $8)\overline{52}$ 10. $5)\overline{19}$ 11. $8)\overline{26}$

12. $9)\overline{25}$ 13. $7)\overline{65}$ 14. $8)\overline{67}$ 15. $6)\overline{51}$

16. $7)\overline{17}$ 17. $3)\overline{22}$ 18. $9)\overline{74}$ 19. $3)\overline{28}$

20. $6)\overline{37}$ 21. $9)\overline{89}$ 22. $3)\overline{16}$ 23. $4)\overline{38}$

24. $5)\overline{49}$ 25. $6)\overline{46}$ 26. $7)\overline{40}$ 27. $9)\overline{79}$

Set A (Use after page 247.)

25
3)75

1. 2)88

2. 5)55

3. 5)80

4. 3)84

5. 2)76

6. 5)85

7. 3)66

8. 3)81

9. 2)94

10. 2)38

11. 7)77

12. 4)72

13. 4)76

14. 6)78

15. 5)95

16. 3)99

17. 4)96

18. 2)90

19. 2)48

20. 2)68

21. 7)98

22. 6)96

23. 8)96

24. 5)75

25. 6)90

26. 7)84

27. 4)92

Set B (Use after page 249.)

12 R2
3)38

1. 6)17

2. 8)78

3. 5)27

4. 4)13

5. 9)12

6. 3)10

7. 7)46

8. 2)91

9. 4)59

10. 5)76

11. 4)89

12. 3)85

13. 5)68

14. 2)73

15. 2)79

16. 6)94

17. 3)56

18. 6)83

19. 8)94

20. 3)76

21. 7)90

22. 7)82

23. 8)92

24. 5)62

25. 7)93

26. 6)99

27. 8)99

Write a fraction to tell how much is colored.

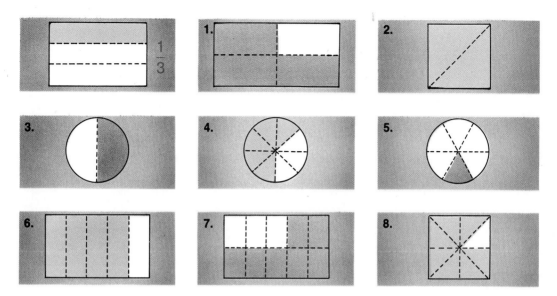

1.

2.

3.

4.

5.

6.

7.

8.

Write a fraction for each ▦.

1. ▦ are green.

2. ▦ are full.

3. ▦ are upside down.

4. ▦ are red.

Set A (Use after page 267.)

Copy and complete.

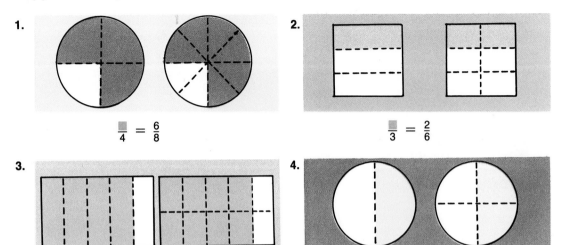

1. $\dfrac{}{4} = \dfrac{6}{8}$

2. $\dfrac{}{3} = \dfrac{2}{6}$

3. $\dfrac{4}{5} = \dfrac{}{10}$

4. $\dfrac{1}{2} = \dfrac{}{4}$

Set B (Use after page 269.)

Write a mixed numeral for each ___.

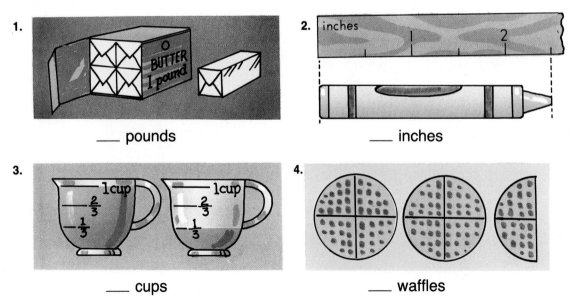

1. ___ pounds

2. ___ inches

3. ___ cups

4. ___ waffles

Write < or > for each ●.

1.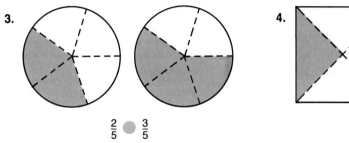

$\frac{2}{3}$ ● $\frac{1}{3}$

2.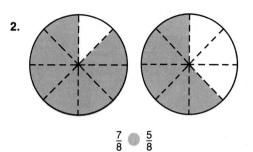

$\frac{7}{8}$ ● $\frac{5}{8}$

3.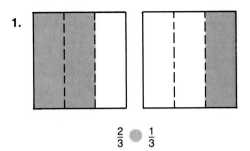

$\frac{2}{5}$ ● $\frac{3}{5}$

4.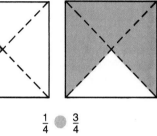

$\frac{1}{4}$ ● $\frac{3}{4}$

Set B (Use after page 277.)

Write a decimal for each fraction.

$\frac{1}{10}$ = 0.1   **1.** $\frac{2}{10}$ **2.** $\frac{6}{10}$ **3.** $\frac{5}{10}$

4. $\frac{3}{10}$ **5.** $\frac{7}{10}$ **6.** $\frac{4}{10}$ **7.** $\frac{8}{10}$

Write as a decimal.

$2\frac{3}{10}$ = 2.3   **1.** $2\frac{8}{10}$ **2.** $1\frac{4}{10}$ **3.** $19\frac{9}{10}$

4. $11\frac{1}{10}$ **5.** $3\frac{7}{10}$ **6.** $26\frac{6}{10}$ **7.** $6\frac{5}{10}$

This graph shows how many pupils chose reading, math, science, and social studies as their favorite subject.

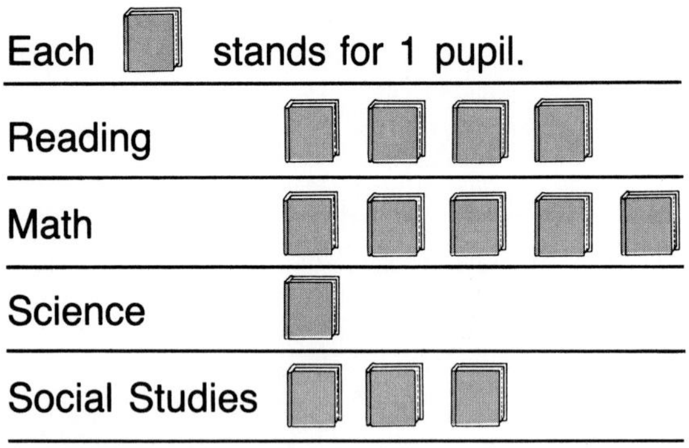

Each stands for 1 pupil.

Reading	
Math	
Science	
Social Studies	

How many pupils chose

1. reading
2. math
3. science
4. social studies

Which subject was chosen

5. by 3 pupils   6. by 4 pupils   7. the most   8. the least

9. Make this on grid paper.

Pets Pupils Have

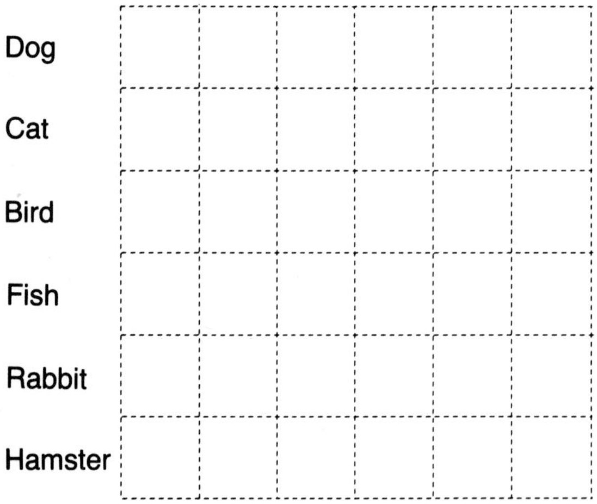

Dog

Cat

Bird

Fish

Rabbit

Hamster

Pet	Number of pupils
Dog	6
Cat	4
Bird	3
Fish	4
Rabbit	1
Hamster	2

Then make a picture graph to show the number of pupils that have each kind of pet. Draw an X to stand for 1 pupil.

Each pair of moves takes you to a letter.
Tell the letter for each pair of moves.

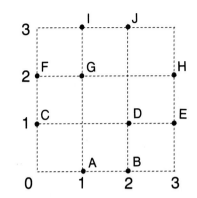

| 1→0↑ | A | 1. 0→1↑ |

2. 2→1↑   3. 1→2↑

4. 1→3↑   5. 3→1↑

6. 0→2↑   7. 2→0↑

8. 3→2↑   9. 2→3↑

Use grid paper.
Make a bar graph to show how many pupils have each color of bicycle.

Color a ⬚ to stand for 1 pupil.

Color of bicycle	Number of pupils
Red	8
Blue	7
Yellow	2
Purple	5
Green	7
Pink	3
Orange	1
Silver	4

Glossary

addend Any of the numbers to be added.

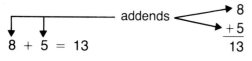

$$8 + 5 = 13$$

angle A figure that looks like this.

area The number of square units that fit inside a figure. The area of this figure is 12 square inches.

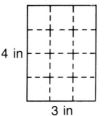

4 in

3 in

average The quotient obtained when the sum of a set of numbers is divided by the number of addends.

centimeter A unit of length in the metric system (one hundredth of a meter).

1 centimeter or 1 cm

circle A curved figure (in a plane) with all points the same distance from a point called the *center.*

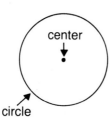

cone A figure that is shaped like this.

cube A figure that is shaped like this. Each of its six faces is a square.

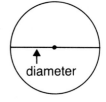

cylinder A figure shaped like this.

decimal A numeral with place values based on ten. The following are decimals:

5.6   12.48   342

denominator The bottom number in a fraction. In the fraction $\frac{3}{4}$, the denominator is 4.

diameter A line segment that joins two points on a circle and passes through the center.

difference The number you get by subtracting one number from another.

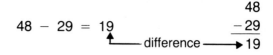

$$48 - 29 = 19$$

digit Any of the symbols 0, 1, 2, 3, 4, 5, 6, 7, 8, and 9.

328

dividend A number that is divided.

$$32 \div 4 = 8 \qquad\qquad 4\overline{)32}$$
dividend

divisor A number by which another number is divided.

$$32 \div 4 = 8 \qquad\qquad 4\overline{)32}$$
divisor

equivalent fractions Two or more fractions that name the same number or amount.

$\frac{1}{3}$, $\frac{2}{6}$, and $\frac{3}{9}$ are equivalent fractions.

estimate To guess a result before doing the computation.

even number Any whole number with 0, 2, 4, 6, or 8 in the ones place.

factor Any of the numbers to be multiplied.

$$6 \times 12 = 72 \qquad\qquad \begin{array}{r} 12 \\ \times 6 \\ \hline 72 \end{array}$$
factors

fraction A name for numbers like $\frac{1}{2}$, $\frac{5}{6}$, $\frac{8}{3}$, and $\frac{4}{4}$.

gram A unit of mass (weight) in the metric system (one thousandth of a kilogram).

graph A diagram that shows how two sets of information are related (bar graph, line graph, circle graph, picture graph).

is greater than A comparison to show that one number is more than another number.

$8 > 5$ is read "8 is greater than 5."

is less than A comparison to show that one number is less than another number.

$7 < 9$ is read "7 is less than 9."

is more than See *is greater than.*

kilogram A unit of mass (weight) in the metric system (1000 grams).

kiloliter A unit of capacity in the metric system (1000 liters).

kilometer A unit of length in the metric system (1000 meters).

line segment Any part of a line that joins two points.

line segment

liter A unit of capacity in the metric system (1000 milliliters).

meter A unit of length in the metric system (100 centimeters).

milligram   A unit of mass (weight) in the metric system (one thousandth of a gram).

milliliter   A unit of capacity in the metric system (one thousandth of a liter).

millimeter   A unit of length in the metric system (one thousandth of a meter).

mixed numeral   A numeral formed by naming a whole number and a fraction. Numerals like $1\frac{1}{2}$ and $54\frac{5}{8}$ are mixed numerals.

multiple   A product of two whole numbers is a multiple of each number. The following numbers are multiples of 5:

0, 5, 10, 15, 20, and so on.

numeral   A name for a number. A name for the number eight is 8.

numerator   The top number in a fraction. In the fraction $\frac{5}{8}$, the numerator is 5.

odd number   Any whole number with 1, 3, 5, 7, or 9 in the ones place.

ordinal number   *First, second, third, fourth,* and so on are ordinal numbers. They are used to tell order.

parallel lines   Two or more lines (in the same plane) that never meet or cross.

parallel lines

perimeter   The distance around a figure. The perimeter of this figure is 16 feet.

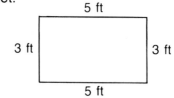

place value   The value of the place or position of a digit in a numeral.

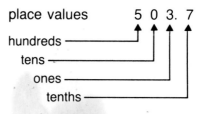

product   The number you get when two or more numbers are multiplied.

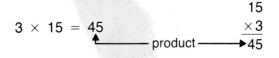

quadrilateral   A figure that has four sides.

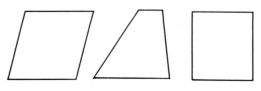

quadrilaterals

330

quotient The number you get when one number is divided by another.

$$42 \div 6 = 7 \qquad \overset{7}{6\overline{)42}}$$

quotient

radius A line segment that joins the center of a circle with any point on the circle.

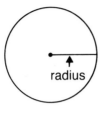

radius

rectangle A figure with four sides and four right angles.

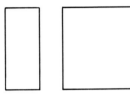

rectangles

remainder The number that is left over, or remains, after a division is completed.

$$\overset{6\ R2}{5\overline{)32}}$$
$$-30$$
$$2$$

remainder

right angle An angle formed by a square corner.

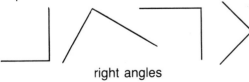

right angles

simplest form (1) A fraction is in simplest form if 1 is the only whole

number factor of both the numerator and the denominator. (2) A mixed numeral is in simplest form if the fraction is in simplest form and names a number less than 1.

sphere A figure shaped like this.

square A rectangle with all four sides the same length.

square

sum The number you get when two or more numbers are added.

$$33 + 28 = 61 \qquad \begin{array}{r} 33 \\ +28 \\ \hline 61 \end{array}$$

sum

triangle A figure with three sides.

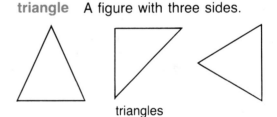

triangles

volume The number of cubic units that fit inside a figure. The volume of this figure is 12 cubic centimeters.

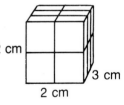

2 cm
3 cm
2 cm

whole number Any of the numbers 0, 1, 2, 3, 4, 5, and so on.

331

Table of Measures

Length

1 centimeter (cm) = 10 millimeters (mm)

1 meter (m) = 1000 millimeters

1 meter (m) = 100 centimeters

1 kilometer (km) = 1000 meters

1 foot (ft) = 12 inches (in)

1 yard (yd) = 3 feet

1 mile (mi) = 5280 feet

Weight

1 gram (g) = 1000 milligrams (mg)

1 kilogram (kg) = 1000 grams

1 pound (lb) = 16 ounces (oz)

1 ton = 2000 pounds

Capacity ℓ

1 liter (L) = 1000 milliliters (mL)

1 kiloliter (kL) = 1000 liters

1 cup = 8 fluid ounces

1 pint (pt) = 2 cups

1 quart (qt) = 2 pints

1 gallon (gal) = 4 quarts

Time

1 minute (min) = 60 seconds (sec)

1 hour (h) = 60 minutes

1 day = 24 hours

1 week = 7 days

1 year = 365 days

1 leap year = 366 days

1 year = 12 months

1 decade = 10 years

1 century = 100 years

Index

334